Acknowledgements

First and foremost, I would like to thank all the research participants, who remain anonymous and who trusted me enough to describe their painful stories. Many of them also entrusted me with some grander notion of trying to improve health care for future generations coming out behind them. This duty will remain as a work in progress. I would also like to thank Lizanne Wilson (Clinical Nurse Specialist HIV and Mental Health), who helped me gain access to potential recruitment sites and who acted as a safety net, offering and providing counseling and support to research participants. Thanks also to Lizanne for emotional support provided to me, which was much needed at times, and also for her belief in the importance of the research study. Lizanne introduced me to two key peer researchers (Sharon and Rosy), whose participation in the project made a real difference in terms of accessing local people who were not the "usual suspects." They also helped me cross the age divide and provided language tuition, which helped me talk to the "youth of today." Thanks also to local youth workers Peter Matthews, Annabelle Hodgson, and Tracey Newman for helping me to connect with young people through their youth services and for helpful discussions.

A particularly tortuous quest to find a second supervisor or an external advisor was supported by Sheila Payne, Rose Whiles, and Mike Hardey. Roger Ingham was incredibly helpful and supportive, and put me in touch with Adrian Coyle at the University of Surrey. I thank Adrian for all his input as an external advisor, for squirreling me into an ESRC (Economic and Social Research Council) research methods course, and for linking me into lesbian and gay psychology networks. I also thank Judith Lathlean,who took over my supervision at Southampton after a period of intermission: Without her, this piece of work would not have reached its conclusion. Also thanks to Jill Macleod Clark, for the initial academic conversation about this project many years ago, and my examiners, Paul Flowers and Andree Le May, for constructive feedback and support. Janice Morse and Moira Calder worked tirelessly to produce the thesis for publication, and I am indebted to both of them.

There are many other people who have supported me in different ways: Bronagh Walsh for her sense of humor, intelligence, and solidarity in the face of adversity; Martin McColl, for joining the Steering Group and offering to pick up any research participants under the age of 16 if they required emergency counseling; Jan Bridget, for saving people's lives while some of us engaged in something more academic and for her contempt as an activist toward armchair social constructionists; Jane Cant, for help traversing the local ethics committee; Richard Ashcroft, for advice about consent in the research process for young people; Jonathon Shepherd, for information about the local peer education project; Robert Power, for a long conversation about privileged access interviewers and incentives; Dale Webb, David Wright, Nick Drey, and Pete Betts, who helped me to understand the local context; Glen Turner and Neil Dacombe at Gay Men's Health Project, for conversations about peer researchers and the use of their premises to interview some participants; Chris Bagley, for a discussion about his random household survey; Hilary Hinds, for pointing out the historical use of the phrase "an unspeakable of the Oscar Wilde sort"; Jacky Stacey, assisted by Hilary Hinds, for an impromptu al fresco tutorial on writing introductory and concluding chapters; Mary Everett, for continuing to ask me how I was getting on with my Ph.D. and telling me it was important to finish it; Lucy Yardley, for keeping me up to date with her draft publications on qualitative methodologies; Mary Gobbi, for corridor conversations about the ineffable and the sixth moment; my sister-out-law Jen and her partner, Joan, for paying my therapist; my therapist; Sally Munt, for recommending key texts by Judith Butler, Anthony Giddens, Victor Seidler, and David Sibley; David Wright, for recommending key texts by David Bell and Gill Valentine, and Nancy Duncan; Chris Gildersleeve and all the other workers at PACE; Helen Jones a nd Rose Hall at Mind in Brighton and Hove, whose daily work made them constantly remind me that any research that would improve the plight of lesbians and gay men with mental health needs had to be finished and put in the public domain; Louise Sprowl, the equal opportunities officer at the University of Southampton, for helping me to recognize and cope with the homophobic bullying I was at the receiving end of while registered as a full-time student; the Workers at Mind in Southampton, particularly Donna Hiscock and Lesley Hall, for publicizing the research to potential research participants; David Longman at Switchboard, for the same; Wessex Medical Trust, for a grant to cover the costs of transcribing interview material; to my sister, Shirley, and my brother in law, Ron, for their railing against homophobes; and to David House, for dragging me back to the St. Peter's band of ringers just when I needed to be distracted with Stedman and Surprise methods.

Finally and most important, I thank my "pretended" family: my partner, Flis, for her continued belief in my ability to complete this piece of work and crucial reminders at critical moments that I had started out as a confident person; also Flis again and our children, Jamie and Lizzie, who put up with some absence on my part during the final push for the frontier.

Preface

This dissertation has its beginnings in a piece of political and professional activism instigated by the British Conservative government's attack on the human rights of lesbians and gay men when they introduced a clause into the Local Government Bill in 1987; this later became Section 28 of the Local Government Act, which was designed to prevent the "promotion of homosexuality and pretended family relationships" (United Kingdom, 1988). On attending local "Stop the Clause" meetings and a lobby of Parliament, I began to realize the serious potential health implications of this proposed legislation. Later, when participating in a lobby of the Houses of Parliament, I was particularly struck by the number of placards demonstrators were holding, which said,

No more teenage suicides

1 in 5 lesbian and gay teenagers attempt suicide

My feeling at the time on seeing these placards was one of dissociation and a sense of anachronism; how was it possible for shame and pride to coexist here? Out, proud, and confident demonstrators were pointing to the shame carrièd within us. In retrospect, this was the first moment of my conscious recognition of and engagement with the binary. However, it has taken me several years of activism, experience, and academic research to understand this moment in a more complete and useful way, involving a journey of contesting and reconstructing binaries. These binaries that shape our lives, our experiences, and our understandings are a product of the dualistic world we live in. One abundantly clear binary at this stage was the heteronormativity of society against the spectre of the pathologization of homosexuality; at this germinal stage of the research, homosexuality was still listed as a mental illness in the World Health Organization (WHO) International Classification of Diseases (1992) and a newly published textbook of social sciences for the first Project 2000 nursing diploma students listed homosexuality as a sexual perversion alongside bestiality (Fisher, 1990).

It has been difficult to step aside from these binaries and not to simply reconstruct another set elsewhere. This journey has involved stepping back from the comfort zone of well-adjusted lesbians and gay men in our communities, and it has involved resisting and contesting the forms of knowledge through which we attempt to understand experience and identities. It has also involved finding nondualistic ways of understanding the resistance to these binaries in lesbians' and gay men's accounts of their mental health care experiences. Furthermore, the project has required an engagement with silence and silencing—a process that defines the health care experience of lesbians and gay men and that further complicates the research endeavor. This erasure was brought into sharp relief by the nursing profession's response to Section 28, and it is worth outlining that history to contextualize this thesis.

As an associate of the Radical Nurses' Group and the London Lesbian Nurses' Group, and as a member of the Royal College of Nursing (RCN), I contrived to use the power of my union to represent concerns about the mental health of this vulnerable group and to oppose the proposed legislation on the grounds that it would be damaging to people's health. I contacted my local RCN branch to propose an emergency resolution to the congress and put a notice in the nursing press urging RCN members to take similar action. The reactions of members of the nursing profession and the establishment of the RCN to this call were salient and informative. This marked the beginning of the trail of a story, a story in which binaries and dichotomies stack up and shore up a particular kind of oppression, which is replicated in health care. In this research, I set out to understand how these binaries assert and reproduce themselves in our experiences, in health care, and in research, mapping onto each other and layering themselves, creating an impenetrable web of power and silence. The injustices in health care are mapped onto the inequalities in research, whereby few people are prepared to sacrifice themselves on the altar of institutionalized homophobia, and the research methods most appropriate to investigating such matters are marginalized and devalued in much the same way as their potential objects of enquiry are.

Those of us who sought to oppose the proposed legislation through our Nursing Union faced a further layer of opposition, one within our own profession, and it became clear that the homophobia behind the proposed legislation was also within the nursing profession. The RCN congress rejected the emergency resolution about the proposed legislation, and so further lobbying took place during congress. It was at this point that the enormity of the struggle became apparent, and the union, which was supposed to represent its members, seemed intent on silencing some of us. Our publicity materials (for fringe meetings and our exhibition stall at the congress) were confiscated by security guards, and we were apprehended when we tried to enter the building. When we demonstrated outside the building, RCN members told us that we were bringing shame on the nursing profession. When we unfurled a banner over the balcony in the congress hall, the General Secretary of the RCN ordered the congress delegates to avert their eyes. I also received homophobic and abusive phone calls at home on several occasions. However, although there was clearly an attempt to shame and silence, on the other side, some RCN activists rallied to the cause, and a long struggle commenced within the organization (for a more detailed history of this, see Platzer, 1992).

What was most apparent during the early stages of this struggle was the silence and the silencing, and this was linked to shame in a profound way (at one point, we renamed the RCN as the Royal Closet of Nursing). By revisiting the message that was on the placards held at the parliamentary lobby it became clear to us, as a group of activists and as nurses, that an emerging body of research evidence showed the vulnerability of lesbians' and gay men's health and also (from North America) a clear evidence base of homophobic attitudes among nurses and other health care professionals, and discrimination in health care (for reviews, see Platzer, 1990, 1993).

It seemed remarkable that attempts to put this on the nursing agenda were so vehemently denied, and "moles" within the RCN reported public chastisement for staff who attempted to break the silence. However, given the cultural taboo about sexuality, the general level of homophobia within society, and the conservatism within the profession, the situation was not totally surprising. Furthermore, in terms of conducting sensitive research, it is well known that researchers avoid the taint of stigma contagion wherever possible (Lee, 1993). There was thus little in the way of "proof" to counter claims that we were merely misguided troublemakers when we claimed that there was evidence of discrimination toward lesbians and gay men in the nursing profession and in nursing care.

Eventually, the RCN set up a working party to investigate these claims and set us the onerous task (with little in the way of resources) to prove the case. It was notable in the discussions that preceded this that entire meetings could be held with RCN staff in which the words *lesbian* or *gay* were never uttered by those who were meeting with us to discuss lesbian and gay nursing issues. Indeed, whole conversations could be had with people occupying the categories of interest without any signifying terms being uttered—hiatuses in the conversation stood in at each unspeakable moment. This was for me the dawning moment of beginning to understand the epistemology of the closet; as the project unfolded, a complex relationship between identity and, at least, education and class, and unspeakability became clear. It seemed we had not moved far from the 19th century, in which the term "an unspeakable of the Oscar Wilde sort" was coined and in which Oscar Wilde himself referred to "the love that dare not speak its name" (Sinfield, 1994). The RCN's tactic of setting up a working party to "prove" discrimination in nursing toward lesbians and gay men could be described under the heading of "new ways to silence troublesome activists"; however, after some time, the working party had interviewed approximately 60 lesbians and gay men about their experiences of nursing care and conducted focus groups or workshops with nurses about the nursing care of lesbians and gay men. The research evidence that we produced clearly showed homophobia in health and nursing care and discrimination against lesbian and gay patients (Caulfield & Platzer, 1998; James, Harding, & Corbett, 1994; James & Platzer, 1999; Platzer, 1995; Platzer & James, 1997, 2000; P. Rose & Platzer, 1993). The working party also produced a number of good practice guides and other RCN publications (1994, 1998a, 1998b, 2000).

Most of the accounts about the nursing care of lesbians and gay men that we collected related to general nursing care, and our findings were commensurate with those that had been published earlier in North America. Among these, however, were a smaller number of accounts about experiences of mental health care and the impact of homophobia in health care on the mental health of lesbians and gay men; it was these accounts, together with that earlier realization outside the Houses of Parliament of our particular vulnerability, that really inspired the further work undertaken in this thesis. I then set out to explore further the mental health care experiences of lesbians and gay men with an understanding that this was a vulnerable group: vulnerable because of homophobia in society generally and with a further vulnerability because of homophobia within nursing and other health care professions.

Another aspect of the research that came to light as a result of the earlier work with the RCN was the difficulty of researching a sensitive topic with a hidden population. It was clear from looking at research into sampling hidden populations, and research on sensitive topics, that tried-and-tested methods for finding research participants tended to produce a class and race bias. In spite of adopting efforts to overcome this, we found, as in many other qualitative studies and studies of hidden populations, that our sampling methods turned in on themselves, leading to a White, professional, and highly educated homogenous group. These biases might have been partly a reflection of the shame and unspeakability around the whole enterprise; on the whole, the lesbians and gay men who participated in the study we conducted for the RCN were not unspeakable: They were mostly positively identified lesbians and gay men with professional jobs who were well and truly out of the closet. However, it was notable even among these people that being "out" in a health care setting was more problematic.

In this study, I set out to develop further the work conducted for the RCN and, in particular, to focus in on mental health care for people who were accessing care at a time when they were struggling with their sexual identity and it was affecting their mental health—in short, those people who were represented in the placards outside the Houses of Parliament. In doing this, it was important to develop innovation in sampling approaches to challenge (or at least understand) the apparent class, race, and education biases in previous studies. I felt at this stage that any investigation into the mental health of lesbians and gay men would need to engage with research participants who were not only at the pride end of the shame/pride dichotomy, that is, to investigate the experiences of lesbians and gay men whose sexual identity was implicated in their mental health. Furthermore, it was important to try to do this in a way that did not reproduce the shame/pride dichotomy, that is, did not repathologize lesbians and gay men in the process of undertaking research but also not to elide the issue of shame.

This point helps to situate the research and make sense of the political and social context that created an absence of research on this topic. Although mainstream researchers might have neglected the topic because of homophobia and heterosexism, it had also clearly been neglected up until this point by academics in the emerging field of lesbian and gay studies and in gay-affirmative psychology. In both of these areas, a great deal of effort had gone into conducting research that refuted pathologizing models of homosexuality, and in the political drive to gain lesbian and gay rights, research that drew attention to mental health vulnerability created a hostage to fortune. It was as if the stigma of mental illness was too much to bear alongside the stigma of homosexuality; gay-affirmative psychology and lesbian and gay studies had to make sufficient inroads alongside gains in human rights before it was tenable to revisit psychopathology. However, certain inroads had been created as the balance of power shifted toward a more tolerant society, and during this time, some research came to the fore that did highlight the specific mental health needs of lesbians and gay men; this came with a shift in understanding that it was minority stress, or the effects of homophobia, rather than sexual identity itself, that was linked to mental health vulnerability.

The findings of such studies have yet to be incorporated into health or research policy, however. Section 28 caused a retrenchment and made it difficult to continue this momentum. Moreover, post Section 28, two key studies were conducted in the United Kingdom that demonstrated that homophobia in mental health care settings was alive and kicking (Golding, 1997; MacFarlane, 1998). In a sense, another binary had been created through the pursuit of gay-affirmative research, which was that of the pathologized homosexual versus the well-adjusted lesbian or gay man. Even in research into mental health care experience, this binary remained intact.

Chapter 1
Disordered Identities

Homophobia in mental health care is alive and well, as recent studies have shown (Golding, 1997; MacFarlane, 1998). In this book, I have set out to go beyond the limits of those studies by disrupting the binary embedded in them—that of the pathologized homosexual versus the well-adjusted lesbian or gay man—which is itself a product of the dualisms and binaries that foregrounded such research. These recent studies highlight homophobia in health care but do not really engage with how this subsequently affects access to health care and health itself. They also elide the problematic relationship between sexual identity and mental health. Furthermore, much of the existing research on lesbians' and gay men's experience of nursing care is atheoretical, which makes it difficult to understand and assess the impact of discrimination in health care. More important, it makes it difficult to engage in any serious debate about what is going on in nursing practice and nurse education that allows such discrimination to go unchallenged. Again, silence and silencing are significant here, and one of the major challenges for this study has been to get beyond the liberal "we treat everyone the same/we treat everyone as an individual" approach. This often seems to be invoked by the nursing profession as a defense against any evidence that discrimination toward lesbian and gay patients does occur. This "treating everyone the same/treating everyone as an individual" is part of the liberal humanism embedded in nursing practice, and, again, is part of the dominant dualistic thinking of modern Western society.

Here, I have attempted to disrupt and problematize the dualisms, binaries, and dichotomies that construct and define identities, nursing practice, and health care experiences: "binary oppositions thus become analytic sites of ongoing struggle and contestation" (Cheek & Rudge, 1994, p. 19). As I do this, I am aware that no clearly defined body of nursing knowledge or nursing theory exists to draw on, and a theoretical framework emerged that drew on a range of disciplines, including psychology (e.g., Mathieson & Stam, 1995; Osborn & Smith, 1998; Parker, Georgaca, Harper, McLaughlin, & Stowell-Smith, 1995; J. Smith, 1991; Ussher, 2000; Yardley, 1998), sociology (e.g., Charmaz, 1987; Clarke, 1996; Henwood, 1993), geography (e.g., D. Bell & Valentine, 1995; Chouinard & Grant, 1996; Duncan, 1996), cultural studies (e.g., Hall, 1997b; J. Hart & Richardson, 1981; Richardson, 1981), and, in some cases, work that claimed to be postdisciplinary (e.g., Butler, 1990). Some of these works were applied to identity, some specifically to sexual identity, and some to health care experience, but at this point no research had been done that brought together the mental health care experiences of lesbians and gay men and their coming-out experiences.

Whatever discipline was drawn on, it tended to be work that was itself at the margins of that discipline and was pushing methodological and epistemological boundaries. This led to further inquiry about the epistemological, ontological, and methodological debates in these disciplines, and this lent a critical lens through which to view previous work that had been done on mental health, coming out, and sexual identity and through which to critique the emerging literature on the mental health care experiences of lesbians and gay men. Within all this, tensions repeatedly arose about how identity and experience could be understood, and polarized positions reasserted themselves, whether in the description of experience, the understanding of identity, the sampling methods to be used, or the way in which data can be analyzed and interpreted. The particular dualisms that asserted themselves during the development of a theoretical framework for this thesis were those of essentialism and social constructionism in terms of how identity is understood, and realism versus relativism in terms of how research is undertaken. These map onto each other, with essentialists tending toward realist methods and constructionists tending toward relativist methods.

The theoretical framework for this study arises as much from methodological debate about how experience can be investigated as it does from any prior empirical studies of experience; in fact, another dualism that created tensions throughout this research project was that between the empirical and the theoretical. Where identity or experience had been theorized, it has rarely been empirically investigated, and vice versa. When identity and experience have been investigated, this investigation often relied on methodological approaches on the positivist side of the dualism and seemed to swing to the social constructionist when the theorization began. Even when researchers have adopted a social constructionist approach to their investigations of sexual identity, they have often seemed to backslide into essentialist definitions of sexual identity when obtaining a sample for empirical investigation. The notable exceptions were in some studies of sexual health in which the relationship between sexual identity, behavior, social class, community attachment, and sampling has been investigated with more intellectual rigor (e.g., Dowsett, Davies, & Connell, 1992; Flowers, Smith, Sheeran, & Beail, 1997b; Weatherburn, Hickson, Reid, & Davies, 1998).

In an attempt to advance knowledge about the relationship between sexual identity and mental heath care experience, I have resisted and sidestepped these dualisms throughout the thesis; this side-stepping is an attempt to bring together the empirical and the theoretical to be able to say something about those experiences in a social-political-cultural context; in other words, to develop a situated and grounded knowledge base that locates the contingent nature of identity and experience without relegating them to the realms of the unreal. This required not only, then, a side-stepping of the dualisms that define our experiences, our identities, and nursing practice but also a side-stepping of the dualisms that limit how we can investigate those experiences, identities, and practices.

In disrupting the dualisms in mental health and sexual identity, I have also disrupted the ontological and epistemological dualisms that determine and limit methods of inquiry. This approach to research is innovative and in its early stages of development with respect to attempting to straddle epistemological divides; in allowing tensions arising from the mixing of methods, it becomes possible to analyze thoroughly tensions that arise in people's accounts of their health care experiences. This approach to conducting research has been referred to by a range of terms, which vary according to the academic discipline from which they arise; thus, both the terms critical realism (see Bhaskar, 1989; Pilgrim & Rogers, 1997; Sayer, 2000) and material-discursive approaches (see Ussher, 1997a; Yardley, 1997c) have been used to describe such approaches. Denzin and Lincoln (1998; 1994) have referred to these paradigm shifts (or, rather, mixing of paradigms) as the fifth and sixth moments in qualitative research and referred to research arising from these approaches as a *bricolage*, and the researcher as a *bricoleur*. This approach "provide(s) distinctive insights into nursing practice and allows us to interrupt the particular historical, situated systems of oppression which inform nursing activities" (Manias & Street, 2000, pp. 50-51).

The approaches I used to undertake this disruption of dualisms in this study are located in both the sampling strategies and the methods of data analysis. The sampling strategies problematized the binaries embedded in how people define and locate themselves in recognition of the unspeakability of some stigmatized existences and experiences. I sought to use a variety of innovative sampling approaches drawn from sexual health research and research with intravenous drug users in an attempt to access a diverse research population whose diversity might map onto vulnerability in mental health and mental health care. I intended to research beyond the "usual suspects," who could be captured relatively easily through lesbian and gay community networks, and to identify a sample of people who were diverse at least in terms of lesbian/gay community attachment, race, social class, age, and educational background. Again, this is part of the attempt to disrupt dichotomies—it seemed to be possible that the shame/pride dichotomy at work might obscure important differences in people's experiences of mental health care and might also obscure how accounts of those experiences were accessed. Through this innovation in the sampling methods, I set out to address these issues and explore the complex relationship between identity, community, mental health, and access to care and to consider how this complex relationship can itself affect the process of undertaking research.

In the attempt to problematize the whole sampling strategy—by undertaking the research that cannot speak its name—further innovation was required in the analysis of data. Because I was entering the realm of the ineffable, both in terms of the research topic and through the deliberate sampling of lesbians and gay men who had been silenced and, perhaps, silenced themselves as a strategy of resistance, it was important to find ways of interpreting and making sense of the data that had been obtained from a large number of research interviews. One way to achieve this was by straddling epistemological divides and treating the data in both realist and nonrealist ways, that is, creating a bricolage by viewing the data through different lenses. Some aspects of people's accounts of their experience could be analyzed through the realist lens of interpretative phenomenological analysis—such analysis was grounded in people's verbatim accounts of their experiences and is presented in Chapters 5 and 6. However, other aspects of people's accounts seemed to be more rhetorical and needed a constructivist, nonrealist lens through which to make sense of those experiences. There were also significant silences and contradictions in people's accounts of their mental health care experiences, and a discursive analysis using positioning theory helped to make sense of and further interpret those aspects of people's accounts

(Chapter 7). By juxtaposing these methods of analysis, I was able to produce not a only a description of homophobia in health care but also to develop a deeper understanding of how homophobia in health care is resisted and negotiated (see Chapter 8); hence, it becomes possible to understand more about the nature of that health care interaction and its impact.

Chapter 2
The Persistence of the Pathologization of Lesbian and Gay Sexual Identities

The rationale for this study emerges from a social context in which prejudice against lesbians and gay men remains commonplace (Citizenship 21, 2003) and in which negative attitudes toward lesbians and gay men are held by a significant number of nurses and other health care professionals (Annesley & Coyle, 1995; Bartlett, King, & Phillips, 2001; Bhugra, 1988; Bhugra & King, 1989; Bond, Rhodes, Phillips, & Tierney, 1990; Eliason, 1996; Phillips, Bartlett, & King, 2001; L. Rose, 1994). An established body of empirical literature demonstrates clearly that lesbians and gay men experience the effects of homophobia and heterosexism in nursing and health care (Eliason, 1996; James et al., 1994; Platzer & James, 2000; Stevens, 1992; Stevens & Hall, 1988, 1990). Homophobia is defined as an irrational fear of lesbians and gay men, whereas heterosexism is a broader term that shifts the focus away from individual attitudes toward a more general understanding of how negative attitudes are embedded in social practices and institutions; through these social practices, heterosexuality is privileged and seen as more normal and desirable, and this contributes to the oppression of lesbians and gay men (Eliason, 1996).

More recently, researchers have begun to focus specifically on lesbians' and gay men's experiences of mental health care. Again, the social context for this is particularly important, as it was only in 1992 that the World Health Organization officially declassified homosexuality as a mental illness (D. Davies & Neal, 1996). In spite of this declassification, however, a number of recent studies have shown that lesbians and gay men experience homophobia in mental health care. In particular, they report that their lesbian or gay identity is still pathologized by mental health care practitioners, in that it is viewed as a mental illness or something that can potentially be cured or changed (Annesley & Coyle, 1998; Golding, 1997; MacFarlane, 1998; G. Proctor, 1994).

The other body of literature relevant to informing the aims of this study is that which looks at the mental health of lesbians and gay men. A significant amount of empirical work suggests that lesbians and gay men have a higher than expected incidence of mental health problems and, in particular, a higher than expected rate of attempted suicide when compared to the general population (for a review, see Rivers, 2002). Furthermore, this empirical research shows that lesbians and gay men are particularly vulnerable to suicide attempts when they are "coming out"; that is, when they are realizing their sexual identity and coping with decisions and consequences related to disclosure (i.e., deciding whether to tell others about their sexual identity). Although some of the literature on health care experience looks at issues relating to disclosure to health care practitioners, none to date has looked specifically at how people manage mental health encounters when they themselves are realizing (or coming to terms with) their own sexual identity.

I have sought to explore this area further by investigating how people experience mental health care when they are at this juncture of their lives. The overall research aim was to conduct an exploratory study to investigate the mental health care experiences of lesbians and gay men when they are negotiating their sexual identity (or "coming out"). To set the scene for this and to develop specific research questions, I reviewed the following literature:

- the mental health of lesbians and gay men,
- the nature of the "coming out" process and how people negotiate and manage their sexual identity, and
- lesbians' and gay men's mental health care experiences.

I found an extensive body of literature about mental health and coming out, and also a growing body of literature on the mental health care experiences of lesbians and gay men. No specific research, however, brought these bodies of literature together. The specific research questions that emerged from this review of the literature were

1. How do homophobia and heterosexism manifest themselves in mental health care encounters when lesbians and gay men are coming out? and
2. How do homophobia and heterosexism affect lesbians' and gay men's access to mental health care when they are coming out?

I will review each body of literature in turn, that is, the mental health of lesbians and gay men, coming out and mental health, and health care experience. Most of the studies reviewed are empirical studies framed loosely within a psychological or sociological framework. The review of these studies will be followed by a discussion of the more theoretical literature, which I drew on to inform the method of the study and subsequently the analysis and interpretation of the findings.

THE MENTAL HEALTH OF LESBIANS AND GAY MEN

Empirical evidence suggests a higher than expected incidence of a number of mental health problems among lesbians and gay men. It is important to note that no inherent psychopathology is associated with lesbian or gay identity (Gonsoriek, 1991), but gay-related (or minority) stress caused by homophobia in society might lead to mental health problems (DiPlacido, 1998). In particular, a relationship seems to exist between the time in people's lives during which they are realizing their sexual identity and higher than expected rates of attempted suicide as compared to the general population or matched controls.

Two large-scale and two smaller scale studies at the end of the 1960s and early 1970s showed a higher than expected incidence of attempted suicide and suicidal feelings among lesbians and gay men as compared to control groups of heterosexuals (A. Bell & Weinberg, 1978; Jay & Young, 1977; Roesler & Deisher, 1972; Saghir & Robins, 1973). In Bell and Weinberg's study, approximately a third of the lesbians and gay men in the sample had attempted suicide compared to about 10% in the heterosexual controls; 20% of the gay men had made a suicide attempt when they were under age 20. Bell and Weinberg also found that of those who reported previous suicide attempts, 58% of gay males and 39% of lesbians felt that their first suicide attempts were related to the fact that they were lesbian or gay. More recent analysis of these data found that among gay men, being troubled over their sexual identity during adolescence was related to subsequent attempts, and "data reveal that for both males and females, negative feelings about one's incipient homosexuality are associated with suicidal feelings and may explain some of the suicide attempts that occur during late adolescence and early adulthood" (Harry, 1989, p. 358). In the Jay and Young study, 39% of the total sample of lesbians of all ages attempted or seriously contemplated suicide, and 33% of these said that it related to their sexual identity; similarly, 40% of the gay men had attempted suicide, and 53% said it related to their sexual identity. In the Saghir and Robins study, 5 of the 6 gay male attempters had made their attempts before the age of 20 during conflict with family members or within themselves over their emerging sexual identity, and 6 of the 7 lesbian attempters had made their attempts during their 20s during a depression following the break-up of a relationship.

It could be argued that these high rates of attempted suicide relate to a historical period when the criminalization and pathologization of homosexuality led to more repression and oppression of lesbians and gay men and that such findings would not be reproduced today. However, more recent studies have continued to show higher than expected levels of attempted suicide among lesbians and gay men as well as an increase in incidence of mental health problems such as depression (Bradford & Ryan, 1987; D'Augelli & Hershberger, 1993; Geraghty, 1996; Hetrick & Martin, 1987; C. Proctor & Groze, 1994; Remafadi, Farrow, & Deisher, 1991; Saunders, Tupac, & MacCulloch, 1988; M. Schneider, 1991; S. Schneider, Farberow, & Kruks, 1989; Trenchard & Warren, 1984; Trippet, 1994). In these studies, the incidence of attempted suicide ranged from 18 to 42%. Bradford and Ryan (1994) found an overall attempted suicide rate of 18% in their sample of lesbians, but in those aged 17 to 24, it was 24%. Where specific lesbian and gay youth populations have been sampled, the rates found were 42% (D'Augelli & Hershberger, 1993), 32% (Geraghty, 1996), 20% of those presenting for services (with a higher incidence amongst those calling the helpline) (Hetrick & Martin, 1987), 40.3 % (C. Proctor & Groze, 1994), 30% (Remafadi et al., 1991), 31% (Roesler & Deisher, 1972), more than a third (M. Schneider, 1991), and 20% (S. Schneider et al., 1989). These rates of attempted suicide in lesbian and gay youth are higher than the rates of 6 to 13% found in high school students (D'Augelli & Hershberger, 1993).

Schneider et al. (1989) compared suicide attempters and non-attempters and found that the attempters were aware of their sexual orientation at an earlier age but did not feel positive about it. Trenchard and Warren (1984) found that 19% of their respondents had attempted suicide because they were lesbian or gay. Harry (1989), in a review of the literature, noted that the average age of coming out coincides with the period when gay men are at the greatest risk for suicide attempts. Some studies have shown that the younger lesbian and gay youth are when the coming-out process begins (in terms of awareness of same-sex attraction), the younger they are when they disclose their sexual orientation to another person, and the more rejecting key social supports are to disclosure, the more vulnerable they are to suicide attempts (D'Augelli & Hershberger, 1993; Remafadi et al., 1991; S. G. Schneider et al., 1989). It is of further interest that in some of the studies, young people report that they had no emotional difficulties and no problems with their families until they themselves became aware of their sexual orientation (Hetrick & Martin, 1987; M. Schneider, 1991). Proctor and Groze (1994), in a survey of 221 lesbian, gay, and bisexual youth, found an association between poor family relations and suicidal ideation and suicide attempts. Another study by Rotherum-Borus et al. in 1992 (cited in Savin-Williams, 1994) of 139 lesbian and gay youths aged 14 to 19 found that suicide attempters and non-attempters were no different in terms of general stressful life events, but the attempters experienced more gay-related stressors, including coming out to parents and fear of being discovered to be lesbian or gay by parents or other family members.

Many of these studies have been criticized on the grounds that they tend to draw from youth groups and will thus inevitably find a disproportionate number of distressed youth who attend the groups for support. Furthermore, the purposive sampling approaches used in most of the studies make it difficult to find a meaningful comparison group. However, Rotherum-Borus (cited by Prenzlauer, Drescher, & Winchel, 1992) compared three groups of minority youths and found that 41% of the lesbian and gay youth had attempted suicide compared to 28% in the other groups.

The most compelling evidence of an association between suicidal behavior and sexual orientation comes from a study that involved probability sampling methods. In addition, the data collection instruments guaranteed a high level of anonymity, and the overall survey had an exceptionally high response rate (Bagley & Tremblay, 1997). Questions about sexual identity and behavior were embedded in a questionnaire with a wider remit than finding out about sexual orientation and suicide attempts. The findings from this study were that gay and bisexual males were 13.9 times more at risk of a serious suicide attempt than heterosexual males.

A number of authors have postulated reasons for an increased incidence of suicide and attempted suicide in lesbians and gay men on the basis that they are a marginalized group subject to the effects of stigmatization and minority status. Saunders and Valente (1987) have argued that Durkheim's theory regarding alienation, as well as an increased risk in interruption of social ties, would predict an increased risk of suicide for lesbians and gay men. Hetrick and Martin (1987) have discussed the effects of social, cognitive, and emotional isolation on lesbian and gay youth, and have argued that the minority status of lesbian and gay youth is worse than for other minority groups, as they are not socialized into or prepared for their minority position by their families or their culture: They have no sense of "we" versus "they" as a minority within their family and community (Hetrick & Martin, 1987). There is also evidence that lesbians and gay men and youth are at increased risk of a number of other factors that could predispose them to suicidal behavior: violence (Hunter & Schaecher, 1987), including from their own families (Martin & Hetrick, 1988); victimization and bullying (Hershberger & D'Augelli, 1995; Hunter, 1990; Remafadi et al., 1991; Rivers, 1997); and rejection by their families, leading to homelessness (Gonsoriek, 1988; Hunter & Schaecher, 1987; Trenchard & Warren, 1984). In addition, the research reports a high incidence of drug and alcohol abuse, which might predispose lesbians and gay men to suicidal behavior (Bradford et al., 1994; Hershberger & D'Augelli, 1995).

The empirical literature, then, strongly suggests that the higher incidence of mental health problems in lesbians and gay men relates to the stress associated with negotiating a marginalized and stigmatized identity. This stress will be particularly salient at that point in people's lives when they are realizing their sexual identity and also trying to cope with decisions and consequences in relation to disclosure of this to others. This time of realization and decisions about disclosure is often referred to as coming out. This term is problematic, however, in that it has various usages with loaded political meanings and sociocultural specificity. Furthermore, much of the literature on coming out assumes that it is a finite process rather than a matter of ongoing negotiation and day-to-day management of sexual identity.

"COMING OUT": NEGOTIATING
AND MANAGING SEXUAL IDENTITIES

The meaning of the term *coming out* is variable and has also shifted over time; pre-Stonewall (i.e., before the Stonewall riot in New York in 1969, which coalesced an emergent gay rights movement), the term referred to a debut within the secretive homosexual subculture or coming out to other homosexuals. (The term *homosexual* is also problematic, associated as it is with a pathological identity—I have used it where it is "historically correct" and when in the context of studies that pathologize lesbian and gay identities. A full discussion about the language assigned to lesbian and gay identities follows in Chapters 3 and 4 and is related to sampling procedures.)

However, after Stonewall, it acquired a political meaning and related to the building of a mass movement, public declaration of one's lesbian or gay identity, and increasing visibility. It can also be taken to mean either identifying oneself as gay or lesbian, or disclosing that self-recognition to others (D'Emilio, 1993; Troiden, 1992). That the term is problematic, and has different meanings, also leads to methodological problems, which are discussed further in Chapter 4, as is the problem of naming identities. Nevertheless, it is necessary at times to use it as a shorthand to stand for something that occurs when people become aware of and subsequently act on (or do not act on) the awareness of their same-sex desire.

A popular idea involves a sequence of stages that lesbians and gay men go through when they are realizing and disclosing their sexual identity. This is reflected in the development of several models derived from empirical data that describe this process (e.g., Cass, 1979; Plummer, 1981; Troiden, 1992; Troiden & Goode, 1980). In addition to this, a certain amount of empirical work seeks to look at the relationship between these stages and mental health. The models

> attempt to organize and interpret...coming out experiences in relation to homosexual identity formation (which) progresses from an initial awareness of same-sex feelings through homosexual behaviour to eventual self-labelling, self-disclosure, and the final stabilization of a positive gay identity. (G. McDonald, 1982, p. 48)

The assumptions built into these stage models are that self-recognition followed by disclosure of one's lesbian or gay identity is directly related to the acquisition of a positive identity and some form of psychological adjustment. A further assumption is that gay/lesbian community involvement or the adoption of a gay/lesbian lifestyle is an intrinsic component of a developmental and linear progression toward resolution of a confused identity to an integrated and stable identity relating to same-sex attraction (e.g., Plummer, 1981).

These stage models, and the assumptions derived from them, have been critiqued in a number of ways. Some authors have put forward empirical evidence to refute the linear and sequential nature of the stages. For instance, G. McDonald (1982) noted that Troiden's (1992) model insisted that gay men formed relationships with each other only when they were in the final stages of the coming-out process, whereas McDonald's study showed that men could be in long-term relationships with other men for years before identifying themselves as gay. Other critiques of these linear and sequential stages have been offered by Markowe (1996) and Rust (1993). Both have reasoned that coming out is not a linear and finite process but an ongoing, lifelong process mediated by changing social circumstances and interactions. Others have said that the models tend to be based on gay and White male experience, and fail to take into account variation relating to gender (e.g., Grammick, 1984), cultural differences (e.g., Herdt, 1992), or social class (Harry, 1993). Many of these biases built into the models probably derive largely from sampling artifact and cohort effects (see Chapter 4 for further discussion).

Some researchers have looked at how different cultural contexts will affect identity development, management, and disclosure (Chan, 1995; Herdt, 1992; Tremble, Schneider, & Appathurai, 1989). It has been suggested that one of the salient differences for minority-ethnic cultures relates to collectivism, family ties, and associated obligations (Abdulrahim, 1998). One particular study found that Jewish gay men's socialization, informed by particular religious doctrines and cultural expectations, created another set of conflicts and difficulties that had to be negotiated and managed. The religious doctrines and cultural expectations also informed the particular homophobic reactions that the participants had experienced (Coyle & Rafalin, 1999).

The sampling bias that is built into many studies of lesbians and gay men reinforces essentialist ideas that sexual identity is fixed, stable, binarized, and universalized. More recent social constructionist approaches to understanding the development of sexual identity have questioned the assumptions of these early simplistic models of coming out. The essentialist models assume a position in which lesbian or gay identity is a "true" identity waiting to be realized. Rust (1993) said that even Plummer (1981), who adopted a constructionist approach to his model of coming out, ultimately adopted an essentialist, goal-orientated view with the idea of acquiring a stable identity. Rust went on to say that from a social constructionist point of view, "identity is the result of interpretation of personal experience in terms of available social constructs...and coming out is the process of describing oneself in terms of social constructs rather than a process of discovering one's essence" (p. 68).

This idea of linear progression, bound in essentialist notions, is linked to ideas that coming out and disclosure, as well as attachment to the lesbian/gay community, are good for one's health and general well-being. Again, in an early developmental stage model of coming out, Plummer (1981) asserted that coming out to the gay community will be a positive experience. However, in another early model, Ponse (1980) argued that the lesbian community would provide both support and pressure for conformity. It is notable that early coming-out models of lesbian identity models adhered less to notions of sequential stages than those exploring the development of gay male identity. A number of studies have shown a relationship between disclosure of sexual identity, a positive lesbian or gay identity, and improved psychological adjustment (e.g., Miranda & Storms, 1989; Schmitt & Kurdek, 1987). Griffin (1991) and Markowe (1996) have defined this more in terms of the need for authenticity. This, together with the available developmental coming-out stage models, has led to assumptions that coming out and disclosure relate to self-acceptance, but these ideas have been questioned in a number of ways. Franke and Leary (1991) found that disclosure was very variable, even in groups that were at least partially out, and that disclosure related more to the imagined reaction of the person disclosed to than it did to self-acceptance. Cohen (1996) also found that disclosure was not always related to feeling positive about one's identity but related more to the availability of support when making such disclosures, especially to family members. Harry (1993) has suggested that disclosure relates more to an individual's circumstances in relation to occupation, income, and area of residence than it is indicative of a late stage of a coming-out process.

However, it seems that ideas about strategies around disclosure have become conflated with ideas about coming-out trajectories. As a number of authors have argued, it is sometimes hard to see what is about developing a lesbian or gay identity and what is about stigma management (Brown, 1995; de Montflores, 1993; Healy, 1993). It is also difficult to disentangle the direction of relationships between variables such as identity formation and psychological adjustment (Miranda & Storms, 1989). The same caveats apply to interpreting evidence that belonging to a lesbian or gay community promotes psychological well-being, which has been found in some studies (e.g., Coyle, 1998; Geraghty, 1996). I have no intention of dismissing findings that coming out can lead to psychological benefits (including coming out in the context of a supportive lesbian/gay community) or the idea that passing (nondisclosure) (see, e.g., Berger, 1990; Cain, 1991) can create psychological strain. However, it is clear that these relationships are more complex than suggested by linear stage models of coming out. To begin to understand these complexities, I will now discuss more recent work on how sexual identity is managed and negotiated on an ongoing basis.

A number of researchers have begun to explore the complex ways in which lesbian and gay identities are managed in different public and private spaces and contexts. They have questioned the idea of linear progression in coming out and have shown quite clearly the ongoing and day-to-day necessity for identity management, and, to a certain extent, the effects of the need for such management on people's lives. Some studies have highlighted the need for ongoing identity management in the workplace and the contextual factors that will affect degrees of disclosure (e.g., B. E. Schneider, 1987), and others have gone further to suggest that such identity management will influence career decisions and opportunities (e.g., Boatwright, Gilbert, Forrest, & Ketzenberger, 1996). A number of researchers have explored identity management strategies and the effects of having to manage one's identity in the work environment of physical education school teachers, where disclosure of a lesbian identity can be especially problematic. Clarke (1996, 1998) found that these identity management strategies and their effects not only pervade the public work space but extend into private and social space. She found that when lesbian women do not feel safe to disclose their sexual identity in the workplace, this has effects on mental health, leading to low self-esteem and self-destructive behavior. Squires and Sparkes (1996) also reported these findings from their research in a similar setting. It can be seen from these studies, then, that coming out is an ongoing process.

The assumptions built into much of the work on the mental health of lesbians and gay men, and associated ideas about coming out, are that lesbians and gay men are most vulnerable when they are coming out in their youth and that once they have disclosed their sexual identity, they will be on a trajectory that leads to lesbian or gay community support, self-acceptance, and improved mental health. Although this might be part of the picture, it is possible that much of this theorizing is limited by the sampling approaches used in many of the studies. Most of those researched have been attached to lesbian or gay communities and have come out during their youth. The need to sample more diversely from the lesbian and gay population is further explored in Chapter 4. The critiques of stage models of coming out, alongside social constructionist accounts of identity management, which take into account the ongoing need to deal with stigma, suggest a need to broaden our thinking about the relationship between coming out and mental health. As Richardson and Hart (1981) have said, coming out is something implicated not only in the *development* of identity but also in its *maintenance*.

THE HEALTH CARE EXPERIENCES OF LESBIANS AND GAY MEN

I have indicated in the previous discussion that the negotiation of a marginalized sexual identity in a heterosexist and homophobic culture will be difficult. It is important to ask how this will map onto a health care setting: How do homophobia and heterosexism operate in health care settings, and how do people manage their identities in such settings? A substantial body of empirical work shows that nurses and other health care professionals share the anti-gay and anti-lesbian attitudes of the wider culture and do not have specific training to counter this (Annesley & Coyle, 1995; Eliason, 1996; Hardman, 1997; Milton & Coyle, 1999; G. Proctor, 1994; Stevens, 1992). Lesbians and gay men experience overt hostility; refusal or withdrawal of care; verbal, sexual, and physical abuse; and voyeurism at the hands of nurses and other health care providers in general health care settings (Eliason, 1996; Platzer & James, 2000; Scherzer, 2000; Stevens, 1994a; Stevens & Hall, 1990). Fear of such reaction affects disclosure of sexual identity and leads to reluctance to seek health care; this has been found to be the case in both general nursing and health care settings (Paroski, 1987; Stevens, 1992, 1994b; Stevens & Hall, 1988) and in mental health care settings (Bradford & Ryan, 1987; Golding, 1997; Hetrick & Martin, 1987; MacFarlane, 1998). However, disclosure of sexual identity is linked to greater satisfaction with health care (Dardick & Grady, 1980).

This issue of nondisclosure is of vital significance to the mental health care setting, but to date, studies investigating experiences of nursing and health care have not focused specifically on what might be happening here beyond an assumption that nondisclosure relates primarily to the avoidance of abusive homophobic reactions from health care staff. Undoubtedly, this is part of the picture. However, it is important to interrogate these findings further and ask what else might be taking place, particularly when lesbians and gay men are coming out and seeking mental health care in relation to this. Although no studies of health care experience have specifically explored nondisclosure, some of the literature on gay-affirmative psychology and the effects of internalized homophobia are relevant to this discussion. These discussions, alongside theoretical writings about identity, help to make sense of these gaps in the empirical literature.

In relation to mental health care, recent studies have shown that lesbian and gay mental health users experience homophobic abuse and that health care professionals continue to work to a medicalized model of homosexuality, in which it is seen as a type of psychopathology (Golding, 1997; Hetrick & Martin, 1987; Koffman, 1997; MacFarlane, 1998). Many studies have shown that people who present to health care providers because they are struggling with their sexual identity often feel unable to disclose this (Bradford & Ryan, 1987; D'Augelli & Hershberger, 1993; Hetrick & Martin, 1987). If they do disclose, they are often met with a pathologizing discourse, in which their identity, rather than the struggle to cope with it in a homophobic society, is construed as problematic, or they are met with a discourse that constructs homosexuality as an immature and temporary phase (Hetrick & Martin, 1987; M. Schneider, 1991). Some researchers have begun to explore the impact of these encounters, as seen in suggestions that experiences of homophobic practice can lead to avoidance of future health care. Hetrick and Martin (1987) have suggested that counseling approaches that trivialize or pathologize homosexuality will delay or postpone the work that has to be done in coping with a stigmatized identity.

Another common experience of lesbians and gay men in mental health care settings is that they are silenced in relation to their sexual identity, that is, they are told they should not talk about it, or the health care practitioners avoid the subject (Golding, 1997; MacFarlane, 1998; G. Proctor, 1994). Little theoretical discussion has taken place, in studies of health care experience, about what is operating when such silencing takes place. However, there has been some discussion about how liberal humanism, as an approach that tends to ignore difference, can have the effect of silencing lesbians and gay men about their sexual identities and associated mental health needs (Annesley & Coyle, 1998). In broader terms, a number of writers have problematized the way in which liberal discourses can mask subtle forms of prejudice and allow heterosexism to erase and deny lesbian and gay identities in mental health care (Coyle, Milton, & Annesley, 1999; C. Kitzinger & Coyle, 1995; Peel, 2002). It is important to be alert to this, as liberal humanism underpins modern nursing philosophies and ethics of care. Hart and Lockey (2002) have argued that the liberal humanism underpinning nursing practice often fails to take account of difference and inequality. C. McDonald and Anderson (2003) argued further, in relation to liberal humanism, that individualism and heteronormativity within nursing have led to "resistance within the discipline to value and research social determinants of health (which) raises questions about our complicity in dominant ideologies of health and healthcare" (p. 698).

Although no empirical research looks specifically at how such nursing discourses affect health care experience, it is important to remain cognizant of the accruing evidence about silencing and explore it further. I have developed a theoretical framework for understanding this, and the way in which it is embedded in dualistic thinking, in the next section. This helps to inform not only silencing but also the silence imposed by lesbians and gay men themselves through nondisclosure of their sexual identity. I will discuss the empirical evidence suggesting that self-silencing is important in the final part of this section. Then, I will revisit both silencing and self-silencing in the final section of this chapter, where I have drawn on more theoretical work to help contextualize this, begin to understand its significance, and begin the process of developing a framework for investigating the mental health care experiences of lesbians and gay men.

Some authors have explored the protective strategies that people can employ to help them cope with potentially threatening health care encounters; in particular, avoidance of further health care encounters has been identified as a protective strategy (MacFarlane, 1998; Stevens, 1994b). Silence, or nondisclosure, has been cited as a strategy of resistance to stigmatization by lesbians and gay men in general social settings in relation to sexual identity (Cain, 1991; de Montflores, 1993; P. Griffin, 1991; Murphy, 1989). The strategy of silence and/or nondisclosure has been less thoroughly investigated in relation to mental health or mental health care, with Martin and Hetrick's work (1982) being a notable exception in terms of raising this for discussion. However, other empirical studies that explore how people manage threatened identities in social situations (Breakwell, 1986; Susman, 1994) and, more specifically, in health care encounters (Abdulrahim, 1998; Bloor & McIntosh, 1990; Heaphy, 1998; Huby, 1997) lend some understanding to how silence is used as a strategy of resistance to that threat. These strategies of resistance map onto those discussed in the previous section on mental health and coming out, and the management of sexual identity in the workplace, where it was noted that "passing" (or nondisclosure) is used as a strategy by lesbians and gay men to avoid homophobic reactions from others. However, none of these studies specifically explored the impact of nondisclosure when it relates, as it were, to the "presenting" issue. More theoretical work on identity and discussion in the gay-affirmative literature help to illuminate this further and also begin to point to how difficult it is to explore such phenomena empirically, embedded as they are in shame, unspeakability, silence, and the ineffable.

THEORIZING RESISTANCE

It is particularly important to ask about the nondisclosure of the very issue that might be part of the reason why a person has "presented" for mental health care. The review of the empirical research to date on health care experience, the development and management of lesbian and gay identities, and the mental health of lesbians and gay men showed that such work has not yet been done. There is an unspoken tension in the existing literature on the mental health care experiences of lesbians and gay men; this tension is between the counterclaims to pathologizing research (i.e., an insistence on the normality of lesbian and gay sexual identities and evidence of the psychological adjustment of lesbians and gay men) and the other body of research, which insists on the mental health vulnerability of lesbians and gay men. This tension is not particularly problematic if it is taken as given that the vulnerability arises from the effects of homophobia rather than being an inherent psychopathology linked to sexual orientation; however, it does not map so easily onto mental health care situations in which coming out is implicated in mental health. In the existing research into mental health care experiences of lesbians and gay men, there is an insistence of the lack of relationship between sexual identity and mental health, so when evidence is reported that a lesbian or gay man has had her or his sexual identity pathologized, the counterclaim is implicitly that such as an approach is just plain wrong. However, it might be more complicated than that.

In turning to the gay-affirmative literature on the counseling needs of lesbians and gay men, we find some discussion of the effects of shame and internalized homophobia in terms of the impact on mental health (D. Davies, 1996; DiPlacido, 1998; Gonsoriek, 1988; Mair, 2000; Meyer & Dean, 1998; Shidlo, 1994; Sophie, 1987; Tasker & McCann, 1999) and the beginnings of discussion about the difficulties of articulating this in a therapeutic encounter (Mair, 2000; Shidlo, 1994). An understanding of internalized homophobia and how it is understood "psychologically" in terms of the coming-out process provides a link to theory that might provide a framework for understanding the ways in which homophobia and heterosexism disrupt mental health care encounters. Garnets et al. (1990) have described the task of coming out as part of the interrelated challenge of overcoming internalized homophobia created by heterosexist stigma, which involves a "process of reclaiming disowned or devalued parts of the self, and developing an identity into which one's sexuality is well integrated" (p. 369).

With respect to theory on how lesbian and gay identities are "constructed," there is much discussion about how identities are formed in relation to, and in opposition to, homophobia and heterosexism. Butler (1995), drawing on the work of Foucault, said,

> even the most noxious terms could be owned, that the most injurious interpellations could also be the site for a radical reoccupation and resignification...Called by an injurious name, I come into social being...I am led to embrace the terms that injure me, precisely because they constitute me socially...As a further paradox, then, it is only by occupying—being occupied by—that injurious term that I become enabled to resist and oppose that term, and the power that constitutes me is recast as the power I oppose. (Butler, 1995, p. 245)

What Butler is referring to here is resistance to being treated as the "Other," where Othering takes place through splitting and binarization (Rutherford, 1990); this splitting into binaries relates to a process of projection wherein all that is bad, devalued, or otherwise undesirable is projected onto one half of that binary (Hall, 1997b; Sibley, 1995). These binaries relate to sexual identity, race, gender, and other categories that are constructed in relation to difference. With sexual identity, these binaries have split people along the heterosexual/homosexual continuum, and the projection of madness and badness on to lesbian and gay identities is seen in the criminalization and pathologization of homosexuality (Butler, 1993; D. Davies & Neal, 1996; Fuss, 1991; Hall, 1997a; King & Bartlett, 1999; McColl, 1994; Rutherford, 1990; Sibley, 1995; Stevens & Hall, 1991). Othering takes place not only through projection but also through erasure and silencing (Butler, 1991); silence and shame are also entwined (Wilton, 2000), and, as noted in the section on health care experience, the liberal humanism underpinning nursing can have the effect of silencing and erasing difference. In terms of identity, the process of Othering, in which a person feels that he or she has not lived up to ideals, can result in a sense of shame (Giddens, 1991).

Resistance to Othering has been identified through the study of lesbian and gay communities (e.g., D. Bell & Valentine, 1995; Duncan, 1996; J. Hart & Richardson, 1981; Munt, 1998; Richardson, 1992; Sampson, 1993; Shotter & Gergen, 1989) and by looking at how people identify in relation to community (e.g., Butler, 1995; Clark, 2002; Clarke, 1998; hooks, 1990; Myslik, 1996; Weeks, 1991). However, to date, such studies have not really explored resistance to pathologizing identities by people who are also suffering from mental health problems; what has taken place has been the study of the celebratory: the study of survivors who have resisted pathologization and made their own identities and communities. In such celebration, the shame/pride dichotomy has unwittingly been re-inscribed, with pride being a place that can be inhabited only by the well-adjusted. However, these studies, through their theorization of Othering, lend an understanding to how resistance can be understood and made sense of. In particular, a theoretical understanding of the process of Othering allows an exposure of the underlying dualisms that shape our identities.

Research methods that help to uncover or side-step these dualisms are the most appropriate ways of analyzing experiences in which these dualisms are at work. Such approaches are identified in Chapter 3, following a detailed methodological discussion about the limits of both realist and constructionist approaches to understanding and interpreting both identities and experiences and to interpreting resistance and silence. The methodological position arrived at following this discussion is that both realist and constructionist approaches lend some understanding to interpreting data about people's identities and experiences, but ultimately, an approach that straddles this epistemological divide (in this case, the use of positioning theory) helps to give a fuller and more complete understanding of how people resist, negotiate, and contest the erasure and pathologization of sexual identities in health care; very little research has been done on illness and identity, or health care and identity, using such approaches, but where it has been done, striking parallels are found between negotiating sexual identities and negotiating other pathologized or stigmatized identities in health care settings (Parker et al., 1995; Ussher, 1997a; Willig, 1999; Yardley, 1997c).

CONCLUSION

The literature clearly points to inadequacies in the delivery of care and the pervasiveness of homophobia and heterosexism in both general and mental health care. In particular, it would seem that the pathologization of lesbian and gay identities, silencing about sexual identity, and issues relating to nondisclosure are especially relevant in mental health care. However, the literature gives little indication of how these processes affect people if they are seeking mental health care at a time in their life when they perceive their mental health issues to be associated with their struggle to negotiate their sexual identity (i.e., coming out). Given the research to date showing the mental health vulnerability of lesbians and gay men who are negotiating and managing their sexual identity, it seems important to investigate further the nature of mental health encounters at such times. A further in-depth exploration of these experiences might usefully point to ways in which access to mental health care can be improved for lesbians and gay men who are coming out. In this study, then, I set out to look in detail at the nature of these mental health encounters with a view to developing understanding about the ways in which homophobia and heterosexism operate in mental health care settings and their impact on people who are presenting with mental health issues in which their sexual identity is implicated. The initial review of the empirical literature helped me to refine the original research aim and to design a study that would build on the existing knowledge base. The theoretical work, much of which came from a broadly poststructuralist perspective, helped to situate those empirical research findings and give a purchase on how descriptive "experience of illness" type studies could be built on to inform understanding about access to care in a more sophisticated way. The theories of identity that were located in a poststructuralist framework highlighted some of the methodological challenges for this investigation. The tensions in the shame/pride dichotomy, which set this research project in motion, were mirrored by tensions in epistemology and methodology arising from a further set of dualisms.

Chapter 3
On Not Grasping the Nettle*

The particular research questions asked in this research and the nature of those questions, together with the lack of a coherent or robust prior theory, demanded an approach to the research that is exploratory and that might enable concept development rather than an approach that is hypothetico-deductive. The research needed to be located within a qualitative paradigm premised on a search for meaning, or *Verstehen*, in which the researcher adopts a phenomenological approach to gain an understanding of experience from the point of view of the research participants. Within the qualitative paradigm, there is also a recognition of the process of interpretation, the negotiation of intersubjective meanings, and the importance of understanding the complexity of experiences in context (Henwood & Pidgeon, 1992, 1994).

The selection of appropriate methods to address the research questions in terms of how to gather data, how to analyze them, and how to assess the status of the research findings requires a consideration of the researcher's positions regarding epistemology and ontology. This consideration can be located within wider debates that have engaged those adopting qualitative approaches in psychology and other human sciences. Qualitative methods and inductive approaches, such as grounded theory, have been used now for

---

* To "grasp the nettle" means to confront and deal with an unpleasant and potentially painful situation. The nettle plant has leaves that sting if they are touched lightly but do not sting if grasped firmly.

some time in the human sciences. However, an increasing dissatisfaction within psychology, with the continued dominance of positivism even within qualitative approaches (B. Davies, 1998; Woolgar, 1996), has led some psychologists at the critical edge of the discipline to call for more attention to be paid to the ways in which a social constructionist or constructivist perspective can inform understanding of social and (broadly defined) psychological processes. This shift has been marked by some as the discursive turn in psychology, leading to the adoption of methods such as discourse analysis (Harré, 1995; Stainton-Rogers, 1996) and contextualist or constructivist revisions of methods such as grounded theory (e.g., B. Davies, 1998; Woolgar, 1996).

Continued methodological debate has led more recently to a position that also questions the usefulness of constructionist approaches and cautions against the exclusive use of this perspective, as it, too, can lead to the loss of a vital perspective on how the world is understood (Gergen, 1998). Increasingly, researchers are developing methodological positions that allow us to view and interpret data through multiple lenses (Denzin & Lincoln, 1998, 1994). Up until recently, such mixing of methods would have been regarded as flawed if the methods or lenses used were underpinned by different and incompatible epistemological positions. However, these approaches are becoming more common, and in epistemological terms, they straddle the polarized and dualistic positions between realism, positivism, and empiricism, on the one hand, and relativism, idealism, and constructionism, on the other. Some have defined this epistemological position as critical realism, and others have characterized it as a material-discursive approach (Pilgrim & Rogers, 1997; Sayer, 2000; Ussher, 1996; Yardley, 1997c).

In this study, I interpreted the data using multiple lenses that belonged within different epistemological traditions. This combination of approaches produced an interpretation within a material-discursive framework; this allowed a phenomenological thematic interpretation of some aspects of the data clearly grounded in people's accounts of their experiences and also allowed an interpretation of other aspects of the data that were more complex and were better informed by a constructionist worldview. I analyzed the data initially using a technique called interpretative phenomenological analysis, which shares many of the assumptions of grounded theory. A further analysis was then conducted using discourse analytical approaches. By combining these approaches, it is possible to begin to see how lesbians' and gay men's experiences of mental health care are mediated by the social context in which these experiences are embedded and the positions that people adopt or are placed in.

To locate the method used in this study, in this chapter, I set out how debates about epistemology regarding the analysis of qualitative data have developed over recent years. I begin by looking at developments from positivism to handle data in a postpositivist light and then examine the contribution of social constructionist approaches. We will see that views on epistemology have polarized; this will be followed by a consideration of how a critical-realist, or material-discursive, approach, which straddles this epistemological divide, might help us to arrive at a more complex understanding of the data collected for this study. The resulting approach is one in which the researcher works as a bricoleur in the way described by Denzin and Lincoln (1998, 1994) in their discussion of the developments of the fifth and sixth moments in qualitative research.

QUESTIONS OF EPISTEMOLOGY AND ONTOLOGY

Questions of method are secondary to questions about the nature of reality and how that reality can be known or the relationship between the inquirer and the world that he or she attempts to understand. Within the natural sciences, a realist ontology is assumed (i.e., of a tangible world out there that can be discovered along with its deterministic laws of cause and effect), and it is assumed that this world can be known through methods of inquiry that emphasize objectivity and control. The application of this positivist paradigm—with its associated empiricist epistemology, experimental methods, and concerns with issues of validity and reliability—to the study of human beings rather than the natural world has long been criticized (J. Smith, Harré, & Van Langenhove, 1995b, 1995c). Henwood and Pidgeon (1992) highlighted the role of the 19th-century philosopher Wilhelm Dilthey, who stated that the human sciences should be premised on a search for meaning or understanding (Verstehen) rather than a search for causal relations and deterministic laws.

The alternative epistemological positions are seen in the interpretative or naturalistic paradigm which has been influenced by hermeneutics, phenomenology, and constructivism (Henwood & Pidgeon, 1992). This paradigm is less concerned with (and sometimes denies the possibility of) detachment and objectivity on the part of the researcher and is more concerned with acknowledging the role of the researcher in interpreting or even co-constructing reality with those who are being researched. The roots of the epistemological positions and associated methods in this alternative paradigm differ according to the discipline and theoretical concerns of those conducting the research. A number of influences include symbolic interactionism, social constructionism, and phenomenology, along with the more recent poststructuralist and postmodernist perspectives (Yardley, 1997b). Although these different traditions share a skepticism about the value of positivism in our understanding of the human sciences and tend to privilege qualitative methods as legitimate modes of inquiry, considerable debate and tension concerning ontological and epistemological positions remain.

Part of the critique of positivism, and its associated realism, has been that it entails the adoption of a dualistic framework for understanding the world, and, in particular, the mind-body dualism limits our ability to understand psychological processes (Yardley, 1999). Other dualisms set up within this paradigm are those between subjectivity and objectivity (Yardley, 1999) and the individual and society (C. Griffin & Phoenix, 1994). The implications of the individual/society dualism will be discussed first.

The individual/society dualism within health psychology has reproduced the medical gaze of the body that is seen in biomedical discourse, and although it has incorporated the mind, this is still at the expense of any understanding of social processes (Murray & Chamberlain, 1999). It has also been argued that positivism has had a strong influence on nursing practice and nursing research through the influence of the patriarchal medical model; this has led to dualistic thought patterns and the intolerance of diversity, which contribute further to the oppressive nature of nursing (Wilson-Thomas, 1995). The individual/society dualism dominates Western, or modernist, thinking, and it is therefore the hardest to register, as it is so thoroughly normalized, underpinning as it does the liberal humanist thinking that represents the dominant value system of our society. Furthermore, Lister (1997) has said that the enlightenment discourse of the primacy of the individual is a central feature of modernist nursing, but, in line with critiques of liberal humanism generally, he asserted that this stance unduly emphasizes personal responsibility for health and fails to take into account the ways in which the sociocultural-political world influences nursing practice. The individual/society dualism implicit within liberal humanism privileges the individual as a rational, unitary subject with free will and free choice (Rothfield, 1990). In this scheme of things, society is no more than an aggregation of individuals, and society, or the social, is absolved of any responsibility for the actions of individuals (Parker et al., 1995).

Further dualisms that map onto the privileged unitary individual are the splits between private and public life and between the personal and the political. Liberal humanism erases difference (Seidler, 1994), but at the same time, it is heteronormative and patriarchal; this means that individuals who are different will be treated as if they are the same as that which is at the centre of this discourse, that is, the privileged subject, who is at least White, heterosexual, and male (Hall, 1997b; Jackson, 1996; Rutherford, 1990). If they are not the same, then they will be construed as deviant and, as Stainton-Rogers (1996) has said,

> Liberal-humanism is not half as benign or egalitarian as it has been made out to be. It can be profoundly ethnocentric, and it can serve to bolster the power injustices that run through the relationships between men and women, the rich and the poor, and indeed anywhere where there are differentials of power. (p. 75)

Furthermore, the discursive practices inscribed by the dominant value system of liberal humanism are only one short step away from victim blaming (Nightingale & Cromby, 1999; Parker et al., 1995).

However, it would seem that the attempt to counter the dominance of the positivist paradigm in the human sciences has spawned its own set of dualisms: the material versus representations (Ussher, 1997b), cognitions versus discourse (J. Smith, 1996a), realism versus idealism, empiricism versus relativism, and foundationalism versus relativism (Maynard, 1994). A further polarization or dualism can be seen in the debates between essentialists and social constructionists. This perhaps can account in part for Yardley's (1996) and Ussher's (1997b) observations that the physical dimensions of health and illness are often missing from accounts about the personal experiences of health and illness. There have been critiques of what has been represented as the nihilistic relativism of discursive and social constructionist approaches, where nothing can be "decided" about the world (Pilgrim & Rogers, 1997).

Attempts have also been made to reconcile the binary divide between material and discursive approaches (e.g., Ussher, 1997b; Yardley, 1997b) and to transcend disciplinary and epistemological boundaries by mixing methods when attempting to address particular research questions (e.g., Boyle & McEvoy, 1998; Gough, 2002; Henwood, 1993; Willott & Griffin, 1997). However, before we attempt to transcend dualisms and disciplinary and epistemological boundaries, it would be useful to look at the contributions and limitations of social constructionist and discursive approaches and the extent to which they can be used to inform this particular inquiry. According to Yardley (1997b), discursive approaches recognize the "socially and linguistically mediated nature of human experience" (p. 1) and are theoretically informed by the perspectives of postmodernism, poststructuralism, and social constructionism. These perspectives have "converged to argue that knowledge and identities are fractured...Hence, they promote a radical scepticism about the possibilities for knowledge" (Henwood & Nicolson, 1995, p. 110). Those advocating for a discursive approach to psychology have challenged psychology's object of study as a bounded individual because of the problems of incorporating social processes. They have argued that discursive psychology can help in an analysis of the diversity and complexity of individual experiences within an account of how that experience is mediated by and lived within a social context (Morgan, 1999).

The underlying ontological and epistemological assumptions of social constructionist and discursive approaches are idealist and relativist; that is, what is taken to be real is seen as a construction in the minds of individuals, and meaningful constructions are multiple and conflicting (Schwandt, 1994). Furthermore, constructivists take an anti-essentialist position. They take what is assumed to be self-evident and question whether the taken-for-granted is actually the product of complicated discursive practices (Schwandt, 1994). Discursive practices are "the different ways in which people, through their discourses, actively produce psychological and social realities" (Spink, 1999, p. 88). *Discourse* can be taken to mean the institutionalized use of language or language-like systems (Spink, 1999), seeing language, talk, and text as constructive of reality rather than a way of getting at an underlying reality (Gill, 1996), or used to refer to a coherent system of meanings (e.g., a "biomedical discourse") (Yardley, 1997a). This latter definition is more Foucauldian than the others, in that it infers more about knowledge and power relations. One further use of the term *discourse* is to refer to the way in which talk and texts function as social practices in local and flexible ways through interpretative repertoires (Potter, 1996), defined as a set of terms, descriptions, and figures of speech, often clustered around particular metaphors, that are used as building blocks for constructing versions of events or for performing specific functions (Yardley, 1997a).

Coyle (2000), in attempting to bring together the disparate ways in which the term *discourse* is used, has suggested that discourses can be seen as "sets of linguistic material that have a degree of coherence in their content and organisation and which perform constructive functions in broadly defined social contexts" (p. 245). It is important to note that any such use of language is not necessarily seen as intentional. The different ways in which the term is used, either to mean local interpretative repertoires or in a wider, more Foucauldian, sense will vary according to whether a micro or macro analysis of discourse is undertaken (Stainton-Rogers, 1996). Some discursive researchers will combine both to show "how people draw on wider systems of meaning to construct and defend their own particular position or perspective" (Yardley, 1997a, p. 32).

Thus, social constructionist and discursive approaches have been used to create alternative ways of seeing things, challenge existing practices and power relationships, publicize suppressed discourses (Yardley, 1997a), and contribute to ideological critique and understanding of the ways in which power relations of "domination and subordination are reproduced and justified" (Gill, 1996, p. 156). Examples of how discursive research has been used in psychology are given by Willig (1998). These include the work of Parker et al. (1995), who have questioned what is taken for granted, such as psychopathology. A further example of how discursive research is used in psychology is given by Potter (1996), who has used it to help to illuminate how racist practice and the blaming of minority groups is legitimated and how blame and responsibility are managed.

Discursive and constructionist approaches would then seem to be particularly useful for looking at how sexual identities are managed and, in particular, how they are negotiated in health care encounters. However, a further set of debates and tensions concerning the utility of this approach have developed. These debates are particularly relevant to this study, as they are concerned with the ways in which constructionist approaches can fail to take into account material conditions, such as oppression and the corporeal dimension of illness. The aim of this study is to explore and understand an illness experience that has a strong social dimension; that is, the mental health problems and mental health care that the participants in this study had received needed to be understood as having a material dimension in terms of how homophobia and heterosexism contribute to both the development of mental health problems and subsequent health care experiences.

A number of authors have questioned the applicability of extreme social constructionist approaches to understanding areas of human activity that have a material or embodied aspect and, in so doing, question the extreme ontological idealism and epistemological relativism of these approaches. Yardley (1996) has argued that such approaches have merely inverted the dualisms of more traditional scientific modes of inquiry, and little account is then taken of what she termed the "material." Ussher (1996) went on to suggest that some of the material aspects of experience that get neglected are the influence of biology, age, social class, race, and sexual identity; Gergen (1998), more dramatically, said that although social constructionism was born of opposition and appealed to the marginalized, "the constructionist axe turned back to gash the hand of the user. There was no power structure, race or gender oppression...that was not itself constructed" (p. 147). Extreme relativists state that their approach challenges the taken-for-granted and have said that this should allow for openness and change (D. Edwards, Ashmore, & Potter, 1995; Potter, 1998). However, it has been argued that extreme relativist approaches are not used to effect social change and that the inherent deconstruction of these approaches makes it difficult to talk about oppressed groups, because the categories themselves are problematized

(Burr, 1998). Ultimately, a number of authors have argued for attempts to reconcile material and discursive approaches, as each on its own limits the ways in which we can usefully know the world (see edited collections by Parker, 1998; Ussher, 1997a; and Yardley, 1997c).

The discussion so far might indicate that researchers can position themselves only on one side or the other of epistemological and ontological dichotomies as either realist empiricists or idealist relativists, but a number of other possible positionings exist (Hammersley, 1996). For example, Schwandt (1994) holds that a constructivist need not be an anti-realist, and B. Davies (1998) has said that critical realists and ontological relativists attempt to straddle the binary divide between realism and relativism. Debate has also ensued about the extent to which researchers must position themselves in consistent and compatible ways. These debates concern the transgression of disciplinary boundaries and appropriate use of methodologies and methods. Some researchers have attempted to reconcile and combine seemingly incompatible epistemological positions and methodologies (e.g., Henwood, 1993; Yardley, 1996). These same researchers have also argued for the need to transgress disciplinary boundaries. It is important to be mindful of this when addressing issues relating to "validity" and note Potter's (1996) caution that such interdisciplinarity can lead to superficial theorizing and loose analysis.

However problematic, this mixing of epistemological positions and methodological approaches is becoming increasingly common within the qualitative paradigm and fits with the general call by Denzin and Lincoln (1998) for the qualitative researcher to be a bricoleur. The researcher-as-bricoleur works within and between competing and overlapping paradigms and perspectives, piecing together multiple methods and strategies in a pragmatic, reflexive, and strategic manner to address particular research questions that are understood to have a context. The result is a bricolage that is a "complex, dense, reflexive, collage-like creation that represents the researcher's images, understandings, and interpretations of the world or phenomenon under analysis" (Denzin & Lincoln, 1994, p. 3). Such a stance is consonant with material-discursive, or critical-realist, approaches to investigating issues relating to health psychology that break away from a necessary link between particular epistemologies and associated methodologies, instead advocating the use of multiple methods, although they would be used in a skeptical manner (Ussher, 1996).

Material-discursive approaches involve an attempt to straddle the divide between realism and relativism. They are an attempt to embrace physical and material aspects of existence and experience in a nonrealist manner and, in so doing, attempt to side-step dualist frameworks (Yardley, 1999). The researcher also attempts to explicate the mutual and reciprocal influence between discursive practices and the material domain (Ussher, 1997b) but in a way that goes beyond a simple notion of interaction, as in the biopsychosocial model, which remains dualistic and mechanistic (Yardley, 1999). However, arriving at a nondualist perspective is not necessarily easy—requiring a profound and disturbing shift—but it would lead to a different research objective, namely,

> to develop a detailed, multi-layered, insightful interpretation of a phenomenon, and to consider explicitly the way in which the context, the participants and the researchers have jointly contributed to the understanding acquired in the course of the investigation. (p. 32)

One way in which this can be achieved, and it is emphasized in critical realist and feminist standpoint approaches, is by accepting, although not necessarily privileging, the legitimacy of lay knowledge and investigating a phenomenon through the participants' eyes (Ussher, 1996). A further advantage of this approach is that it has the potential to produce explanations that are less pathologizing or victim blaming than many of the models produced by mainstream research (Stoppard, 1997). Such an approach is consonant with the aims of this project, which are to investigate the health care experiences of lesbians and gay men while taking into account the material conditions of homophobia and heterosexism without blaming or further pathologizing those whose experiences are being investigated.

Adopting a material-discursive position, together with the particular objectives of the research, requires, then, a consideration of the most appropriate way of gathering data and analyzing them. I took the approach to data collection of in-depth semistructured interviews to engage with the meanings and complexities of personal experiences of health care. This epistemological commitment to the qualitative paradigm also required a method of analysis that explicitly acknowledged the interpretative role of the researcher while attempting to gain an "insider" perspective on the participants' worlds (J. Smith, Flowers, & Osborn, 1997). Furthermore, though, in adopting a material-discursive approach, I also required another method of analysis that took into account the social context of individual experiences and discursive practices that constructed those experiences. The method used initially in this study was developed by Smith and colleagues (1997) and is known as interpretative phenomenological analysis, or IPA. Following this analysis, a discursive analysis was also conducted, and the two methods of analysis were juxtaposed to produce a material-discursive understanding of participants' mental health care experiences. I will now discuss the method of IPA in detail, leading to an explication of the limits of this method of analysis for this particular study, followed by a discussion of how it was juxtaposed with a more discursive approach.

INTERPRETATIVE PHENOMENOLOGICAL ANALYSIS (IPA)

Epistemologically, Smith (1995, p. 10) adopts what could loosely be viewed as a critical realist perspective, in which it is

assumed that what a respondent says in [an] interview has some ongoing significance for him or her and that there is some, though not a transparent, relationship between what that person says and beliefs or psychological constructs that he or she can be said to hold. (p. 10)

Using IPA, a researcher seeks to engage with the way participants think and act to reflect their perspectives through allowing them to tell their own stories in their own words. It is thus concerned with personal accounts rather than objective statements, although these personal accounts are seen as representing some sort of psychological reality (Flowers, Smith, Sheeran, & Beail, 1997a; J. Smith, Flowers, et al., 1997). It is thus underpinned theoretically by phenomenology and also by symbolic interactionism, itself influenced by Husserl's phenomenology, which, in turn, leads to an emphasis on interpretation in elucidating the negotiated meanings of participants (J. Smith, Flowers, et al., 1997).

In terms of where IPA is situated in the debates about ontology and epistemology, J. Smith (1995) stated that his approach is consonant with the grounded theory of Charmaz (1995). However, the position that both Smith and Charmaz take is not all that clear. Charmaz has said that grounded theory can bridge positivistic and interpretative methods and is credited with a constructivist revisioning of Glaser and Strauss's (1967) grounded theory (Henwood & Pidgeon, 1994), However, Charmaz ultimately argues for an empiricist position. Smith has also said that the underlying ontological position of IPA is realist, assuming a chain of connection between accounts, cognitions, and behaviors (Flowers et al., 1997a) but also, paradoxically, claimed that phenomenological and discursively oriented approaches could potentially be combined (J. Smith, 1996a).

Where Charmaz (1995) and J. Smith (1995, 1996) concur, however, is in the idea that the data are actively co-constructed by researchers and their participants. Researchers traveling this particular route invariably invoke the idea of reflexivity to try to address the problems arising in this interpretative process from the researchers' own preconceived ideas and the effects of prior experience (Flick, 1998; Henwood & Pidgeon, 1994). What becomes apparent in this exploration of epistemological and ontological positioning is that one can either try to grasp one of the nettles or move around in the middle and get stung from all sides. The idea that it is not a matter of grasping nettles has perhaps been best put by Henwood and Pidgeon (1994), who said that there is

> an epistemological tension at the heart of the naturalistic paradigm, which Hammersley (1989) calls the "dilemma of qualitative method." Put simply, this arises from a simultaneous commitment to, on the one hand, realism (and inductively reflecting participants' accounts and naturalistic contexts), and on the other, constructivism, which includes, amongst other things, actively encouraging the researcher in the creative and interpretative process of generating new understandings and theory. Philosophically speaking, theory cannot simply emerge from the data. Observation is always set within pre-existing concepts, and this then raises the question of what grounds grounded theory?" (p. 232)

Henwood and Pidgeon's (1994) solution to this dilemma is to work with a more constructivist version of grounded theory, which they have characterized as a process of "flip-flop" between data and conceptualization, which they link to Charmaz's (1995) constructivist revision. This explicitly acknowledges the role played in the analysis by the researcher's prior frameworks derived from schools of thought, disciplines, and personal experiences. Ultimately, a number of ways of working with this tension exist, but what is fundamental is that the tension must be worked with, not against (see, for example, Fine, 1994; Hammersley, 1996; Holland & Ramazanoglu, 1994). It is perhaps only through using particular methods and realizing their limitations that one can arrive at a position of beginning to work with that tension. It would seem appropriate, then, to take some time to consider the use of IPA in more detail and then explore ways of dealing with the tensions that arise in the interpretative process.

IPA AS A METHOD

The aim when using IPA is to undertake a detailed exploration of the participant's view of the topic being investigated through the analysis of verbal material derived from in-depth semistructured interviewing in which the researcher attempts as much as possible to enter the psychological and social world of the person interviewed (J. Smith, 1995; J. Smith, Osborn, &

Jarman, 1999) (see Chapter 4). It is recognized that in the attempt to get close to the phenomenal world of the participant, the researcher's own conceptions are necessary but complicate access to and interpretation of that world. Smith et al. (1999) stated quite clearly that there should be no prescriptive way of conducting analysis, as the process of interpretation is ultimately personal, but they do suggest working in detail with one initial interview transcript before incorporating other interview material, with the gradual and cautious build-up of theory or more general categorization. This falls within a more general idiographic approach (J. Smith, Harré, & Van Langenhove, 1995a; J. Smith, Osborn, et al., 1999). I will discuss this in more detail later in this section.

The analysis of verbatim transcribed interview material requires a "sustained engagement with the text and a process of interpretation," which is an iterative rather than linear process (J. Smith, 1995, p. 18). Each of the many rereadings of the initial material analyzed is likely to produce new insights, and as new themes emerge from later material, the earlier material must be revisited to test out the new themes, which can "enlighten, modify or become subordinate to [those] previously elicited" (p. 21). Smith has suggested a close reading of and engagement with the text, against which analysts should note anything that strikes them as interesting or significant; these might be emerging themes, connections between themes, or preliminary interpretations. This is followed by an attempt to cluster themes into some sort of hierarchical order of super- and subordinate categories, with an instance given for each master or superordinate theme identified (J. Smith, 1995). This process is repeated cyclically and with additional interview material until a final coherent list of master or superordinate themes is produced. This ultimately requires a process of selection, not on the basis of prevalence but based on the richness of the data and the extent to which each theme illuminates other aspects of the account (J. Smith, Osborn, et al., 1999).

This method of analysis can be applied to a single case study, or an initial interview can be analyzed in this way and used as a starting point for subsequent analysis of a small number of interviews, which might lead to cautious generalizations. The method can also be used to analyze larger data sets, either following the same procedures or starting with the analysis of a small subset of cases to generate themes, which are then searched for, elaborated on, and refined in the larger data set (J. Smith, 1995). Smith, Osborn, et al. (1999) also suggested that handling large data sets might require a more exploratory analysis, in which one or two themes of mutual relevance across the data are identified early on and theorized at a group level. These are then focused on in more detail, allowing consideration of how these themes interrelate as well as of personally distinct experiences within those themes. This approach still requires an in-depth engagement with one initial interview or subset of interviews, but the researcher undertakes a broader level of coding than in the case study approach. The analyst is then primed or oriented to looking for previously identified clusters of themes in subsequently analyzed interviews. This method also allows for a greater degree of freedom with respect to the initial selection of themes to focus on for further analysis (J. Smith, Osborn, et al., 1999). A larger data set can also be used to begin generating grounded theory (J. Smith, Flowers, et al., 1997).

Regardless of the approach used in relation to the size of the data set, J. Smith, Flowers, et al. (1999) suggested that as part of the iterative process, the analyst should continually return to the original transcript material to check that as themes are clustered or organized, the connections work for the primary source material or what the person actually said as a way of reducing the researcher's bias in the process of selection. A further point is the insistence with the use of IPA that themes should be seen to "emerge" from the data; that is, material should be introduced by participants without cues or prompts from the interviewer, and such material should be clearly reflected in verbatim content (J. Smith, 1995). This method has been used in a number of studies to access the phenomenal worlds of people in relation to health care and illness experience (e.g., Flowers et al., 1997a; Golsworthy & Coyle, 1998; Jarman, Smith, & Walsh, 1997; Osborn & Smith, 1998), but it relies on people's being able to articulate that experience, as the analysis must be grounded in the participants' own words (Osborn & Smith, 1998).

Herein lies a tension that arises when we attempt to interpret ambiguities and silences in people's accounts and also in exploring further the impact of their experience. J. Smith and colleagues (Smith, Harré, et al., 1995a; Smith, Osborn, et al., 1999) have said that the method can be used to explore ambiguities and complexities. Rennie, Phillips, and Quartaro (1988) made this point regarding grounded theory. Smith (1996a) has also made the suggestion that IPA could be used with discursive approaches, but as yet, no publications have explored this possibility. Osborn and Smith (1998) have argued a place for both types of analysis, in that despite seemingly incompatible theoretical perspectives and epistemological positions, people's accounts can be seen both as indicative of people's underlying beliefs and as linguistic devices that people use to account for themselves in particular ways. They noted that people's accounts do both things, not one to the exclusion of the other, and they went on to argue for an intermediate position, in which people's accounts are seen as "complex, dynamic and shifting entities formed and reformed, in this case, as patients struggle to make sense of their condition and to articulate that struggle to the listener" (p. 80).

However, there remains a tension in adopting this position and using IPA when attempting to interpret omissions, silences, and contradictions, partly because of the previously mentioned insistence on grounding analysis in the participants' words but also because of the relationship between IPA and prior theory. Although J. Smith (1996b) said that developments need to be made to see how phenomenological and discursive approaches can be integrated, this work remains to be done.

This study is an attempt to resolve the dilemma by juxtaposing IPA with a more discursive analysis, following the recent call to adopt the use of mixed methods, complementing phenomenological analyses and grounded theory approaches with discursive analyses and tolerating multiple viewpoints (Yardley, 1997a, 1997b). Yardley (1997a) has been critical of the "experience of illness" approach arising from a phenomenological perspective that has been slow to recognize the sociocultural processes in the construction of shared meanings. In a similar vein, Pilgrim and Rogers (1997) have been critical of the individualism intrinsic to interpretive humanism or Verstehen approaches. Therefore, although J. Smith (1996b) has said that IPA could be used in a more discursive way, in practice, published studies, which adhere to the methodological insistence on thoroughly grounding findings in verbatim accounts, tend toward analyses that are more phenomenological than interpretative. Researchers might take into account the local social context but not the broader social and discursive practices in which the subject of inquiry might be embedded. However, approaches such as IPA and grounded theory are particularly useful at beginning exploration of areas where there is little in the way of prior formal theory to draw on.

This use of grounded theory and IPA to explore undertheorized areas of research needs further discussion in terms of both their contribution to research and the limitations of the approaches. They allow the exploration of a field where formal theory or grand theory is either lacking or inadequately explains the problems of interest to the researcher (Henwood & Pidgeon, 1992, 1995; J. Smith et al., 1997), or is confining because existing theory or models are, for example, androcentric (Henwood & Pidgeon, 1995). Furthermore, J. Smith (1995a) has argued for the need in psychology to build theory from case studies using an idiographic rather than a nomothetic approach. These methods are thus particularly useful in nascent disciplines (Archer, 1988), such as nursing, health psychology, and lesbian and gay psychology, as they allow an openness to exploring complex problems (Flick, 1998) with recognition of the "extent to which we share with our participants all the problems of and possibilities of making sense of the world" in a way that quantitative approaches obscure (Grbich, 1999, p. 23). They can also "represent context-specific understandings, as well as guarding against overwriting participants' internally structured subjectivities with externally imposed 'objective' systems of meaning" (Griffin, 1986, cited in Henwood & Pidgeon, 1995). However, this position forces a return to the question posed earlier: What grounds grounded theory?

Henwood and Pidgeon (1995) and Charmaz (1995), in their call for a constructionist revision of the method of grounded theory, have explicated more fully the relationship between prior theory and grounded theory. The grounded theory approach has been characterized as purely inductive, and Morse and Field (1996) have noted that some researchers would not even conduct a review of the literature before entering the field. However, Flick (1998) claimed that this is a misrepresentation of grounded theory and that the postponement relates not to theoretical structuring but to hypothesizing. Charmaz (1990) argued that the researchers' perspectives should be informed by their discipline, personal experiences, and values, leading to a set of sensitizing concepts. Pidgeon (1996) went on to argue for a more discursive form of analysis within grounded theory that leads to "the 'everyday' being interpreted in terms of wider social contexts and power relations" and said that the method of constant comparison "with its emphasis upon exploration of variety and difference in meaning, might potentially serve as a vehicle for a deconstructive form of analysis" (p. 83).

Henwood and Pidgeon (1995) also discussed how a feminist research perspective can move us on from a purely phenomenological approach or pure induction through highlighting the centrality of women's accounts, but these accounts are, nevertheless, mediated by social and cultural frameworks. Stoppard (1997) explicated further this relationship between women's accounts and available discourses, arguing that an understanding of women's depression must start from the perspective of women, but women's uses of dominant discourses might obscure the social relations of depression. She did go on to argue, though, that these accounts might reveal the limitations of contemporary conceptualizations of depression. J. Smith, Flowers, et al. (1997) have been less forthcoming than Henwood and Pidgeon on how IPA might be applied in a more discursive way, and it would seem that both methods, IPA and grounded theory, cannot adequately account for silence and omission in texts. Although this ultimately might say something about the limitations of relying on interview material, it would seem most appropriate at this juncture to juxtapose IPA with another method of analysis. In this case, a discourse analysis was also undertaken following in the trend to mix methods in this way when exploring complex issues. I also thought that a discursive analysis might help to explicate the interpretative framework of the researcher as well as the researched (Fine, 1992, 1994; Gillett, 1995).

THE (RE)TURN TO DISCOURSE

The necessity of combining discourse analysis with IPA emerged through an engagement with the texts (when I was analyzing the interviews using IPA), in which it became clear that participants often seemed unable to articulate certain experiences or remained silent. Gill (1996) said that discourse analysis requires sensitivity to language but also to what is not said. One of the central procedures of discourse analysis is deconstruction, which is a process of revealing the ideological constraints on what can and cannot be said through searching for dichotomies. These dichotomies reveal dominant discourses and subordinate discourses that are hidden or stifled (Yardley, 1997a). In one particular study, a grounded theory and discursive analysis of women's experiences of abortion, prior theory, including what is known about currently available discourses about abortion, was used to interpret some of the silences, contradictions, and apparent uncertainties in women's accounts (Boyle & McEvoy, 1998). Heaphy (1998) has also argued that we must listen beyond what is explicitly voiced in interviews to understand silences and to arrive at possible interpretations. Such interpretations relate to power relations between the researched and researchers as well as between the researched and health care providers implicated in the health care experiences being researched.

What was required in the analysis of the data for this project was an explicit recognition of the power relations between the researched and their health care practitioners. This required a prior theoretical commitment to locating these experiences in wider discursive practices relating to medicalization and the effects of homophobia and heterosexism. This necessitated using a macro discourse perspective, in which it was possible to interpret and understand the accounts of the research participants about the ways in which they positioned themselves in relation to discursive practices.

DISCOURSE ANALYSIS

The decision to undertake a discursive analysis requires a further discussion about types of discourse analysis (DA), their theoretical roots, and epistemological differences between proponents of different perspectives. Ultimately, all proponents of discourse analysis adhere to a social constructionist epistemology (Coyle, 2000), but within this there are different perspectives about degrees of constructionism and the uses to which DA can be put (Gillies, 1999). What discourse analysts have in common is that they understand language to be constitutive of reality. This can be seen in broad social terms, whereby the power to define something in a particular way produces knowledge and power. Such a position arises from the influences of the French philosophical traditions of structuralism and poststructuralism, and most notably from the work of Foucault (Burr, 1995). Another way of seeing language as constitutive of reality focuses on the performative aspects of discourse and what people do with their talk (Burr, 1995). This approach has its roots in work on conversation organization and rhetoric (Potter & Wetherell, 1995). Potter and Wetherell have made the distinction between different types of DA as a difference in focus on either discourse practices (what people do with their talk) or on discursive resources (the devices people draw on when engaged in discursive practices). They have argued that although these two approaches can be distinguished, they can also be used together, depending on the nature of what is being investigated.

Burr (1995) has also argued that the two approaches are not incompatible but that they have different concerns, and said that the macro discourse perspective tends to be more theoretical and less empirical than the micro discourse perspective. However, Potter et al. (cited in Burr, 1995) have said that what they do can rightly be termed DA, whereas those such as Parker are engaged in something that should be termed "analysis of discourse." Deconstructive approaches are subsumed within "analysis of discourse" (Burr, 1995). Lying beneath this are epistemological differences; Potter and others have adopted an extreme relativist position, whereas Parker and others, in resisting this slide into relativism, have taken a critical realist position (Burr, 1995; Gillies, 1999). Although we must be mindful of these epistemological tensions, it is possible to say something about what is being engaged in when analyzing discourses, whether at a macro or micro level; it is possible to develop hypotheses about the purposes and consequences of language (i.e., its functions) (Wetherell & Potter, 1988) and look at how people construct their versions of the world and what they gain from these constructions (Coyle, 2000). Although DA is not strictly a method, there are tools and approaches that can be used to assist in the process of analysis. Ultimately, these approaches are not markedly different, whether one is in engaged in a macro or micro discourse analysis. However, with the latter, more stringent methods are used with transcribed material (Burr, 1995).

Another way in which concepts such as identity can be analyzed through discursive practices is to look at how subjects are positioned. This approach comes from a different tradition within discourse analysis and relates to the work of Davies and Harré (1990). In this understanding of identity, individuals are constructed through discourses, which they can accept, with their attendant obligations, or resist. Furthermore, people's accounts of themselves require some sort of cooperation and, therefore, negotiation with others in terms of how they are positioned or position themselves. Identities are thus produced in relation to culturally and socially available discourses (Burr, 1995). These positions provide us with our subjectivity, and we come to experience the world from that perspective (B. Davies & Harré, 1990). Furthermore, how positions are "offered, accepted or resisted in everyday talk are the discursive practices by which discourses and their associated power implications are brought to life" (Burr, 1995, p. 147). Willig (2000) has argued, however, that even these approaches do not go far enough to enable us to understand people's experiences. She indicated that positioning theory has thus far tended to offer an explanation of subject positions offered by current discourses but has failed to explain how these are implicated in the constitution of subjectivity, experience, and identity: "Our focus needs to shift from the *availability* of discursive resources in the culture to the individual's *appropriation* of (some of) these over time" (Willig, 2000, p. 560, emphasis added).

Willig (2000) went on to say that positioning theory can be used to explain how some subject positions become internalized (in contrast to social constructionist approaches, which view discursive formations as transient and contextual) and actually come to structure an individual's private experience and subsequently define and constrain possible ways-of-being.

DA, then, is an important tool for understanding and interpreting the mental health care experiences of people who are negotiating their sexual identities in a context in which dominant discourses pathologize those identities. It also allows an interrogation of the data in terms of the way in which participants position themselves and the ways in which they might be positioned by health care practitioners. Furthermore, one of the few ways of resisting the dominant discourses around lesbian and gay identities is through silence, and DA and deconstruction in particular provide useful ways of theorizing, contextualizing, and interpreting such silences and resistance. In this study, then, a discursive analysis was used as an adjunct to the more grounded and phenomenological approach of IPA. This allowed an initial analysis of data that thematized shared experiences of health care grounded in verbatim data. The discursive analysis allowed another layer of interpretation with particular attention being given to contradictions and silences in people's accounts.

The methods used in this study all fall within the qualitative paradigm, and many concerns have been voiced about the "validity" of these methods. The term *validity* is specific to methods used within the positivist paradigm, and alternative terms and criteria are evolving for qualitative research (Elliott et al., 1999; Henwood & Pidgeon, 1992; Lyons, 1999; J. Smith, 1996b; Yardley, 2000). I will now discuss these as they relate to this study.

CRITERIA FOR EVALUATING THE WORTH OF QUALITATIVE RESEARCH

Once a nonrealist epistemological position is adopted, the relationship between the knower and what can be known is immediately problematized (Henwood & Pidgeon, 1992). The traditional criteria for evaluating rigorous research in the positivist paradigm, (i.e., validity, reliability with associated notions relating to objectivity, and generalizability), then become untenable (Guba & Lincoln, 1994). Constructionists' attempts to address the issue of how to evaluate qualitative research with alternative criteria such as trustworthiness and authenticity have not yet resolved the issue, as "their parallelism to positivist criteria make[s] them suspect" (Guba & Lincoln, 1994, p. 144). Henwood and Pidgeon (1992) have presented a number of good practices in this area, as have Elliot et al. (1999) and J. Smith (1996b). Smith and Elliot et al. have stated that alternative criteria can be presented only as work in progress at this stage. Lyons (1999) also made the point that any such guidelines will vary with the paradigm in which different qualitative researchers locate their work. Yardley (2000) argued that criteria cannot be fixed for establishing the worth of nonrealist and nonpositivist research where meanings are negotiated and communally co-constructed. Instead she argued for the adoption of criteria that are open to flexible interpretation, as otherwise, "we would limit the criteria for truth (which) would mean restricting the possibilities for knowledge, and would also privilege the perspective of the cultural group whose criteria for truth was deemed 'correct'" (p. 217).

The criteria offered by Henwood and Pidgeon (1992), J. Smith (1996b), and Yardley (2000) have a considerable degree of overlap save for some criteria specific to particular methods, such as grounded theory (e.g., theoretical sampling and negative-case analysis). However, the criteria offered by Yardley are more comprehensive and will therefore form the framework for this discussion. Yardley has suggested four key dimensions that can be used to assess the quality of research using qualitative methods:

1. sensitivity to context,
2. commitment and rigor,
3. transparency and coherence, and
4. impact and importance.

The concern with sensitivity to context concerns the importance of prior theory; although prior theory will influence interpretation and might even be necessary, a need to remain sensitive to the data remains (Yardley, 2000).

Henwood and Pidgeon (1992) suggested making explicit how the researcher arrives at the categories and called this sensitivity to the data "the importance of fit," meaning the fit between interpretation and data. Another component of sensitivity to context, discussed by Yardley, is the need to be aware of the sociocultural setting of the research and its impact on the meaning and function of phenomena. As Altheide and Johnson (1998) have stated, "a valid interpretation without a context is impossible, and an account needs to "point out the multiplicity of meanings and perspectives, and the rationality of these perspectives, by setting forth the contexts(s)" (pp. 306-307). Context is important here in terms of the research setting and the researcher: "The listener contributes to what is said...by actively or passively invoking the relative identities and shared understandings which provide the framework for speech" (Yardley, 2000, p. 221).

Denzin and Lincoln (1998) have discussed how postmodernist and poststructural thinking has attacked the notion of objectivity and have also attacked the idea that the subjective meanings of individuals' experiences can be accessed:

> There is no clear window into the inner life of the individual. Any gaze is always filtered through the lenses of language, gender, social class, race and ethnicity. There are no objective observations, only observations socially situated in the worlds of the observer and the observed. Subjects, or individuals, are seldom able to give full explanations of their actions or intentions; all they can offer are accounts, or stories. (p. 25)

Yardley (2000) went on to argue that the design of a study must take into account the positioning of the researcher. How this can be worked toward is discussed further in relation to transparency and reflexivity. Although Yardley's focus here is on the researcher, Elliot et al. (1999) also said there was a need to situate the sample. This entails giving sufficient background information about research participants to enable the reader to judge the relevance of the findings.

An additional element to evaluating sensitivity to context is to consider participant involvement (Yardley, 2000). Henwood and Pidgeon (1992) said that it is frequently suggested that theory that has a good fit should be recognizable to participants. They argued that this can be problematic but went on to say that some researchers might seek to negotiate interpretation and meaning with participants. This dimension to assessing the quality of research they termed sensitivity to negotiated realities. J. Smith (1996b) also argued that this approach can be problematic and is not always viable but, although not able to reach an absolute truth, can lead to fuller understanding. In one particular study, he argued that this approach led to richer data (Smith, 1996b).

Further dimensions to judging qualitative research are commitment and rigor (Yardley, 2000). Commitment concerns a prolonged involvement with the topic through immersion in the data and the use of methods in a skilled and competent manner. Rigor refers to the completeness of the data collection, not in terms of sample size or representativeness but "in terms of its ability to supply all the information needed for a comprehensive analysis" (p. 221). This relates to the coherence of the analysis, discussed subsequently. Rigor also relates to the completeness of an interpretation, which should address complexity and variation. One way in which complexity can be addressed is through the use of triangulation (Yardley, 2000), although Yardley (1997a) has suggested that such a stance implies weak realism. Another way in which rigor can be worked toward is through a recognition of the inherent limitations of any perspective and instead the adoption of a combination of analytic approaches (Yardley, 2000).

A transparent and coherent account of a research study should be convincing and meaningful to the reader, with a fit between theory and method and clear exposition of the analysis (Yardley, 2000). Such an account should disclose all relevant aspects of the research process, perhaps through a paper trail (Yardley, 2000). Such a paper trail allows others to check that the account is credible or warrantable (Smith 1996b). That is not to say that only one definitive account is possible, nor is there an attempt to suppress alternative readings or reach consensus, but it allows an attempt to "validate one particular reading" (J. Smith, 1996b, p. 193). Others have argued for the need to provide credibility checks through, for example, having more than one analyst, conducting member checks, or using an "auditor" (Elliott et al., 1999). A transparent account will address concerns about the importance of fit (Henwood & Pidgeon, 1992) and, by keeping close to the data, will "allow the reader to interrogate the interpretation that is being made" (J. Smith, 1996b, p. 192). However, providing a transparent account is a far more problematic and complex achievement than is normally acknowledged (Reicher, 1994). Attempts to theorize our position and consider our impact as researchers in terms of how we interdependently shape and constitute the object of inquiry (Henwood & Pidgeon, 1992) come under the rubric of reflexivity, which has received considerable attention from qualitative researchers.

Yardley (2000) has described reflexivity as a kind of disclosure that is necessary for researchers who believe that their assumptions, intentions, and actions profoundly affect our experience of the world and will therefore also affect the findings from a research study. Altheide and Johnson (1998) have adopted an analytic realist perspective, in which they reject the conceptual dualism of realism and idealism; from this perspective, the social world is an interpreted world, and a dualistic approach is incompatible with interpreting the nature of lived experience and its interpretation. What follows from this is that all knowledge is perspectival, and it behooves researchers to show their hand, write for an audience, and specify their perspective (Altheide & Johnson, 1998). Altheide and Johnson argued that the authority of an account can come only through paying attention to context and through reflexivity—that is, through a recognition that researchers are part of whatever it is that they are attempting to understand and represent. A more radical position on reflexivity is that the researcher is producing a purposeful construction and that this should be made explicit to make the researcher more accountable (Coyle, 2000).

A number of ways of providing a reflexive account have been developed, and it is common for authors to write themselves in through some kind of biography. Although this is necessary, it might not be sufficient, and many authors have suggested that such attempts can be at best tokenistic (Ahmed, 1999; Bola et al., 1998). Fine (1994) has been particularly instructive on reflexivity, arguing that we must continue to worry about relationships in the research process and "work the hyphen" by keeping discussion open about what is and what is not "happening between" researchers and informants and the negotiated relations of whose story is being told. She went on to say that we must mine our own experiences to interpret and that we have a responsibility to position ourselves in relation to our data (Fine, 1994; Kidder & Fine, 1997). Others have also argued that ultimately, researchers must take responsibility for their own interpretations and the assumptions behind them (e.g., Holland & Ramazanoglu, 1994; Maynard, 1994; Reicher, 1994). This relates to the discussion in the next section of this chapter on the crises of representation and interpretation. The data do not and cannot speak for themselves; it is not possible to capture the informant's voice, but it is possible to "elucidate the experience that is implicated by the subjects in the context of their activities as they perform them, and as they are understood by the ethnographer" (Altheide & Johnson, 1998, p. 296).

However, as Altheide and Johnson (1998) went on to say, these endeavors are not easy, and the attempt to locate the author and her or his perspective cannot be achieved through heroic diligence or empathic virtue. In a similar vein, Holland and Ramazanoglu (1994) said, "We cannot break out of the social constraints on our ways of knowing simply by wanting to" (p. 133). Thus, any attempt at reflexivity can be only "partial (and) temporary" (Kidder & Fine, 1997) but must acknowledge the intersubjectivities between the researcher and the researched implicated in the interpretative process (J. Smith, 1996a).

Yardley's (2000) final dimension to judging qualitative research is impact and importance. She argued that the worth of a piece of research can be judged by its theoretical impact in terms of developing understanding of a topic, as well as by its impact in a more political sense, either by being useful to a local community or, through wider social effects, by influencing the beliefs and actions of others. Henwood and Pidgeon (1992) discussed the impact and importance of research in terms of theory that "works" (p. 106) and in terms of transferability, arguing that such theory will suggest its own sphere of relevance.

If a transparent account is presented, it should be possible for the reader to make some sort of judgment about coherence and the relevance of the research as well as the researcher's commitment, rigor, and sensitivity to context. As Potter (1996) has noted, readers are themselves skilled interactants, so they can make judgments about claims. As one of the key components of providing a transparent account is reflexivity, the authors must write themselves into the research account. The discussion of what a reflexive approach entails, however, raises implications not only for analysis but also for how data are collected (see Chapter 4). A further issue that a reflexive approach requires consideration of concerns representation once data have been collected and analyzed. The debates about these concerns in the literature have been referred to as the crisis of representation and the crisis of interpretation.

THE CRISES OF REPRESENTATION AND INTERPRETATION

The earlier discussion on epistemological differences foregrounds a debate about how we interpret and represent those we seek to understand through the process of research. Denzin and Lincoln (1998) have characterized five moments, or periods, in qualitative research. Denzin (1998) also marked a current crisis in interpretation, in which, following postmodern and poststructural sensibilities, no privileged claims for authority or knowledge can be made. Denzin and Lincoln argued that a crisis of representation followed challenges to the application of the positivist paradigm to the human sciences and its associated realist stance of an objective ethnographer distanced from the observed subject (Fitzgerald, 1996). This crisis of interpretation led to challenges to realist and modernist approaches, which claimed to provide authentic accounts through narrative devices using the "voice of the other" accompanied by personal accounts to convey the author's honesty (Fitzgerald, 1996). The challenges were to the authority of the author to claim the voice of the other, and to the notion of the possibility of an objective account (Denzin & Lincoln, 1998; Fitzgerald, 1996). Denzin and Lincoln proposed that the fifth moment in qualitative research is characterized by tensions and diversity in which observations can never be objective, only situated. Coffey (1999) stated, however, that this characterization of five moments is overly simplistic and obscures the history of ethnographers' struggling with tensions, including those relating to representation. The struggle with these tensions does have a long history and is ongoing: Denzin and Lincoln (1994) suggested a developing sixth moment characterized by reflexive, experimental texts that are "messy, subjective, open ended, conflictual and feminist influenced" (p. 560). It is worth spending some time discussing these tensions, as they relate to representation and interpretation. Some of them have been discussed in earlier sections on the criteria for evaluating the quality of qualitative research, status of the data, and reflexivity. A further issue of particular importance for this study is the status of the researcher as an "insider."

Particular issues regarding representation arise when conducting sensitive research on vulnerable populations, including concerns about perceived colonization by academic researchers investigating the lives of "others" (e.g., hooks, 1990). Some of the ways in which this dilemma has been addressed are through an insistence on insider research, calls for participatory research and cooperative enquiry, and letting the data speak for themselves. There are arguments for insisting on insider research, but although this might be necessary in terms of access to hidden populations (discussed further in Chapter 4), this can also be problematic. It is problematic but it restricts researchers to studying their own kind (Lee, 1995) and, furthermore, is almost always inevitably incomplete (Oguntokun, 1998). Some, such as Fine (1994), have even gone so far as to argue against insider research on the grounds that it leads to essentialism. Others have claimed that only an outsider can create the distance, or Otherness, needed to make data productive during the analytic task (Pujol, 1999). Furthermore, a case can be made for reversing the process of Othering and "writing back," as when, for example, lesbians have written about heterosexuality or Black women have written about Whiteness (see C. Kitzinger & Wilkinson, 1996). However, Ahmed (1999) says that even from a relativist perspective, there is something to hold onto in the claim that insider status (albeit partial) not only permits access and facilitates data collection but can also be vital to the interpretative process. She argued that shared cultural membership, shared language, and tacit reasoning can help or even be a requirement for discursive analysis.

Whatever one's sympathies about insider research, there is always likely to be something "outside" about the researcher, and, once again, a way of working with rather than against the arising tensions must be found.

Edwards (1996), drawing on arguments by the Black feminist Patricia Hill-Collins, suggested that it is possible for White women to understand Black women's experience through empathic dialogue, although she remained skeptical about how such understandings can be represented in academic inquiry. Oguntokun (1998) has also suggested, drawing on Goffman's (1963) work, that one can be "wise" and become knowledgeable about and sympathetic to the accounts of others. Such wiseness can also lead to action. However, Oguntokun was speaking from a partial insider perspective in relation to her research participants, and the extent to which a more complete outsider or insider status affects the interpretative process is unclear. Fine has convincingly argued that researchers must find ways of working with the tensions that arise in the process of representing others and says that researchers cannot somehow let the data speak for themselves (Fine, 1994; Kidder & Fine, 1997).

A further issue in terms of representation and interpretation are the limits of verbal data and written analysis. The difficulties of interpreting silence in people's accounts were discussed in an earlier section ("The (Re)turn to Discourse", p. 38); a related issue is the extent to which people are able to articulate their experiences verbally, which brings into question reliance on the method of interviewing. Huby (1997), drawing on Rosaldo, argued that people cannot always describe what matters to them most; Foster (1998) found that people do not always have a readily available language to express their experience, particularly when that experience involves loss, trauma, and powerlessness. This is of particular relevance to this study, where for many participants, coming out was experienced in a traumatic way that involved loss. Furthermore, lesbian and gay identities are often lived through silence (Sedgwick, 1994), and many people have problematic access to a language to describe or negotiate these identities. Foster (1998) has argued that if such experiences can be articulated, they are more likely to be represented as stories or metaphors, which serve to distance the narrator from the horror and reality of that lived experience.

Holland and Ramazanoglu (1994) reasoned that interview material should be supported by field notes, saying "the unvoiced can never be fully grasped in an interview, and we can only negotiate recognition of what may be hinted at" (p. 140). Altheide and Johnson (1998) also discussed the limits of language in describing experience, noting that it is important to acknowledge the "realm of *tacit knowledge*, the ineffable truths, unutterable partly because they are between meanings and actions," and they also argued for ethnographic work that reflects that "tacit knowledge, the largely unarticulated, contextual understanding that is often manifested in nods, silences, humor, and naughty nuances" (pp. 296-297). Again, the use of discourse analysis, field notes, and observations allowed an engagement with and interpretation of ineffable aspects of the material in this study. Final methodological considerations that also relate to representation concern sampling and how the meaning of terms in relation to sexual identities and coming out are negotiated with potential research participants. These are discussed in detail in Chapter 4.

CONCLUSION

I have set out in this chapter an argument for mixing methods to investigate aspects of identity and experience. It is particularly important to find methods that disrupt the dualisms that not only construct identities and experiences but also constrain the possibilities for investigating those experiences. It is important to be able to find ways of interrogating data through different lenses that will allow an exploration of experience without further essentializing it (Cosgrove, 2000). In using a phenomenological approach to interrogate experience, we should be able to disrupt the subjective/objective dualism of positivism (Cosgrove, 2000). However, on its own, phenomenology becomes essentialist, as it does not allow an interrogation of the sociopolitical realm, resulting in a "backslide into empiricist notions of truth" (Burman & Parker, 1993, p. 161).

By also using the lens of social construction and, in particular, the tool of deconstruction, it might be possible to interrogate data further, taking account of the sociopolitical context. However, again, on its own, this approach might result in a failure to take into account experience and, most important, resistance (Cosgrove, 2000). Of particular relevance to this study is that social constructionist identity theories rely ultimately on the binaries they seek to destabilize (Butler, 1993) and fail to take into account those who refuse these binary positions (Fine, 1994; McDowell, 1996). Only by using phenomenological and constructionist approaches together is it possible to develop an understanding of resistance and to begin to theorize resistance and resilience (Cosgrove, 2000). In this study, I attempted this through the use of IPA as well as deconstructive approaches and the positioning theory, which itself attempts to disrupt the dualism created by extreme constructionist approaches.

Chapter 4
The Research That Cannot Speak Its Name

Two factors largely determined the design of the study and the methods used. The first related to the overall aim of capturing accounts of people's experiences and the meanings they attribute to such experience. The second factor related to the hidden nature of the population under study and the sensitive nature of the research topic. These two combined to make the use of qualitative interviews with lesbians and gay men about their experiences of mental health care the most appropriate way to gather data.

It is common practice with studies of lesbians and gay men to recruit through lesbian and gay community sources. However, this approach, along with approaches in general to studying hidden populations, tends to lead to samples with a race and class bias. Given some of the points noted in the review of the literature, it is likely that class and race differences are theoretically significant, so I paid considerable attention to finding ways of accessing hidden populations that reduce such bias.

Another bias that tends to be built into studies of lesbians and gay men is the degree to which research participants are "gay-community attached." Again, the review of the literature suggests that this might be theoretically significant, and I have considered this, too, in relation to sampling techniques. Alternative methods to sampling hidden populations, drawing on work done with intravenous drug users and, more broadly, peer education programs, are explored, as well as the use of advertising. I have also included a discussion about the importance of attending to issues such as the use of language, access to research participants, insider status, and approaches to interviewing when conducting sensitive research, followed by a description of the sampling approaches I used and the recruitment and profile of the sample obtained. The aim was to obtain a diverse sample that matched the demographic characteristics of the wider local population in the area in which the study was conducted. I then discuss the relative success of the different sampling approaches used in this study. Following this discussion of sampling procedures, I will explore the method of conducting qualitative interviews alongside the ethical considerations that were built into the study. Finally, I discuss the approaches used to analyze the interview data.

ROUNDING UP THE USUAL SUSPECTS: THEORETICAL BACKGROUND TO SAMPLING ISSUES

Research on lesbians and gay men necessitates finding ways of accessing and sampling a hidden population. Not only is the population under study hidden, it is also rare (i.e., it is estimated that only about 6% of the total population identifies as lesbian, gay, or bisexual), and the research is generally considered to be sensitive. Two modes of recruiting this population have evolved. Historically, research into lesbians and gay men drew on prisoners and psychiatric patients, many of whom were incarcerated or hospitalized in relation to the criminalization and pathologization of homosexuality. That such samples would be unrepresentative of the wider lesbian and gay population hardly needs to be said, but a fuller discussion of the implications of such sampling strategies can be found in Gonsoriek (1991).

Once the political climate had moved toward depathologizing and decriminalizing homosexuality, and had shifted toward a more gay-affirmative psychology, sampling strategies also had to change. Initially, to disprove the assumed absolute relationship between homosexuality and psychopathology, it was necessary only to find cases of lesbians and gay men who were not psychologically maladjusted (Gonsoriek, 1991). In these circumstances, a convenience sample drawn through lesbian and gay community networks, rather than a clinical population, would probably be sufficient to address the aims of the research. This was the case in Hooker's (1992) classic and groundbreaking study, which was conducted almost 50 years ago. In this study, a sample of gay men drawn through gay networks was compared to a matched sample of heterosexual men, and no significant differences between the two groups in terms of psychological adjustment were found. This seriously challenged the position taken up until that point that homosexuality was a mental illness. The subsequent use of convenience samples drawn from lesbian and gay networks, social organizations, and clubs and bars to study lesbian and gay lifestyles can be understood in the historical context of a drive to depathologize homosexuality.

Problems in the Use of Convenience Sampling

The continued use of such convenience samples is problematic, particularly when research questions broaden beyond such a limited depathologizing agenda and more diverse samples are required. They restrict respondents

> not only to those groups who identify as gay, but to that subset which is more articulate, more ready to respond to published appeals, more likely to join social and political organisations, in short the middle class. (P. Davies, 1990, p. 23)

Many convenience samples of lesbians and gay men are also biased toward those with higher education (e.g., Bradford & Ryan, 1988; P. Davies et al., 1993) and do not have sufficiently large subsamples of minority ethnic groups to enable meaningful comparisons (P. Davies et al., 1993; Wyatt, 1991). This class and race bias is not confined to studies of lesbians and gay men but tends to be a feature of qualitative studies and survey-type research (Cannon, Higginbotham, & Leung, 1991; Fassinger, 1991; Kalton & Anderson, 1986; Patrick, Pruchno, & Rose, 1998; Research and Decisions Corporation, 1984). Given that a number of studies have demonstrated the important theoretical differences to attend to within the lesbian and gay population on the basis of social class (Dowsett et al., 1992; Flowers & Buston, 2001; Flowers et al., 1997b; Weatherburn, Davies, Hickson, & Hartley, 1999) and ethnicity (Anzaldúa, 1990; Bradford et al., 1994; Chan, 1995; Cochran & Mays, 1994; Coyle & Rafalin, 1999; Doll et al., 1992; Greene, 1994; Rotherum-Borus et al., 1992; Tafoya, 1997), it is important to find approaches that increase the likelihood of achieving a diverse sample.

There is also evidence that the degree to which lesbians and gay men are attached to lesbian and gay communities and the degree to which they are "out" can have implications for their health (e.g., Coyle, 1998; Geraghty, 1996). These degrees of attachment and outness interact in a complex way with ethnicity and social class and need to be understood more fully (Bradford et al., 1994; Doll et al., 1992; Dowsett et al., 1992; Weatherburn et al., 1996). As well as degree of community attachment and outness, a complex relationship probably exists between how people identify themselves, if at all, in terms of sexual identity and the relationship between self-definition, social class, and attachment to lesbian and gay communities. Doll et al. (1992) and Weatherburn et al. (1996) found that few in their predominantly working-class sample used gay pubs and clubs or the gay media and that many of them did not identify as gay. Flowers et al. (1997b) have argued that these differences in sexual identities are important in relation to sexual decision making, and Dowsett et al. (1992) have indicated that these differences influence the effectiveness of sexual health promotion.

It is also, therefore, important to consider sampling in ways that are not totally dependent on convenience sampling through lesbian and gay community networks. Allowing sampling bias to persist can seriously threaten the validity of theory emerging from studies. For example, Cannon et al. (1991) found from analysis of their results that had they failed to recruit Black women raised in middle-class families and White women raised in working-class families, this would have seriously distorted their conclusions about how race and class affected current occupation and class position.

Difficulties in Obtaining Random Probability Samples of Lesbians and Gay Men

If the need for and utility of convenience samples has passed, then the logical starting point would be to consider the feasibility of obtaining representative probability samples for further studies. However, it is generally agreed that it is extremely difficult to generate a sampling frame for such populations from which a representative sample can be drawn (P. Davies et al., 1993; Fish, 2000; Lee, 1993). The authors of the largest sex survey conducted in the United Kingdom, using random probability sampling by residential address, have conceded that their methods result in an underestimation of the prevalence of homosexual behavior and lifestyles (Copas et al., 2002; Fenton, Johnson, McManus, & Erens, 2001; Johnson, Mercer, et al., 2001; Johnson, Wadsworth, Wellings, & Field, 1994). Further corroboration of the likelihood of such an underestimation comes from research with Sigma's[1] (P. Davies et al., 1993) sample of gay men. Respondents in this sample were asked if they would have participated in the national survey had they been approached, and 50% said they would not have participated. The Sigma authors suggested that given that their sample comprised largely out and confident gay men, the actual refusal rates in the national survey were likely to have been much higher.

A number of approaches have been developed to adapt random sampling methods to find rare and hidden populations. These methods include multiplicity sampling (Rothbart, Fine, & Sudman, 1982), which relies on members of randomly selected households nominating members in the sought-after population. However, this method is unlikely to work when trying to generate a sample of lesbians and gay men, as many are not out (e.g., G. McDonald, 1982) and because of the sensitivity of the information. Another potential way of generating a random sample of a rare or hidden population that is less resource intensive than household sampling is to undertake telephone screening (McCann, Clark, Taylor, & Morrice, 1984). It has been suggested that this could be used to access a lesbian and gay population (Harry, 1990), but it has met with limited success when it has been used (Hatfield, 1989). The samples obtained shared the characteristics of more easily generated convenience samples in terms of race and class bias and the extent to which people are out (Fassinger, 1991; Martin & Dean, 1993). This sampling method also tends to underrepresent people on low income, people from ethnic minorities, and those who are single or divorced (Kalton & Anderson, 1986). Thus, multiplicity sampling and telephone screening do not always overcome the sampling bias of convenience sampling, and they are more resource intensive.

The only exception known in which probability sampling methods seem to have been used with success to identify homosexual behavior and gay identity was in Bagley and Tremblay's (1997) study. They found that the incidence of homosexuality or bisexuality on the basis of self-identification was 12.7%, and the incidence of reported current homosexual activity was 9.2%. This suggests a higher rate of disclosure than is normally found. It is noteworthy that the main purpose of the study was not to identify a gay population; the questions were inserted into a questionnaire asking young men about previous childhood sexual abuse. The study also had an unusually high participation and completed response rate. The authors attribute this to the use of "peers" to collect the data and the use of a laptop computer for self-completion, which assured an unusually high degree of anonymity and no possibility of follow-up. Although this methodological breakthrough is exceptionally encouraging, it precludes gathering any qualitative data. Although it might help to enumerate a hidden population, it could not be reproduced to explore issues specific to lesbian or gay identity. A study on this scale was also beyond the scope of this study. Compelling arguments can be found against the use of probability sampling methods, and it remains possible only to explore the extent to which nonprobability sampling methods can be used to study lesbians and gay men.

THE DEVELOPMENT OF SNOWBALL, OR CHAIN-REFERRAL, SAMPLING

Historically, snowball, or chain referral, sampling was developed to study people with drug addiction and the even more hidden population of people who had recovered from opiate addiction without treatment (Biernacki & Waldorf, 1981; Waldorf & Biernacki, 1981). Snowball sampling shares many of the features of theoretical or purposive sampling, which tend to be used in grounded theory approaches (Glaser & Strauss, 1967). Snowball sampling approaches have also been applied to the study of other hidden populations, such as active burglars, including those who have never been apprehended (Wright, Decker, Redfern, & Smith, 1992). They are also commonly used to study lesbian and gay populations, including studies specific to understanding the epidemiology of HIV infection (P. Davies et al., 1993; Martin & Dean, 1993).

Snowball sampling relies on using insiders to locate others who share some knowledge or characteristic of relevance to the research (Biernacki & Waldorf, 1981). It is based on a technique whereby the first set of research participants refers the researcher to another set of participants through their personal contacts. This next set of participants then refers the researcher to another set, and so on. These sets of participants are called waves, or generations. However, it is not self propelling, as the term *snowball* might imply, but requires active initiation and control with pacing and monitoring. Biernacki and Waldorf have also recommended the use of multiple starting points, or seeds, and monitoring the eligibility of respondents in terms of the research criteria. Another recommendation is to use some respondents as paid or unpaid key locators, who will require at least minimal training. They referred to these individuals as de facto research assistants. They are similar to the significant informants, sponsors, patrons, or guides used in sociological field studies. Such people, once convinced of the trustworthiness of the researcher and the worthiness of the research project, can act as a bridge to other key individuals and gatekeepers and can indirectly facilitate the acceptance of the researcher by others (Lee, 1993). They can relatively easily contact data sources and are therefore more efficient in recruiting participants than the researchers are (Biernacki & Waldorf, 1981).

Martin and Dean (1993) used chain-referral sampling in their research into the epidemiology of AIDS in a community sample of 746 gay men. They noted how by generating this community sample, lower estimates for alcoholism and HIV prevalence are obtained than from the usual convenience samples drawn from bars or clinics. Martin and Dean (1993) found that they had obtained a clearer picture of the gay community than they would have had, had they "simply advertised for volunteers, [or] relied on a single recruitment strategy" (p. 96), and when conventional probability sampling is not possible, these alternative methods "can result in samples that approach representativeness of the population of interest and can be considered scientifically valid by virtue of their explicitness and replicability" (p. 97).

Martin and Dean's (1993) study is noteworthy, in that it followed guidelines for best practice in snowballing. It had multiple starting points and continued for five generations. Whereas many smaller qualitative studies have use snowballing but generated little more than a convenience sample of the researcher's immediate personal contacts (e.g., Coyle & Rafalin, 2000), Martin and Dean's study should be more robust. However, neither Biernacki and Waldorf's original (1981) study nor Martin and Dean's study managed successfully to recruit the expected numbers of minority ethnic group participants to reflect the overall population. This also seems to be a feature of snowball sampling in studies of lesbians and gay men (e.g., P. Davies et al., 1993; Troiden & Goode, 1980).

Other researchers using this technique, trying to find quite different populations and with regard to less sensitive topics, have found that the snowball method is less effective than other recruiting methods in accessing members of ethnic minorities (Patrick et al., 1998). Part of the problem of using snowball sampling to access lesbians and gay men is that the initial seeds, or starting points, should be, but are not usually, randomly obtained. The initial seeds are usually obtained through lesbian and gay community sources, and these networks have a habit of turning in on themselves and are unlikely to be able to recruit lesbians and gay men who are not attached to lesbian and gay communities.

It is difficult to establish whether race, education, and class differences in samples of lesbians and gay men derived from snowball sampling are the result of sampling bias or evidence of some naturally occurring skew in the population. There are often few meaningful data to make comparisons with, given that discussion about the difficulties of obtaining a representative probability sample, as noted by Kalton (1986):

> Distributions of important background variables are seldom known for a rare population: the use of hypothesised distributions in place of known distributions introduces its own potential biases. (p. 79)

However, with snowball sampling it is occasionally possible to compare the sample obtained with official statistics, as in the case of Lee's (1993) work on mixed Catholic-Protestant marriages in Northern Ireland. He found a disproportionate number of middle-class couples in the snowball sample as compared to census data, which revealed the numbers of working-class couples in mixed marriages. Little information is available to make such comparisons about samples of lesbians and gay men, but Lee's observation should caution us against settling for samples that do not reflect the diversity of the wider population. A case in point here relates to the numbers of minority ethnic groups in lesbian/gay community–derived samples. Some of this can be explained by White lesbian and gay in-migration to cities where research is conducted (Scott, 1998; Snape, Thomson, & Chetwynd, 1995). However, in the U.S. census, in which same-sex cohabiting couples were able to declare themselves, the number of couples from minority ethnic groups was representative of the wider population (Black, Gates, Sanders, & Taylor, 2000). These discrepancies suggest, once again, that it is necessary to work harder to recruit some subgroups than others, and, as P. Davies et al. (1993) have said, any minority group needs to be oversampled to allow comparisons to be made.

It is clear that although snowball sampling can be successful up to a point in recruiting hidden populations, as a method it tends to underrecruit those groups least likely generally to participate in social research: people with less education, those from lower socioeconomic groups, and those from minority ethnic groups. Adaptations to snowball sampling are much more successful in reaching populations that generally have low participation in research studies. Snowball methods have been further developed in response to the need to understand, and respond to, changing patterns of drug abuse (Kaplan, Korf, & Sterk, 1987). Further developments or adaptations to this technique to overcome some of its limitations have included the use of indigenous interviewers (Power & Harkinson, 1993), privileged access interviewers (Griffiths, Gossop, Powis, & Strang, 1993), peer-driven interventions (Broadhead, Heckathorn, Grund, Stern, & Anthony, 1995b; Grund, Broadhead, Heckathorn, Stern, & Anthony, 1996), and incentive schemes and respondent-driven sampling (Heckathorn, 1997; Watters & Biernacki, 1989). These approaches develop the potential to use insider status and build incentives into research.

The Use of Insiders and Incentives

One method for increasing participation in research with groups who are typically underrepresented or hard to reach is to include members in the research team who are indigenous in relation to the targeted population. These approaches are used not only for research purposes but also to recruit people into health education programs. In terms of conducting sensitive research, such approaches often come under the heading of using "insiders" as researchers, as they are more likely to be trusted by potential research participants (Lee, 1995). This was a feature built into Biernacki and Waldorf's (1981) original approach to snowball sampling in their use of de facto research assistants. In the practice-related field, many similarities with outreach efforts exist (Wiebel, 1996; Wiebel, Biernacki, Mulia, & Levin, 1993). Where research is sensitive, it is often extremely difficult to recruit participants into a study, and insider status might be the only way in which access can be gained (Lee, 1993). There are many clear examples of potential research participants' refusing to cooperate with researchers perceived to be outsiders (e.g., Edwards, 1996; Farquhar, 1999; Sophie, 1987). The use of insider status of openly gay and lesbian research teams to gain access to lesbian and gay populations has been demonstrated (P. Davies et al., 1993).

However, the use of insiders as research workers does not always increase access to minority participants (e.g., Biernacki & Waldorf, 1981; Phoenix, 1994a). This might partly be because insider status is unlikely to be unitary, and other ways in which we differ from our potential research participants affect access (Heaphy, Weeks, & Donovan, 1998; Phoenix, 1994a). Insider status is important but not sufficient for gaining access, and it can be more successful if used alongside other more labor-intensive approaches to sampling (Cannon et al., 1991; Patrick et al., 1998) and with an outreach worker approach (Wiebel et al., 1993). This might be because outreach workers are offering a service and/or have more of a peer relationship with research participants. However, as with snowball sampling, outreach workers tend to only recruit people with whom they share characteristics and the process tends to stagnate or lose momentum (Broadhead, Heckathorn, Grund, Stern, & Anthony, 1995a; Broadhead et al., 1995b).

Thus, the use of insiders as paid research workers or outreach workers is limited by the number of diverse people who can be employed on a project. The diversity of the research team can be extended by enrolling peers to help recruit, collect data, or conduct health education programs (Broadhead et al., 1995a), and these approaches have been found to increase the diversity of the sample obtained for research or the group reached for an intervention (Griffiths et al., 1993; Kuebler & Hausser, 1997; Power, 1994). Such methods will reach a more diverse audience or create a more diverse sample simply because the research team itself has expanded on its own diversity. The extent to which such methods rely on the peer relation between participants is unclear; although it might help if they share certain characteristics such as ethnicity, ultimately what matters is that those who are reaching the hidden population have privileged access (Griffiths et al., 1993). However, the use of indigenous interviewers (Kuebler & Hausser, 1997; Power, 1994) rather than outreach workers or research assistants will allow for greater diversity, simply because resources can be spread further. Such methods combine the advantages of diversity and privileged access.

Approaches that involve the use of peers, privileged-access interviewers, or indigenous interviewers are particularly successful when incentives are built in, in terms of keeping snowball samples moving through waves or generations and of producing a diverse sample. Griffiths et al. (1993) paid 22 interviewers for each interview that they conducted, and through this method reached a diverse group of 400 drug users who were members of a range of local drug subcultures. With a similar design, Kuebler and Hausser (1997) paid 31 privileged-access interviewers to conduct 917 interviews. Heckathorn (1997) has argued that a dual-incentive scheme will be more effective in recruiting members of a hidden population, whereby those who are recruited, as well as those who recruit, are given a reward and each person who has been recruited can go on to receive further rewards by continuing to recruit. He also opined that this design overcomes the inherent bias of snowball sampling that does not commence with an initial random sample. Instead, the dual incentive scheme produces a final sample with characteristics that are independent of the characteristics of the initial seeds.

In Heckathorn's (1997) study, the dual incentive scheme produced a sampling method that did not stagnate and produced a diverse sample that was representative of the wider population in terms of local demographic data. Grund et al. (1996) also used this method to generate a sample of drug users in which the first 50 interviewees had never been interviewed before. In another study of active residential burglars, one initial seed who was an ex-offender led to referral chains through which 105 participants were recruited into the study (Wright et al., 1992). Again, a dual incentive scheme was operating in this study, although it evolved through the innovation of study participants rather than being inherent in the original design.

It is hardly surprising that incentives will increase participation in research, and this has often been demonstrated to be the case in survey research (Willimack, Schuman, Pennell, & Lepkowski, 1995). In addition, incentives have been found to be effective when accessing hidden populations (Cottler, Compton, & Keating, 1995; Deren, Stephens, & Davis, 1994). With the peer-driven and respondent-driven approaches discussed previously, it is worth considering the nature of incentives offered. Although the appeal of a monetary incentive might seem obvious, not all members of a hidden population will find this sufficient or necessary. Other incentives include the desire to talk to a researcher (Lee, 1993; Wright et al., 1992); the desire to help one's own community and protect one's own health, as in peer-driven programs to prevent HIV infection among intravenous drug users

(Heckathorn, 1997); and the need for practical help (Watters & Biernacki, 1989; Wright et al., 1992).

Although all of these adaptations to chain-referral sampling might improve on the class and race biases of previous studies, it remains unclear to what extent such network-dependent methods can reach isolates. This is particularly important when sampling lesbians and gay men, as theoretically, the degree of community attachment and patterns of identifying might influence health. Claims have been that peer educators drawn from gay-attached sources can begin to penetrate the hidden population and reach more isolated, less gay-attached individuals (Shepherd, Weare, & Turner, 1997), but this remains to be explored further. One way in which the potential sample can be broadened to reach such people is to use publicity and advertising in media, which will reach people who are not attached to lesbian and gay communities.

The Use of Advertising

One final approach to reaching hidden populations is through the use of advertising and publicity through the media. However, studies advertised in the lesbian and gay press have found that very few people respond to such advertising (e.g., Annesley, 1995; Webb, 1999). Historically, prior to the existence of the lesbian and gay press, ads were placed in the mainstream media. Harry (1986) noted that those men who answered ads for Bell and Weinberg's (1978) study, in which data were gathered between 1969 and 1970, were different from the men recruited through homosexual organizations. They were more likely to identify as bisexual rather than homosexual, had lower self-esteem than men obtained through homosexual organizations, and were less likely to be part of a gay network. This suggests, once again, that attachment to lesbian and gay communities, and the way in which people identify in terms of sexual identity are theoretically important when considering mental health and need to be considered in sampling approaches.

Further evidence that advertising in mainstream media will reach a less gay community–attached population comes from a more recent study by Weatherburn et al. (1996). These authors recruited 745 behaviorally bisexual men but estimated that 20,000 to 34,000 men responded to the advertising and attempted to get through to the phone line during an 8-week period. The demographic characteristics of the sample more closely matched those of the general population than any other study of men who have sex with men, and most of the sample was not gay community attached.

Furthermore, when asked about their sexual identity, many of the men did not see themselves or define themselves in such terms:

> This suggests that a high proportion of behaviourally bisexual men do not see their sexual practice as central to their sexual identity or, that when they do, the catch-all terms that describe broad sexual preference (bisexual, homosexual, gay) are not appropriate to the way they view themselves. (Weatherburn et al., 1996, p. 20)

Weatherburn et al. (1996) used a form of wording in their advertisement that involved a behavioral definition of bisexuality rather than relying on self-definition. The ad was also targeted at bisexually active men. The fact that Weatherburn et al.'s sample differs so markedly from many snowball-generated samples of lesbians and gay men in terms of socioeconomic status, levels of education, lesbian/gay community attachment, and self-definition of sexual identity suggests that considerably more attention should be paid to how researchers define the population they are targeting and the words they use to do this.

The Use of Language in Sensitive Research

Weatherburn et al.'s (1996) study focused on a group of behaviorally bisexual men for the purposes of studying sexual behavior. They used explicit language in their advertisements that referred to sexual activity between men; this language was embedded in a behavioral definition of sexual identity. However, if a researcher is interested in mental health, then narrow behavioral definitions might not be adequate. Bagley and Tremblay's (1997) study showed that one of the most at-risk groups for suicide attempts, suicidal thoughts, and depression was celibate, gay-identified men. This should caution us against using behavioral definitions of sexual identity, particularly when researching mental health. A tradition in recent studies of lesbians and gay men allows people to select themselves into studies through self-definition (e.g., Fish, 1999; C. Kitzinger, 1987; Kitzinger & Wilkinson, 1995). This was partly a response to, and rejection of, the use of behavioral definitions, which had been associated with the pathologization of homosexuality. However, Weatherburn's (1996) study also showed that not everyone identified with terms such as *gay* or *bisexual*, and thus self-definition can also be problematic for recruitment of lesbians and gay men into a study. Paul (1996) has argued that "nominal categories based on sexual preferences may say more about the individual's socio-political affiliations than about her or his erotic experiences and desires" (p. 436). That such labels are derived from sociopolitical affiliations might go some way toward explaining the persistent race, class, and age bias of so many studies of lesbian and gay lives.

There has been debate about how problematic such labels are, whether they are arrived at through self-definition or cast on us, as it were, by external behavioral definitions (Fox, 1995; Herdt, 1990; Plummer, 1981, 1992b; Tafoya, 1997). A recognition of the need to problematize these categories exists, for they fix people into inappropriate concrete and binarized categories (Jenness, 1992; C. Kitzinger & Wilkinson, 1996; Mills & White, 1997; Plummer, 1992a). However, there is little evidence in the empirical literature of this being translated into applied research. One recent development is the use of the term *nonheterosexual* in Weeks et al.'s (2001) study, even though they continued to recruit only through lesbian and gay community networks.

Resistance to the use of particular terms or reluctance on the part of research participants to identify with terms used by researchers is not confined to studies of lesbians and gay men but is generally a feature of sensitive research. Examples of this come from studies of sexual harassment and violence (e.g., Brannen, 1988; Fine, 1989; Herek & Berrill, 1990). However, in studying lesbians and gay men, an extra hurdle has to be overcome, which is that lesbian and gay lives have a long history of being unspeakable and unnameable (Sinfield, 1994; Ussher, 1997b), and this is still reflected in recent coming-out stories (e.g., Markowe, 1996; Troiden, 1993). It has also been noted that people with emergent sexual identities are unable to associate with the terms *lesbian* or *gay* until they feel positive, or at least neutral, about adopting such a term for self-definition (Sophie, 1987; Watney, 1993). Furthermore, language is often unstable and can cause serious misunderstandings in the research process (Davies et al., 1993; Harvey, 1997; Harvey & Shalom, 1997; Healy, 1993; Mills & White, 1997; Wellings, Field, Wadsworth, Johnson, & Bradshaw, 1990).

This all points to a need to consider seriously how to present a research topic to potential research participants, paying close attention to the use of language when trying to recruit people into a study. Brannen (1988) noted that in sensitive research, the researcher is faced at the outset with whether and how to name the topic under investigation and said, "it is important not to pre-judge the research problem by labeling it or defining its boundaries too closely; respondents may thereby define the problem in their own terms" (p. 553).

One way of trying to progress with this agenda is through the use of focus groups to empower participants to help conceptualize strategies to access hidden populations and conduct sensitive research (Ayella, 1993). Focus groups can also be used to access the colloquial or subcultural language, with which participants might be more at ease (Andrade, 1995). Power (1994) also recommended using focus groups and training sessions to explore the knowledge and experience of indigenous or peer researchers to help conceptualize the research.

SAMPLING APPROACHES USED IN THIS STUDY

Given the theoretical issues discussed, I considered it important to obtain a sample that was diverse and broadly representative of the local population in terms of social class and ethnicity. It was also considered important to not sample only through the lesbian and gay community because of the theoretical significance of lesbian/gay community attachment. It was clear that for the purposes of this study, it would be impossible to draw a representative probability sample or to use methods such as multiplicity sampling or telephone screening. However, it was also clear that a convenience sample would be inadequate. Ultimately, if a probability sample cannot be generated, it would seem to be good practice to use a range of approaches. As van de Goor et al. (1994) have stated,

> in studying hidden populations no best or worst method exists ...Rather, diversity is a strength and different approaches are complementary. It is unlikely that totally new methods in the study of hidden populations will arise. (p. 34)

I therefore decided to use a range of approaches to sampling, which included

- conventional snowball sampling through lesbian and gay community networks,
- the use of sponsors or key informants to gain access,
- peer researchers who were offered incentives to recruit through their privileged access to research participants, and
- advertising and publicity in media not targeted at the lesbian and gay community.

I used a number of methods of gaining access to key groups and individuals within the local lesbian and gay community to provide initial seeds for snowballing and to recruit peer researchers. The term *peer researchers* is used in this study to mean people who were enlisted to help recruit participants into the study to be interviewed about their experiences of health care. They were involved only in recruitment, not in interviewing, but they were similar in other respects to privileged-access interviewers and indigenous researchers. Incentives and training were built into this use of peer researchers. In addition to this, I attempted to access lesbians and gay men who were not part of the local lesbian and gay community through publicity and advertisements in the local mainstream press and in the local community. These ads and publicity invited participation as an interviewee or as a peer researcher. I made further attempts to recruit lesbians and gay men from minority ethnic groups through targeted publicity and advertising. Incentives were also offered to those targeted through such advertisements and publicity. By confining the sampling to a specific geographic area rather than obtaining a national sample, I hoped to see a great degree of penetration of the hidden population to reach isolated individuals and a diverse group. I will discuss sampling methods used for this study in detail, with a discussion of how effective these were in terms of my aim of achieving diversity within the sample.

The first stage of recruitment involved gaining access to key figures in the local lesbian and gay community who, by virtue of their position, act as gatekeepers to outside communities, including the research community. I had a degree of insider status but was not part of or familiar with the local scene or community. I identified four key points of contact in the local community that would provide potential initial seeds for snowball sampling and recruitment of peer researchers:

- local lesbian and gay friendly youth services and the local lesbian and gay youth group,
- local lesbian and gay student groups,
- the local gay men's sexual health project, and
- user groups run by the local branch of the mental health charity MIND.

I made contact with a local health worker who as part of her professional work and her social life was connected to the first three areas. This person, known from here on by her pseudonym, Maggie, was central to gaining access, and she could be regarded as a sponsor or patron, as discussed by Lee (1993). Maggie helped me to gain access to the three previously mentioned areas and helped to locate many other points of contact within the local lesbian and gay community in which to publicize the project and try to recruit initial seeds for snowballing. She also offered to provide a free counseling service to any research participants. This was within the remit of her job description, and it also worked as an indirect incentive for some participants.

Some of the individuals to whom Maggie introduced me also acted as sponsors, allowing further introductions and facilitating access. These were, again, people who were well networked, and had local knowledge and the respect of many members of the lesbian and gay community.

The Use of Focus Groups

Once I had made initial contacts with gatekeepers, the next stage was to set up focus groups among existing groups. There were several purposes to this approach. The first was that it was a less threatening and more informative way of contacting individuals who might be willing to participate in an individual interview and/or to act as peer researchers; it also allowed a relatively informal opportunity to introduce the purpose of the research and the individual researcher and begin to build trust and rapport. This use of focus groups has been recommended by others conducting sensitive research (Andrade, 1995; Farquhar, 1999). Furthermore, the gatekeepers were keen for me to give something to their existing groups. The youth group leader and the student group leader felt that their groups would benefit from a discussion about coming out and health. The focus groups were therefore run in such a way that participants had a chance to discuss these issues and receive resources to facilitate their own coming-out processes.

I designed the focus groups using Krueger's (1994) guidelines. Focus groups are formed to bring people together who have something in common (in this case, sexual identity) to tap their real-life interactions and get in touch with their perceptions, attitudes, and opinions to identify trends or patterns rather than arrive at consensus. They are used to identify major themes rather than to analyze subtle differences. However, the moderator is interested in getting people to disclose their opinions, which might differ from those of others in the group. Of the many reasons for using focus groups, the ones of relevance to this study are that they are used

1. as part of a needs assessment;
2. when insights are needed as part of a preliminary study;
3. when there is a difference in levels of power, for example, between users and professionals;
4. when the researcher wants ideas to emerge from the group; and
5. when the researcher wants to capture open-ended comments.

To facilitate disclosure rather than presentation of the public self, the moderator needs to create a permissive environment. This involves bringing people together who have something in common and deemphasizing any differences in status while encouraging difference of opinion. This is partly to encourage participation but also because people form their opinions through interacting with others. Attention must be paid to the size of the group, its structure, and the wording and style of questions (Krueger, 1994) as well as to the way in which participants interact (J. Kitzinger, 1994).

Krueger (1994) recommended a structure to the group that has a strict order of types of questions to help participants to focus gradually on the topic under study and to explore their opinions, as follows:

1. Icebreakers and opening questions should be quick and factual, and show what participants have in common. They should not reveal differences in status.
2. Introductory questions should provide participants with an opportunity to reflect on past experiences and see their connection with the overall topic. They should foster conversation and interaction.
3. Transition questions should help participants envision the topic in a broader scope, linking the introductory and key questions and making participants aware of how others view the topic.
4. Key questions drive the study, and there should be two to five of them. In my focus groups, I gave some self-completion items to facilitate disclosure of sensitive information by all participants.
5. Ending questions bring closure to the discussion but allow reflection on what has been discussed. They might, therefore, include summary questions and give participants a chance to say what is most important to them or to add anything they think has been missed.

I used this structure to develop a focus group interview schedule.

I intended originally to conduct four focus groups, but attempts to set up two of these were unsuccessful. In the first case, a worker for women's user support groups at the local MIND sent out a letter inviting interest in the research to 105 women, but it yielded only two responses from people who were not eligible and unlikely to network with other participants. In the second case, an attempt to run a focus group with a young gay men's peer education sexual health project was unsuccessful, as the Gay Men's Health Project denied access. In this case, the project leaders felt that the population under study was being overresearched locally. However, this project later invited me to recruit individual participants following the sponsorship of Maggie. There are a number of possible explanations for this initial denial of access. One is that I might have lacked sufficient insider status to access the community through these particular gatekeepers. Another contributing factor was that the peer education group was itself not functioning well and was unable to support such research activity.

Attempts to set up focus groups with the local lesbian and gay youth group, and a lesbian and gay student group were successful. The first one, with the local lesbian and gay youth group, was attended by 2 workers (1 man and 1 woman), 2 volunteers (both women), and 9 young people (6 young men, 1 young woman, and 2 young transgender people). The second was conducted with the lesbian and gay group at the local college of higher education. This was attended by 15 students: 8 men and 7 women. The two focus groups were attended by 26 young people, of whom 10 agreed to participate further in the research. Eight of these were interviewed, and all of the 10 volunteered to act as peer researchers. The age range of the focus group participants was 18 to 30, with a median age of 20.5 years.

Of the 10 original focus group participants who agreed to become peer researchers, 5 actively recruited. Between them, they recruited a further 9 participants. In terms of snowballing, there were no further referrals from these participants; that is, only one wave was generated. The first aim of setting up the focus groups, to gain access, establish rapport and trust, and invite further participation in the research, can be said to have been met. The second aim of conducting the focus groups was to get participants to help conceptualize strategies for accessing hidden populations or for conducting sensitive research (Ayella, 1993), and to access the colloquial or subcultural language with which they might be more at ease (Andrade, 1995). Participants were asked about how they were defined by others, how they defined themselves, and how they preferred to be defined or referred to with regard to their sexual identity. In the focus groups, the participants articulated how lesbians and gay men are represented in dominant discourse as sinful. They described popular images of lesbians and gay men as corrupting of children, as having uncontrollable and undiscriminating sexual urges, and— in the case of gay men in particular—as dirty or disgusting.

Although the participants' discussions about images of lesbians and gay men can be understood as part of the dominant discourse, what was more revealing in the focus groups was the lack of any consensus on acceptable alternatives that would allow for self-definition. The focus group participants were almost uniformly ill at ease with the use of terms such as *lesbian* and *gay*, and where there was consensus, it was to say that they preferred to be called by their own names, hated labels, and wished to be seen as human. The participants were also ill at ease with the use of the term *coming out*, which some felt had an overly confessional ring to it. These themes continued to be discussed and explored in subsequent training sessions with peer researchers, who were helping to recruit others into the study.

The focus groups provided no easy solution to finding an inclusive and nonthreatening way of naming the project, but it served to alert me further to the need to pay attention to the use of language. As a result of this consultation and consideration of the available literature, we decided not to rely exclusively on the terms *lesbian* and *gay* in the publicity about the project; instead, we used the following wording: "Are you lesbian, gay, bisexual or don't like to define yourself?" As the project proceeded, I confirmed early observations about the problematic use of the terms *coming out* and *lesbian/gay*, and in later advertisements, both were played down, with the project title changing to "Mental health and sexual orientation." These later advertisements were placed in the local non-gay press. The aim of using the focus groups to help conceptualize strategies for accessing a hidden population were met in part, and this work continued in the training sessions given later to peer researchers.

Preparing the Peer Researchers

The next stage of the research was to train the peer researchers so that they could recruit more participants for interviewing. The model for conducting this training followed guidelines set by those using indigenous interviewers and peer education programs (Broadhead et al., 1995a; Griffiths et al., 1993; Power, 1994; Power & Harkinson, 1993; Shepherd, 1997). This involved offering incentives that were not only financial but also social and community based. Thus, a £10 incentive was offered to cover expenses for each participant recruited into the study, and the training was offered as an incentive. I gave guidelines to the participants to show them how they could use the training opportunity for their personal development, and the training also provided a social space with refreshments in a lesbian and gay community venue. A further incentive was an altruistic one, in that participants might believe that the research was of potential benefit to their community in terms of improving access to mental health care. Another incentive was the potential for immediate access to a lesbian- and gay-friendly counseling service, following Lee's (1993) suggestion that providing a service can help to access participants where the research is sensitive. This, and the interview itself, was for some participants an opportunity for catharsis, which, again, Lee has suggested can motivate people to participate. Unfortunately, a key feature of the intended research design was not possible, as the Local Research Ethics Committee refused to allow permission to follow Heckathorn's (1997) model of respondent-driven sampling with dual incentives. In this case, as well as my offering a financial incentive to the peer researcher for recruiting, I would have also offered participants a financial incentive for agreeing to be interviewed. This refusal was unfortunate, as feedback from peer recruiters suggested that such dual incentives would have initiated and perpetuated referral chains.

In addition to using peer researchers, who were offered incentives, I tried conventional snowball sampling, with participants recruited through other channels. Other recruitment methods used in the study involved approaching established groups in person or in writing and distributing flyers about the research; leaving publicity about the research in health clinics and with health projects, and lesbian and gay projects; press releases and advertisements in the local free press; posting on lesbian and gay Internet sites; and personal networking.

Recruitment and Profile of the Sample Obtained for This Study

The aim of the sampling methods used for this study was to obtain a diverse sample in terms of socioeconomic background, ethnicity, and degrees of lesbian/gay community attachment. Overall, I conducted 49 interviews, of which 48 were eligible and fit the criteria for the study. Of the 48 interviewees, 22 were women and 26 were men, and they were aged between 17 and 55. The sample was more diverse than that found in many comparable studies and had a closer match to the local population in terms of demographic characteristics than many similar studies. Each of the recruitment strategies used varied in the extent to which it enabled recruitment of different subgroups within the lesbian and gay population. The advertisement in the mainstream press was particularly successful at recruiting men and women from lower socioeconomic groups and men with lower educational attainment compared to all the other approaches. Although the numbers are small, conventional snowball sampling, without incentives, led to recruitment of more middle-class participants, as has been found in other studies. The peer researchers varied in their capacity to locate a diverse range of research participants. The advertisement in the mainstream press was more successful than other approaches in recruiting lesbians and gay men who were less lesbian/gay community attached than other sources, and more of these people identified as bisexual than as lesbian or gay. I will now discuss each of these differences in more detail, alongside a discussion about the different recruitment strategies and how the comparisons were made.

Comparing Social Class and Educational Attainment

Many studies of lesbians and gay men (e.g., Creith, 1996; Henderson et al., 2002; Hickson, Reid, Weatherburn, Henderson, & Stephens, 1998;

Markowe, 1996; Martin & Dean, 1993) have not collected data about occupation or income on which to base an assignment of social class. This might be because such data are difficult to collect because of their sensitive nature. Many researchers do, however, collect data on educational attainment, which might serve as a proxy for social class. However, evidence is increasing that there is not a straightforward relationship between socioeconomic status and educational attainment in the lesbian and gay population, with higher than expected levels of education in people living in poverty or on low incomes (Black et al., 2000; Calandrino, 1999; Klawitter & Flatt, 1998). For this reason, I attempted to gather data on the educational attainments as well as occupations of participants in this study.

These data on occupation and education were then compared to other studies of lesbians and gay men and to census data. From census data, one would expect approximately a third of the age group studied to come from social classes 1 and 2, or to be in professional and managerial occupations (Office of National Statistics, 2000). In terms of education, using the same sources, we would expect between 13 and 24% of the working population to have a university degree. Most studies of lesbians and gay men have samples in which 50 to 70% of the participants are in managerial and professional occupations (e.g., Bradford & Ryan, 1988; Davies et al., 1993; Dunne, 1997; C. Kitzinger & Wilkinson, 1995; Webb, 1999). In this study, approximately a third of the participants were in professional and managerial occupations (or, if they were too young to have started work, their parents were in such occupations). There were no differences between the men and women in the study in this respect. In terms of education, many published studies have samples in which between 34% and more than half of the participants held a degree qualification (e.g., P. Davies et al., 1993; Dunne, 1997). In this study, 19% of the men and 40% of the women held a degree qualification. In this study, then, I obtained a sample that had a closer match to expected demography from census data than many other published studies. It is particularly useful to compare this sample with Webb's (1999), as they were obtained in the same geographical area. Webb obtained a sample of 544 gay men, of whom 53% were in professional and managerial occupations (data on educational attainment were not collected). Webb recruited only through gay community sources and snowballing, which confirms that such approaches tend to produce a class bias. I obtained a closer match to the general population with regard to social class and, to a certain extent, to education in my study. The conventional snowball sampling approach used through gay community sources reproduced the trends toward middle-class recruitment found in other studies, but my use of advertisements in mainstream media and, to a certain extent, my use of peer researchers produced more diversity within the sample. I will now discuss the effect of each of the sampling strategies in more detail in relation to the social class and educational background of participants.

The use of advertisements and publicity in the local (non-gay) press led, as in Weatherburn et al.'s (1996) study, to a subsample that matched the demography of the national population much more closely in terms of socioeconomic position than the subsample obtained through lesbian and gay community sources. One ad in the free weekly paper distributed in the city where the study was conducted led to 17 inquiries. These led to the recruitment of 11 interviewees as well as 1 peer researcher, who recruited 1 further interviewee. All of the men recruited through this ad were in working-class occupations (or came from working-class backgrounds but had never worked), and only 1 out of the 9 men had a university degree. The women recruited in this way closely matched the general population in terms of occupation but were more likely to have a university education than women in the general population.

The subsample obtained through conventional snowballing and through the peer researchers was more variable in terms of the social class of the participants, and overall, this subsample was more educated and disproportionately from social classes 1 and 2 compared to the general population. This might be because the seeds or starting points were more likely to be middle-class. However, some peer researchers and individual snowball seeds were much better able than others to recruit working-class participants. The reasons for this are unclear: Obviously, the process is network dependent, which is variable. However, it might also be that some individuals were more comprehending of my aims regarding diversity.

As well as the effect of the peer researchers and the location of publicity, other factors might have increased working-class participation. The use of an incentive in the form of a reimbursement might have had the effect of conveying to potential participants that their story was of interest and value to an academic researcher. This is not something that has received much attention in the methodological literature on sampling, but it would be worthy of further exploration. Another factor might be my tenacity, as it is commonly reported that reaching underrepresented groups often requires more labor-intensive approaches. For example, Phoenix (1994a) reported that considerable effort was required on her part as a researcher to recruit women into a study of teenage mothers. On many occasions, appointments for interviews were broken, including one instance in which the interview was not conducted until the 27th attempt. Phoenix is wary of such data's being used to reinforce stereotypes of an already stigmatized group and has argued that for people living in unpleasant and cramped conditions, waiting in for a researcher is not a priority. Similarly, in my study, a number of participants repeatedly failed to arrive for appointments, and in each case, they were in low-paid, unskilled occupations, were unemployed, or were single mothers with children. Two of these were interviewed on the second attempt, 1 could not be contacted again, and another 2 had appointments rescheduled four times but had still not been interviewed by the end of the period of data collection.

The Ethnicity of the Sample Recruited

The recruitment methods used were less successful regarding the participation of people from minority ethnic groups. The percentage of minority ethnic participants in this study was 6.25% (i.e., 3 out of 49 participants) as compared to 4.7% of the local population. Again, it is useful to compare this with Webb's (1999) local study using gay community sources and conventional snowballing, in which only 1.5% of the participants were from minority ethnic groups. However, the aim of oversampling this subgroup to be able to make meaningful comparisons was not met. Advertising and publicity were not successful in recruiting minority ethnic participants into the study, but the use of peer researchers and key informants was.

As stated before, recruitment of minority ethnic groups into research studies often requires more labor-intensive approaches (Cannon et al., 1991; Patrick et al., 1998; Phoenix, 1994b). In this study, I used a number of approaches. All of the peer researchers were White, and there were no obvious starting points in the local area to recruit peer researchers or to snowball from, which would have corrected this imbalance. As with the peer researchers, I had no insider status in relation to minority ethnic status. However, I asked the peer researchers to make special efforts to recruit typically underrepresented groups. One minority ethnic participant was recruited in this way, but she was unable to recruit other lesbian or gay minority ethnic participants, as she had no such community attachments. Another minority ethnic gay man, who worked for a Gay Men's Health Project, was recruited through professional networking, and he was able to recruit one other minority ethnic participant. This participant, although he knew other Asian gay men, was unable to recruit them into the study because of a high level of fear of exposure within his ethnic community.

However, as P. Davies et al. (1993) have stated, where the overall proportion of minority ethnic groups is small, we must oversample if meaningful comparisons are to be made. Other attempts to recruit ethnic minorities included a race-targeted advertisement in the local press, publicity in the African-Caribbean community centre, and publicity in a health center that served the geographic area with the highest density of minority ethnic groups in the city. None of these yielded any participants from minority ethnic groups.

Gay and Lesbian Community Attachment of the Sample

I noted earlier that lesbian and gay community attachment is probably related to both mental and sexual health and that many studies of lesbians and gays tend to recruit only those attached to lesbian and gay communities. I also noted a complex relationship between community attachment, sexual identity, social class, and educational background. Some have reasoned that community leads to identity (Kramer, 1995; Rothenburg, 1995) and that lack of gay attachment can be because of economic disadvantage (Binnie, 1995; Dowsett et al., 1992). Thus, it seemed to be important to account for lesbian and gay community attachment and variation in sexual identities when conducting this study, but this raises questions about how to assess these variables.

In Weatherburn at al.'s (1996) study, gay community attachment was indirectly inferred from where men found their sexual partners. However, such an approach would not be adequate for a study into mental health. Dowsett et al. (1992) have a more sophisticated approach to understanding gay community attachment, which was more useful in this study. They noted that this can include both social and sexual engagement (what would be referred to as the "scene" in the United Kingdom) and also politicocultural involvement, with the latter being a more middle-class terrain than the former. A further dimension to gay attachment that Dowsett et al. (1992) made is to distinguish between participation in the gay community versus integration into it, with politicocultural involvement being more likely to lead to integration in the form of stable and enduring social networks and friendships.

Another dimension to lesbian and gay community attachment and lesbian and gay identity is to consider at what point participants were or were not attached to the lesbian/gay community. It might be that if lesbian/gay community attachment has an impact on mental health, it does so at key times in a person's life, when any support from that community is particularly important. Coyle (1991) has reasoned that high levels of gay community involvement might relate to early stages of awareness and construction of a gay identity, when the support that can be derived from such communities is most needed. Coyle noted that it is important to know whether participants in studies looking at psychological well-being are, or ever have been, involved in a gay community. This is not always clear when trying to make comparisons. For instance, Seidman et al. (1999) said that they obtained a sample in their study that was not gay attached. However, most of their participants reported that they felt that they were part of a gay community and that they had participated in gay community group activities when they were at an earlier stage of gay identity formation and when they were more closeted. Seidman et al. (1999) indicated that many of their participants were "beyond the closet" and had postidentity sexual politics, whereby their sexual identity had become routinized and normalized and was no longer a core part of their identity. At the other end of the spectrum, Watney (1993) has also argued that emergent or pre-gay identities are not established as gay identities until there has been some kind of engagement with a gay community or the "scene." These differences in degree of gay-community attachment and when it takes place, which might relate to stages of identity development, suggest a need to be sensitive to this in research. In this study, I attempted to explore this in research interviews using the criteria adopted by Dowsett et al. (1992) in terms of participation versus integration into a lesbian or gay community and whether participants had ever had such involvement. It was not possible to obtain any kind of accurate measure of attachments to communities, but I considered it important theoretically to attend to these nuances when gathering data and to consider sampling strategies that were more likely to produce a diverse sample in terms of degrees of lesbian and gay community attachment.

Some trends in the effects of different recruitment strategies could be noted in the sample obtained for this study. The lesbians and gay men recruited through the advertisements and publicity placed in the non-gay local newspapers were less lesbian and gay community attached than those recruited through other means. One of those who did describe himself as "part of the scene" was very much of the type described by Dowsett (1992), "on the scene" but not integrated into it. The people who answered the advertisement were also more likely to have been unaware of the existence of the gay scene when they were coming out and more likely to have used contact ads in "straight" newspapers to meet same-sex partners. They were also more likely to describe themselves as bisexual than those recruited via lesbian and gay community networks and via (most of the) peer researchers. The peer researcher recruited via the advertisement was not gay identified, and two of the interviewees had had the advertisement shown to them by heterosexual friends.

These trends can be only tentatively suggested from the data, and their possible significance and interrelationships with other factors, such as social class, will be explored further in the analysis of the data. However, they are trends that are consistent with larger published studies (e.g., Weatherburn et al., 1996) and that raise issues not only about sampling but also about associated theoretical considerations. Another related theoretical consideration is the significance of how people do or do not identify in terms of sexual identity. The trend toward more bisexually identified people responding to advertisements and publicity in the non-gay press might have to do not only with location but also with the wording used. In the advertisements, I deliberately avoided the terms *lesbian* and *gay*, using instead the term *sexual orientation*, a practice developed partly in response to the lack of universal comfort with the terms *lesbian* and *gay* even among the lesbian and gay community–attached focus group participants.

Interviewing and Ethical Considerations

The aim of this project was to gather rich data that could be used to explore and illuminate the meanings of the participants' worlds. An approach was required, then, that would allow participants to tell their stories in as much depth and with as much complexity as possible. A structured interview schedule would not be consonant with such an approach (Smith, 1995) and would run the risk of overwriting the participants' meanings and subjectivities with my prior theoretical assumptions. A less structured approach allows for the development of trust and empathy, and opens up the possibility of the interview's entering previously uncharted territory and the production of richer data (Smith, 1995). Any attempts to structure the schedule in advance should be for the sake of making one's research agenda clear and anticipating possible ambiguities and sensitivities in relation to question wording. Furthermore, as in analysis, this should be an iterative rather than a linear process, with ongoing adaptations to the schedule (Smith 1995).

It is noteworthy that thus far, the term *richer* rather than *better* data has been used. In keeping with the epistemological and ontological positions taken in this study, the data produced in interviews can be regarded as somewhere between a veridical ("truthful") account and a rhetorical account, and the way in which one goes about conducting the interview will have some bearing on what is produced. Sapsford and Abbot (1998) have discussed how the depth interview should give rise to an account that gets underneath people's public rhetorics. Although some research approaches aim to explicate these public rhetorics, in research with a more phenomenological purpose, there is a need to consider how and whether the interview reflects the personal worlds and meanings of participants. Much attention has been paid to how quite subtle wording changes to questions can dramatically alter the response of the person interviewed. For instance May (1991) has discussed how unskilled questioning, in which questions are framed within prior knowledge, can lead to the interviewees' merely reproducing the received lay or scientific view on a topic rather than presenting their own experience of it. Jones (1985) also discussed how we are likely to receive a rehearsed script, rather than a depth interview, if participants feel threatened. This raises many issues concerning the conduct of sensitive research, including insider status, how best to develop rapport and trust, and ethical issues, including consent, support, and representation.

Notwithstanding this discussion about the multiple realities that can be co-constructed between different researchers and those they interview, consideration should be given to the ways in which interviewing techniques will affect the quality of data produced. Considerations need to be made about ways of getting past the rehearsed scripts, public rhetorics, and defensive postures, mentioned before, through attention to issues of trust and rapport as well as questioning styles. Although a number of techniques exist, the epistemological position taken thus far would indicate that it is not possible to know fully whether such techniques are effective. However, again through reflexivity, we can interrogate our analyses to see if we have learned anything new from our participants. If we have, then we might be assured that, to some extent, we have conducted "good" interviews and subsequent analyses rather than merely having succeeded in getting our informants to reproduce what we already know. With respect to the earlier discussion on the validity of qualitative research, Flick (1998) suggested that researchers must adopt an attitude of evenly suspended attention; otherwise, they might be blind to the structures of the persons they are studying. It can be argued that this applies as much to interviewing as it does to the subsequent analysis.

May (1991) has suggested that one way of not superimposing our own or popular theoretical frameworks onto the participant is to use her or his language as much as possible. The use of focus groups to access the street language and conceptual devices of hard-to-reach and hidden populations prior to conducting in-depth work (Andrade, 1995; Ayella, 1993; Power, 1994) has already been discussed in relation to this study. A number of tried-and-tested techniques for producing depth interviews relate to questioning style through the use of open-ended rather than closed or leading questions; avoiding jargon; and the use of prompts, probes, and funneling (J. Smith, 1995). The schedule for semistructured or open interviews should serve as a guide, allowing for a build-up of rapport, in which the order of questions can be flexible, and should allow the interviewer to pursue interesting areas that arise during the interview and follow the concerns and interests of the individual being interviewed (Smith, 1995).

Furthermore, it has been suggested that researchers should attempt to be fairly explicit about their research agenda, so that the participant knows what to focus on (Jones, 1985). However, with sensitive research, there are caveats, and this must be done in very broad terms (Brannen, 1988). A related issue here is that participants might not be committed to giving a detailed account unless they can see some purpose for or value in the project (Lee, 1993, Jones, 1985). A further point to consider is that it might be beneficial to unload certain sensitive questions through the use of presupposition questions or by making a statement that other interviewees have divulged a range of extreme positions on the subject (Patton, 1990). A presupposition question embeds a statement that other people have revealed sensitive information in a research context. Another recommendation is that in long interviews on sensitive topics, researchers should use ending questions, which allow the interview to end on a positive note (Charmaz, 1990). Such questions, aside from ethical considerations, might also generate more useful data (Charmaz, 1990). Furthermore, the use of ending questions in focus groups, although not designed to be uplifting, also has the purpose of generating further data (Krueger, 1994).

Interviews rely on conversational practice (Cunningham-Burley, 1985), and no hard and fast rules can be made about the use of leading, loaded, and open questions, as their use depends ultimately on the relationship with the person being interviewed (Jones, 1985). A case in point is Potter and Wetherell's (1995) suggestion that it might be more analytically revealing to argue with research participants. This latter position throws into relief the need to consider ethical issues in relation to interviewing when researching a vulnerable population on a sensitive topic, as in this study.

The potential exploitation of research participants has been one of the main concerns of feminist researchers. A further concern for feminist researchers has been the ease with which women can get other women to talk about private and upsetting aspects of their lives. Some have felt that in its own way, this ease of access is potentially abusive and exploitative (Finch, 1984; Leonard, 1993), but the potential exploitation can be minimized by having a reciprocal relationship with the interviewees and disclosing something of oneself (R. Edwards, 1993). Fears that research participants will be unnecessarily traumatized by disclosing emotionally disturbing events and memories are also countered by participants, who often claim that the interview was useful and cathartic (Brannen, 1988; Edwards, 1993; Renzetti & Lee, 1993). A further way of attending to ethical concerns arising through interviewing is to use basic counseling skills within interviews to support interviewees and facilitate cathartic disclosure; however, this is not intended to "do therapy" in an explicit or purposeful way (Coyle & Wright, 1996). An additional dimension to ethical considerations following interviewing is how the data are analyzed and how participants are represented. This has been discussed in the previous chapter in the section on "The Crises of Representation and Interpretation" (p. 45).

Local policies meant that approval for this study had to be sought from the Local Research Ethics Committee, even though participants were not being recruited through the health service. The application included protocols for obtaining informed consent and maintaining confidentiality, and for providing support and resources for participants. The committee required specialized support to be available for any participants under the age of 16 from whom parental consent could not be obtained, and this was arranged. I also sought approval for making payments to peer researchers and those they recruited. Approval was obtained for all aspects of the study, except, as noted earlier, the payment to participants recruited via peer researchers.

METHODS OF DATA ANALYSIS

The goal of the data analysis was to arrive at a detailed, multilayered interpretation (Yardley, 1997b) of lesbians' and gay men's accounts about their mental health care experiences. The necessity to break away from strict disciplinary and epistemological divides was discussed in Chapter 3, with the conclusion that it is sometimes most appropriate for the researcher to work as a bricoleur (Denzin & Lincoln, 1994). This requires using whatever methods are most suitable to make sense of the data and working with the epistemological tensions that such mixing of methods might engender. This should enable the researcher to escape both the limitations of positivism and the tyrannies of relativism. In this study, I used an approach similar to grounded theory (interpretative phenomenological analysis) to interpret some of the data, juxtaposing this with a more discursive analysis to interpret other types of data for which the first approach was inadequate. The first approach is situated in a realist epistemology, whereas the second is situated in a more relativist epistemology.

This combination of two types of analysis would until relatively recently been seen as combining epistemologically incompatible viewpoints (Denzin & Lincoln, 1998, 1994; Fine, 1994; Guba & Lincoln, 1994). However, some recent studies have taken this approach of combining grounded theory with more discursive forms of analysis (e.g., Gough, 2002; Henwood, 1993), involving what Yardley (1996) would call a material-discursive analysis. This allows us to analyze the data using different lenses and to explore the mutual and reciprocal influence between discursive practices and the material domain, but in a way that goes beyond a simple notion of interaction as in the biopsychosocial model, which remains dualistic and mechanistic (Ussher, 1997c; Yardley, 1999). In this study, it allows us to understand how dominant discourses, such as the pathologization of homosexuality, and associated power relationships, directly and indirectly mediate lesbians' and gay men's experiences of mental health care.

Following data collection and the preliminary analysis, it was clear that there were two kinds of data that lent themselves to different forms of analysis and that needed to be viewed through different lenses. To begin with, there were clear accounts of people's shared experiences of homophobia in health care and experiences of being silenced, so that they were unable to bring concerns about the effects of homophobia on their health into a health care encounter. These accounts were grounded in the data and could be analyzed using IPA, a method underpinned by a realist epistemology, in which participants are able to articulate their experiences (Osborn & Smith, 1998). The approach has been used to analyze people's accounts of coming out, bereavement, chronic pain, eating disorders, transitions in identity in relation to motherhood, and sexual risk taking (Flowers, Smith, Sheeran, & Beail, 1997a, 1998; Golsworthy & Coyle, 1999; Jarman et al., 1997; Osborn & Smith, 1998; J. Smith, 1991). The underlying epistemology of IPA and its relationship to grounded theory was discussed in detail in Chapter 3.

Within the data, there were also many ambiguities and silences, which were more complex to interpret and which did not lend themselves to such a phenomenological analysis. Some of this interpretive work related to what participants could not or would not say. This seemed to point toward some sort of resistance to the pathologizing and silencing identified in the first part of the analysis using IPA. To explore these silences and ambiguities, I used a discursive approach that situated such silences and ambiguities within wider discursive practices and allowed an exploration of how participants attempted to position themselves in relation to such discourses when they were negotiating their sexual identity in a mental health care encounter. Such approaches allow us to move away from the individualism inherent in phenomenological approaches and situate people's experiences in a broader social context (Pilgrim & Rogers, 1997; Yardley, 1997b).

Of the many approaches to discourse analysis, discussed previously, some take an extreme relativist or social constructionist position (e.g., D. Edwards et al., 1995). The most useful approach to understanding the data in this study was one that enabled an understanding of the way in which participants were positioned by dominant discourses in their mental health care encounters. This approach (sometimes termed analysis of discourse) takes a macro discourse perspective and is characteristic of much of the work of Parker (1996, 1998a, 1999, 1993, 1995) and B. Davies and Harré (1990). It is very different from the more empirical micro discourse analysis characteristic of much of Potter and Wetherell's work (e.g., Wetherell & Potter, 1988, 1992). Analysis of discourse, or macro discourse perspectives, are embedded in a critical realist epistemology and allow us to understand, through a process of deconstruction, how people negotiate and resist the positions offered to them within broad social practices (Burr, 1995, 1998; B. Davies & Harré, 1990). These approaches are particularly useful for interpreting silence and resistance (e.g., Boyle & McEvoy, 1998). Each of the approaches to data analysis used in this study will now be discussed in more detail.

Interpretative Phenomenological Analysis

The analysis commenced with a technique known as IPA, allowing an initial engagement with the data that focused on the thoughts and feelings that participants had about their experiences and the meaning of those experiences. This technique was particularly useful for exploring an area in which there was little prior theory in relation to health care experience to draw on, and it helped me to develop conceptual work grounded in the data. This conceptual work could then be related to broader social theory to locate these experiences within a wider framework. IPA is used as a method to look for shared experiences particularly, as in this study, which produced a large data set (J. Smith, 1995). One potential problem with this type of approach, however, is that it can purge variability from the data, but such variability might be important (Potter & Wetherell, 1987; Wooffitt, 1993). Again, by combining different approaches to analysis and viewing the data through different lenses, the strengths and weaknesses of different approaches can be used to complement each other.

Prior to analysis, the interviews were transcribed verbatim with a level of detail that included relatively gross features such as corrections, hesitations, and pauses, which provided sufficient detail for the IPA. It was also sufficiently detailed for a discursive analysis that focused on content themes and ideological practices on a broad scale rather than interactional specifics (Potter, 1996; Potter & Wetherell, 1995). The data analysis then commenced with the method described by J. Smith, Osborn, et al. (1999) for analyzing large data sets. The method is more exploratory than the idiographic or case study approach used with smaller data sets, focusing instead on broader conceptual categories with an emphasis on discovering shared experiences among participants. All of the interviews were scrutinized, with annotations made in the margins to note preliminary interpretations, emerging themes, associations, and connections, as well as anything else striking or of interest. These early codes tended to be used to mark chunks of text rather than in a detailed, line-by-line approach to keep the coding at a broad level. However, at times, I also noted small amounts of text or silences and pauses, as I had already made a commitment to engage in a more discursive analysis. In addition to this, the preliminary coding involved simply marking out and grouping chunks of text that might be relevant at a later stage purely for the purpose of making the analytic task more manageable (Potter & Wetherell, 1994). As each transcript was coded in turn, new preliminary themes emerged, and I revisited earlier texts to check for connections that might not have been salient previously. Initially, the first six interviews were coded in this way, following the procedures recommended by Smith and colleagues.

I used these preliminary themes as a template as the sequential analysis of each interview proceeded, and each of these themes continued to emerge in other interviews. Although I was therefore primed for or oriented toward looking for these themes in subsequent transcripts, I attempted to remain open to the possibility of further themes' emerging. Following this initial preliminary coding of each interview, I tried to cluster the emergent themes into meaningful groups. Although Smith et al. (1999) have suggested that this should be undertaken after the preliminary coding of each interview, the analysis of such a large data set precluded this. This clustering was an attempt not to develop higher order themes, as might be undertaken in a case study approach, but to look for patterns of shared experience in the data that could be grouped together to form broad categories. Once the themes had been clustered, the data extracts were grouped together under each of these headings, allowing a closer inspection of a corpus of data. I then reexamined this with a more focused lens to explore patterns and interrelationships. The aim of this process was to arrive at a superordinate organizing device to understand the shared aspect of these experiences (Smith et al., 1999).

Analysis of Discourse

As noted earlier, some elements in people's accounts did not lend themselves to a method of analysis grounded in verbatim data. Silence has been noted as a strategy of resistance to pathologizing and disciplining strategies both in the research interview and in actual health care encounters (Heaphy, 1998; Huby, 1997). Silence is also a feature of sensitive research, in which participants might not have a language to describe their experience or might deny it (Brannen, 1988). It became important to find a way of interpreting such data that allowed a consideration of the context of the described health care encounters and also the context of the research interview. A method of analysis that paid heed to such power relations and allowed an engagement with the silences, contradictions, and rhetorical functions of the accounts was required, and thus a deconstruction, or discursive analysis, of the texts was juxtaposed against the IPA. Deconstruction has generally been used to examine texts in which expert and dominant discourses are embedded; for instance, in relation to the pathologization of homosexuality, deconstruction would be used to look at the way in which psychiatrists talk or write about homosexuality rather than examining how lesbians and gay men experience health care. Similarly, with discourse analysis of the Potter and Wetherell (1982) school, the material most likely to be subjected to analysis is that in which dominant discourses are taken up; thus, Wetherell and Potter used DA to understand how people draw on discourse to justify and maintain racism, but this approach has not been used to explore how people experience racism. Other researchers adopting a similar approach have looked at how homophobic discourse is maintained and justified (e.g., Gough, 2002) but have tended not to use it to explore how homophobia is experienced.

Exceptions to this are to be found in work by Yardley (1998) and Boyle and McEvoy (1998). Yardley used deconstruction to examine how people with chronic dizziness attempt to negotiate and resist dominant discourses and identities in relation to illness and coping. Boyle and McEvoy explored how dominant discourses about abortion affect the ways in which women experience abortion. Other researchers have attempted to look at how dominant discourses are implicated in the maintenance of certain kinds of health-related behavior in the areas of smoking and sex education (e.g., Gillies, 1999; Willig, 1999b; Woollett, Marshall, & Stenner, 1998). Again, in common with earlier uses of DA, these studies tend to focus on the uptake of dominant discourses to justify certain kinds of behavior. However, these researchers go further (as do Yardley, and Boyle and McEvoy), in the sense that they try to say something about the relationship between discourse and experience or behavior. Willig (1999b) has argued that we need to use deconstruction to do more than offer a critical commentary if we are to challenge discourses that constrain or limit behavior. Gillies, Willig, and Woollett have done this by using positioning theory to help explain these relationships.

Positioning theory has been developed in the works of B. Davies and Harré (1990), Hollway (1989), and Parker (1992). As discussed in Chapter 3, positioning theory involves an attempt to account for subjectivity in the ways in which discursive resources constrain and enable what can be thought, said, and done by individuals. Individuals are constructed through available discourses, which they can accept or resist. These positions provide us with our subjectivity, and we come to experience the world from that perspective (Davies & Harré, 1990). Individuals might be positioned by the discursive practices of others, or they might position themselves in relation to available discourses. Thus, Gillies and Willig (1999) analyzed interviews with women smokers in terms of how the women positioned themselves in relation to available discourses about smoking behavior. Harden and Willig (1998) explored the ways in which young women were positioned in relation to discourses about contraception to explain the subjective experience of contraception, so that they could gain a (non-individualistic) understanding of what influences contraception use.

I noted in Chapter 3 that among the varied approaches to DA, those in the "analysis of discourse" tradition or macroanalysis tend to be more theoretical than those within the microanalysis tradition, which tends to be more empirical. I also noted that the two approaches were not incompatible. Given that in this analysis, I was more within the analysis of discourse approach but was attempting to analyze empirical material, it made sense to borrow tools or methods from both micro and macro discourse analysis. These tools and methods encompass both tangible and concrete methods, such as thematic coding of data, as well as more conceptual approaches to looking at data. It has been argued that there are no recipe-like instructions for engaging in discourse analysis (Coyle, 2000). Willig (2000) has commented on the limitations to the degree to which discourse analysis has been operationalized, which makes it more difficult to analyze experiences. However, in spite of these limitations, some key pointers and tools can be used when conducting discourse analysis and deconstruction. What is required is the development of scholarship or an analytical mentality, in which beliefs about what is normally taken for granted about language use are suspended and in which we look at how people construct their version of the world and what they gain from these constructions (Coyle, 2000). Variations or contradictions in people's accounts can be used as a lever to analyze discursive practices and provide clues as to what function is being performed (Potter & Wetherell, 1994). Such an analysis requires a close reading of the text, with the researcher mindful of the action orientation of the text and the wider context in which it is embedded (Coyle, 2000; Wetherell & Potter, 1988). A close reading requires attention to details such as pauses, repairs, and word choice, which can be made possible by having a detailed transcription of texts such as interview material (Potter & Wetherell, 1994).

On being mindful of the action orientation of talk and its context, it is important to consider what that talk might be designed to counteract (Coyle, 2000). Alternative versions are not always mentioned explicitly, making awareness of the context all the more important in the analytic task (Parker & Burman, 1993). Silences and omissions might signal dichotomies that support ideological positions and dominant discourses imposing limits on what can and cannot be said (Feldman, 1995). It is here that deconstruction becomes an important tool for analyzing polarities and dualisms. Here, language is understood to be a self-referent system, in which meanings and concepts such as identity can be understood only by what they are not; such oppositions are often forgotten or repressed and can be revealed through deconstructing texts (Burr, 1995). Yardley and Beech (1998), in their deconstruction of accounts of dizziness, suggested examining interview transcripts for inconsistencies, omissions, and moments of conversational awkwardness.

Thus, silences and contradictions alert the analyst to the presence of dominant discourses and subordinate discourses that might be brought to the fore. Part of my analytic task was to look for variability and omissions in the interview data to begin to uncover these subordinate discourses. Notes in my diary signaled inconsistencies early on in the research process. A 2- to 3-hour interview might proceed with good rapport and disclosure of intimate details, only to be followed by a short conversation on leaving, in which material was introduced that seemed to contradict the overall account given during the interview. Such apparent contradictions often related to how the participants revealed themselves in the interview as being "out" to all of the significant people in their life and feeling comfortable about their sexual identity. However, after the interview, they said they did not feel safe enough to disclose their sexual identity to people they lived with or that they had reservations about discussing their participation in the research project with a parent. This early observation suggested the possibility that participants' accounts served a rhetorical function or had an action orientation to present lesbian and gay identities in a positive light during the research interview. During interviews, other inconsistencies were noted, where participants claimed that lesbian and gay lifestyles were as good as and similar to heterosexual lifestyles but would then say that they believed that lesbians and gay men should not have children because their relationships were inherently less stable than heterosexual ones.

Parker et al. (1995) have said that we need to move beyond the text to deconstruct the polarities that underlie and structure power relations. They also argued that psychiatric knowledge and practices are intertwined with institutions and power. A material discursive approach to the data helps us to move beyond the text by considering the role of material factors intersecting with discursive practices in medicine and psychiatry. Clearly, sexual identity, and its discursive construction as psychopathology, was operating as a material factor in the health care encounters. In addition to this, there were the further material factors of age, social class, race, and religious and cultural differences operating that further affected the power relations in health care encounters. These discursive practices led to material consequences for participants in the form of affecting access to health care and further identity work. Parker et al. have suggested that a practical deconstruction can overturn polarities in favor of the less privileged or subordinate term and can allow the construction of less pathologizing or more emancipatory "realities," open up new spaces of resistance, and arrive at new concepts and new practices (Parker, 1998a; Parker et al., 1995). Further deconstructive work, then, was required in the analysis, as I needed to consider further how other material differences affected the negotiation of sexual identity in mental health care encounters. This requires sensitivity to what is not said against my knowledge of the potential significance of such silences in relation to dominant discourses and local cultures and politics (Gill, 1996; Yardley, 1997b).

In this study, I conducted the analysis of discourse using the techniques discussed, within a framework based on Parker's (1992) steps in DA. This involved initially reading and rereading the interview transcripts and organizing the material according to themes; this first part of the discursive analysis had already been achieved in the initial analysis using IPA. However, it also involved a process of "exploring the connotations, allusions and implications which the texts evoke" (Parker, 1992, p. 7) to identify the discursive meanings constructed in relation to the mental health care encounters of lesbians and gay men. In this framework, discourse means a system of statements that construct an object, and text refers to the interview transcripts. Silences within the interviews were also treated as text (Morgan & Coombes, 2001). When I noted silences during the course of an interview, I needed to take ethical considerations into account, so as not to force participants into discussing topics with which they did not feel safe. However, at other times, probing could lead to further discussion about some of the contradictions and difficulties experienced. In this stage of the analysis, I also paid attention to dissimilarities, or the contrasting nature of what was said (Gillies & Willig, 1997). The next stage, following Parker's steps, was to look at the way in which discourses contain subjects and to consider the ways in which subjects were positioned by the discourses so far identified; Parker (1992) stated that in Althusserian terms, we have to ask how a discourse is hailing us and what rights we have to speak when positioned by a discourse. Thus this approach to discourse analysis involves

> specifying what types of person are talked about in this discourse...and speculating about what they can say in the discourse, what you could say if you identified with them. (p. 10)

Parker's (1992) steps were developed to give clearer guidance than that offered in other descriptions of DA, which tend to suggest that the process is intuitive or implicit. However, Parker suggested that these steps need not be followed in a rigid or mechanistic way, and for this study, I adopted those steps that enabled a focus on discursive positioning and the identification of polarities.

CONCLUSION

In the undertaking of this study, an opportunity arose to pay attention to sampling strategies and map them to theoretical discussions about identity and analysis of experience. To begin with, the commitment to try to obtain a more diverse sample arose from unreconstructed positivist reasons concerning notions of generalizability but also for political reasons concerning ideas about inclusivity (although, of course, at this time, this latter term had not been invented). In doing this, I used peer researchers, alongside key informants, incentive schemes, and advertising for recruitment for the study outside lesbian and gay community locations and media. As the recruitment work progressed, discussions took place with peer researchers and key informants about different aspects of the insider status of the main researcher. It also became clear that the farther away I was from lesbian and gay recruitment sources, the more diverse the sample became in terms of social class, ethnicity, and educational background. The significance of lesbian and gay community attachment and the terms or categories people used to signify their sexual identity also came to the fore. Clearly, I was identified by the research participants, either via the peer researchers or through their own inquiries, as an identifiable lesbian, and feedback from participants suggested that this was important to them. Although in some cases, it will have helped me to gain access in a sensitive area, there could be other cases where recruitment failed for the very same reason. Such cases are, of course, unlikely to have come to the attention of either me or others engaged in the recruitment process, but to an extent, the insider/outsider dualism in sensitive research was disrupted.

By taking a different approach to sampling a hidden population, I overcame some of the problems of class and education bias, which enabled further theoretical development about identity, community, and health. The approach taken problematized the essentialist thinking built into many sampling approaches with this population, whereby research participants have to subscribe to particular identity politics and affiliations before they are likely to be included in a study. Such approaches to research reproduce assumptions about the group studied, because arguments about identity and community become self-fulfilling. The basis on which research participants are generally recruited into such studies is through self-identification as a lesbian or gay man, or through lesbian/gay community affiliation. Both identification and community attachment are related to social class and community in ways that do not become apparent if homogenous groups are sampled. The essentialism built into these sampling strategies rests on the unproblematic adoption of *lesbian* and *gay* as self-referential terms of sexual identity. By definition, then, such an approach will tend to recruit lesbians and gay men who are proud, thus re-inscribing the shame-pride dichotomy through the exclusion of those who are ashamed.

Although the usual approaches to sampling in studies of lesbians and gay men approach might suffice in the study of lesbians and gay communities or in the study of the development of lesbian and gay identities, the extrapolation of these approaches to applied research in either sexual health or mental health is clearly flawed. Curiously, even though a critique of such essentialism has come from social constructionists, when social constructionists conduct research into the lives of lesbians and gay men, they, too, fall prey to ill-considered essentialism in their sampling strategies. In this study, by questioning the usefulness of the terms available for people to construct their stigmatized and threatened identities, I developed sampling strategies that allowed a degree of side-stepping of the dualism built into essentialist sampling strategies (i.e., those that rely on a positive [affirmative] lesbian or gay identity and the adoption and use of these terms). Thus, in advertising in particular ways and in particular places, in using peer researchers who might or might not be lesbian or gay identified and who were trained to be sensitive to this issue of language and identity, a more heterogeneous sample was obtained than is usually the case in studies of this kind.

To evaluate the success, or otherwise, of the sampling strategies used in this study, it is useful to return to the question of whether my assumptions had been challenged. In a sense, the success of the bold recruitment strategy was the very thing that disrupted my worldview; as the sample became more diverse, more participants entered the study who gave accounts of being, and remaining, conflicted about their sexual identity. This took me well outside any comfort zone and yet allowed a better engagement with the tension identified early on about the relationship between sexual identity and mental health. The comfort zone was to hear accounts that were told like Damascene conversion stories, which would read something like this:

I was screwed up about my sexuality for a while, I had some mental health problems, was pathologised along the way but then I realised my true sexual identity, accepted it, came to terms with it and joined a lovely caring sharing lesbian and gay community.

To make this story complete, if participants were asked at the end of the interview whether they would take a pill to make them straight, they would answer a resounding "NO." Clearly, though, as the study progressed and as the sampling strategy developed, more people came in who would have taken that pill or at least given it some consideration. As will be seen in Chapters 5 and 7, it was from these accounts that some of the richest data emerged in terms of the second research question. As the sampling strategy progressed, my insider status was dislocated and disrupted, and as this happened, I arrived at new insights. Again, no claim will be made here that such knowledge was complete, and I am offering it as a partial and situated perspective. I do claim, however, that certain important boundaries were pushed, but I also recognize that they could have been pushed further. However, the boundaries were pushed beyond essentializing frameworks that would have reproduced circular arguments and self-fulfilling prophecies. In doing this, I reached a more vulnerable group, and the analysis and interrogation of their accounts will lead to further insights about how homophobia and heterosexism operate in mental health care encounters and how they affect access to care.

ENDNOTE

1 Sigma Research is a social research group in the UK specializing in the policy aspects of HIV and AIDS and they have undertaken more than 50 research and development projects in the past 7 years.

Chapter 5
Identity Parade:
Experiences in the Line-up
for Mental Health Care

In this chapter, I thematically analyze part of the data set from the 49 in-depth interviews that were conducted using interpretative phenomeno-logical analysis (IPA). In the first section, I set out how this first data set was extracted for this analysis with a view to conducting a further layer of analysis using more discursive approaches. Following this, I describe the procedures for using IPA alongside presentation of the data according to the themes that emerged from the analysis. Further discussion of these thematic categories follows in Chapter 6.

THE DATA CORPUS EXTRACTED FOR INITIAL ANALYSIS

As described in Chapter 4, 49 interviews were conducted, of which 48 fit the criteria for the study. One interview was not included in the analysis, as the participant did not identify as lesbian, gay, or bisexual. The difficulties associated with being clear about eligibility criteria when conducting research with hidden populations have been noted by Biernacki and Waldorf (1981) and were discussed in Chapter 4. A further element to this issue of eligibility, which also arises from issues discussed in Chapter 4 about conducting sensitive research, was that not all of the 48 remaining participants had experienced mental health issues or had any related mental health care. In fact, 36 of the 48 identified that they had experienced mental health problems that they attributed in some, but not necessarily a total, way to their struggle with coping with their sexual identity. Of these 36, 32 had related experiences of mental health care. The mental health problems identified ranged from mild and untreated anxiety and depression through to hospitalization for severe depression and eating disorders. Many participants had been treated or had been referred by their general practitioners (GPs) for depression, panic attacks, self-harm, or misuse of alcohol, and many had been referred for counseling. Others had accessed counseling privately or through student services.

There were methodological reasons for keeping the brief about the criteria for the project fairly loose when recruiting participants for the study. This was because of the sensitive nature of the research and also because of the recruitment strategy, in which one participant might snowball to further participants. For example, Anthea had experienced no mental health problems, but she did recruit further people into the study who had relevant experience. Furthermore, Brannen (1988) has noted that participants in sensitive research do not always talk readily about the research topic, even though they have volunteered to participate. Thus, the use of peer researchers and chain referral meant that this had to be taken into consideration, and it was important to allow some latitude about the degree to which recruiters could be expected to determine the eligibility of participants in relation to the specific aims of the study.

There were also theoretical reasons for keeping the brief wide when recruiting that, again, relate to the difficulties of defining sensitive research in advance. Again, these difficulties have been noted by Brannen (1988) and were discussed in Chapter 4. Brannen argued that participants should be allowed to define the problem in their own terms and that they might have difficulty in expressing their experiences or even deny them; keeping the brief wide to include general exploration of issues relating to coming out, and then later on making it even more broad, so that it was defined in terms of "sexual orientation and mental health," facilitated this. This initial approach to allowing participants to discuss their sexual identity and coming out to friends and family allowed time for rapport to develop in the interview before I honed in on more sensitive and threatening issues relating to mental health and mental health care.

This strategy toward the recruitment and the interview process was labor intensive but worthwhile, in that a diverse sample was achieved. This diversity produced data that could further our understanding about the experiences of coming out and the nature of related mental health issues and health care experiences. The wide range of data also allowed some insights into factors associated with mental health issues and coming out experiences and allowed these experiences to be set in a wider sociocultural and interpersonal context. My purpose in this study was not to investigate the relationship between coming out and mental health but, rather, to focus on mental health care experiences. However, it could be seen from this large data set, which included some people who had not experienced mental health problems, that there were probably many other significant factors in people's lives that contributed to their mental health problems. Many participants, in fact, attributed their struggle with their sexual orientation as the "last straw" in a chain of events leading to mental illness. It was striking during the preliminary analysis of the data that a large proportion of those who had suffered mental illness had experienced significant stressful life events, many of which were unrelated to their sexual identity, such as the death of a parent during childhood; childhood abuse, including sexual abuse, witnessing a murder, or other stressful events; rape; and the loss of a child. Other events more directly related to sexual identity included being evicted from the family home and other kinds of family rejection, homophobic violence from family members and peers, and bullying. The interviews also contained a wealth of material about coping with sexual identity for those participants who were part of religious communities. However, as noted earlier, it was not the purpose of this study to examine these in detail, but the context can be illuminative; for instance, some participants described how members of their family viewed homosexuality as a mental illness that should be cured, and this had some bearing on participants' expectations and experiences of mental health care.

Another factor to consider in relation to the total sample was that 4 participants identified that they had experienced mental health problems that they associated with their sexual identity but did not have any related mental health care experience. This lack of health care experience did not appear to be related to the severity of mental illness but might have been related to factors such as age, culture, and other sources of support. Such an investigation was not the main purpose of the study but does illustrate the potential strength of the recruitment methods used, as this diversity might be theoretically important. Some of these cases in which participants experienced mental health problems but did not seek health care help to illuminate our understanding of factors affecting access to care. These are brought into Chapter 7 and build on the understanding developed in this chapter and Chapter 6 about nondisclosure of sexual orientation during mental health care encounters.

For the purposes of this study, then, to address the specific research questions about mental health care experiences, of the original sample of 49, I analyzed a subsample of 36 interviews. Eighteen of the participants are presented in this chapter and discussed further in Chapter 6. These 18 interviews included material about mental health care experiences that lent themselves to a method of analysis grounded in the verbatim data describing participants' experiences and in which these experiences could be thematized, that is, IPA. However, not all of the material in these 18 interviews could be analyzed using this method, and a further, more discursive approach to the analysis follows in Chapter 7. In that analysis, I used additional material from the 18 participants presented in this chapter as well as introducing more material from the remaining participants in the subsample of 36. This subsequent analysis is situated within a more constructionist epistemological framework than IPA. It uses a different lens to view those aspects of the data that were more contradictory and that participants seemed to find harder to articulate. In this further analysis, I subjected those aspects of people's experiences, and their accounts of those experiences, to further interrogation and paid particular attention to the silences, omissions, and contradictions in those accounts.

INTERPRETATIVE PHENOMENOLOGICAL ANALYSIS (IPA) OF THE INTERVIEW DATA

For the IPA, the interviews were transcribed and subjected to a thematic analysis involving the procedures described in Chapter 4. The approach taken to the IPA was that recommended by J. Smith, Osborn, et al. (1999) for use with large data sets. To begin with, I scrutinized the first six interviews. From this preliminary interpretation, I noted emerging themes and anything else striking or of interest. Preliminary themes that emerged from these first six interviews were

- experiences of health care in which health care practitioners seemed to view lesbian identity as an abnormality caused by childhood sexual abuse,
- concerns about being viewed as abnormal and therefore not disclosing sexual identity or associated concerns to health care practitioners, and
- feeling that health care practitioners did not want to discuss issues relating to gay identity.

The first preliminary theme of lesbian identity's being viewed as abnormal and linked to childhood sexual abuse can be seen in Mandy's account.[1] In the following extract, she refers to the childhood sexual abuse by identifying herself as a survivor:

> I went to see my doctor and he sent me to a counsellor and I was seeing a counsellor because I'm a survivor and my counsellor ( ) definitely was turning round and telling me the reason why I was gay was because I was a survivor.

The second preliminary theme was nondisclosure of sexual identity in mental health care encounters because of fears of being seen as abnormal. This can be seen in Josh's account of why he could not bring himself to tell the clinical psychologist he was seeing that he felt that his depression was linked to his negative feelings about his emerging gay identity:

> I just thought (...) if I did say "I'm worried about my sexuality," they might go (...) I probably thought that they would um (...) they would just think that I was some sort of I (...) freak.

The third preliminary theme of feeling that health care practitioners did not want to discuss issues relating to gay identity can be seen in Alec's account. Alec had sought counseling when he ended his relationship with his girlfriend at the time that he was realizing his gay identity, but he felt that the counselor was reluctant to discuss his concerns about his sexual identity:

> I perceived her to be skirting around certain issues and not wanting to talk about certain things that I wanted to talk about because I considered it to be an issue. A lot of it was revolving around sexuality and lifestyle and things like that. Things that I wanted to talk about and speak my mind on but things that I don't think that she was quite prepared to have at her table, as it were.

Alec felt that the counselor wanted to concentrate on his previous heterosexual relationship and would not pursue topics relating to his gay identity:

> It always used to somehow pan back to (my ex-girlfriend) which I think is perfectly natural because that was the initial problem I went to her with, so it would seem logically that a lot of things would stem

from that. But it generally did try (...) or she tried like "What about when you were with (your girlfriend) or what about when you did this or that?" Sort of almost like rebuffing me basically.

I used these three preliminary themes of experiences of mental health care, in which lesbian or gay identities were seen as abnormal, were ignored, or were difficult to disclose because of participants' fears of being seen as abnormal, as a template when analyzing the rest of the interviews. Further examples of all three emerged from the data, demonstrating that these were shared experiences. Although I was primed to look for these preliminary themes in the larger data set, new themes also emerged. These were

- experiences of health care in which health care practitioners seemed to view lesbian or gay identity as a phase that was immature or attention seeking,
- experiences of health care in which health care practitioners seemed to view lesbian or gay identity as the cause of mental illness,
- potential causes of mental illness unrelated to sexual identity not considered by health care practitioners,
- feeling that issues relating to sexual identity were trivialized by health care practitioners,
- feeling that issues relating to sexual identity were ignored by health care practitioners,
- feeling rejected by health care practitioners following disclosure of sexual identity, and
- feeling that health care practitioners distanced themselves following disclosure of sexual identity.

Following this initial preliminary coding of each interview, I then attempted to cluster the emergent themes into meaningful groups. Although J. Smith, Osborn, et al. (1999) have suggested that this should be undertaken after the preliminary coding of each interview, the analysis of such a large data set precluded this. This clustering was not an attempt to develop higher order themes, as might be undertaken in a case study approach, but to look for patterns of shared experience in the data that could be grouped together to form broad categories. At this stage of the analysis, three broad categories were developed:

1. *nondisclosure of sexual identity* because of fears about being pathologized or receiving homophobic abuse;

2. *experiences of being pathologized*, in which lesbian and gay identities were seen as indicative of arrested development and therefore potentially curable; and

3. *experiences of being silenced*, which included having issues relating to sexual identity ignored or trivialized or in which health care practitioners became hostile or rejecting.

The data extracts will now be grouped together under these the three broad theme headings to allow a closer inspection of the corpus of data. This allows a reexamination with a more focused lens to explore patterns and interrelationships (J. Smith, Osborn, et al., 1999). The data clustered under the three broad category headings will be presented in this chapter, and in the following chapter I will discuss how these findings relate to existing research findings and literature. The aim of this process of analysis was to arrive at a superordinate organizing device to understand the shared aspect of these experiences (J. Smith, Osborn, et al., 1999). This will also be discussed in the next chapter alongside a discussion of how such an understanding is informed by existing theory.

Nondisclosure of Sexual Identity

Several participants did not disclose their sexual identity to mental health care practitioners, even though they felt that some of their mental health problems were related to their anxieties about coming to terms with it. The preliminary analysis of the first six interviews revealed how Josh felt that he could not disclose to the clinical psychologist who was treating him for depression in case he was seen as a freak. Other participants also described this fear of being seen as abnormal or being pathologized:

I thought there was too much potential to have the GP thinking "God, you're some kind of freak, or whatever" ( ) it seemed too risky as much as anything.

I was worried the counsellor would think that "you're abnormal," that there's something wrong with you. Or that you're disgusting.

I guess it was about confirmation of my worries that I was abnormal, that if somebody at the time it didn't matter particularly whether it was the counsellor or my mum had a bad reaction or confirmed that it was something to be ashamed of or that was abnormal in society or that was bad or that was an illness, any of those things it was fear of that ( ) My fears with the GP is that they would only see it in terms of the medical model.

I remember sitting there and thinking I know what the problem is but I can't tell you. I can't tell you what it is. And so I'm sat there saying I really don't know, I just, I always feel low in the winter, and you know, and I, I couldn't tell him.

I just don't want to feel like I'm under stud(...) As a freak or some-thing, you know. It's one thing (...) but I don't know I think maybe it's also just the homophobia, afraid that I'm going to get their homopho-bia.

For Simone and Claudia, this was expressed not in terms of being seen as abnormal but as a fear that health care practitioners would see only their sex-ual identity as an issue and not be able to look beyond that to see the whole person:

I guess it's about them thinking less of me or seeing that as the only issue and not seeing me underneath. Not being able to get past me being gay and that's it.

And I thought as well the whole emphasis of the counselling is going to be on that issue. And because that wasn't the only thing I made it so we didn't talk about it at all which was wrong whereas it was an issue but not the only one. That's probably one of the things I worry about most is that it is going to be the only thing people can see. Any other attributes of your personality will go because there—there's Claudia and she's—however people term me—that's going to be the only thing they can talk about and their only thing of interest. And I think that was my fear with the counsellor really.

Some participants gave their concerns about receiving general homopho-bic abuse as a reason for nondisclosure rather than specific fears about being pathologized:

I would always (say I was) heterosexual because I thought it's easier. Otherwise it's like in a hospital you know there's this kind of (...) where all the staff know about you, everything you ever do is passed on to all the staff, regardless of whether or not they're on duty. Everybody knows then. ( ) Also your treatment can depend so much on how the staff see you. If they like you, you get an easy run; if they don't, you can be sedated, sectioned, you know, kept in a room on your own, put in the intensive care unit, denied leave—anything can happen. They can make your life hell. ( ) And when you're there seven days a week, 24 hours a day, and you've got no way out, you just don't want to give anybody any more ammunition.

You know there's, there's homes, hospitals that you can go to and be locked away in, that kind of thing, that's what worries me and that there's people out there that would still try and do that, and it, it still scares me.

These fears about being seen as abnormal, or being seen not as a whole person but only in terms of sexual identity, were realized by many of those who did not disclose their sexual identity, as can be seen in the next section. Finally, in this section, Len's account gives an insight into what practitioners need to do to make care more accessible. This links to later theoretical discussion about how heterosexism makes lesbian and gay identities invisible, so that people accessing care have no indication of whether it would be safe, or even appropriate, to disclose:

Had there been literature around the place, maybe I would have felt that I could talk to the GP because there are leaflets saying that you can talk to your GP about all sorts of other things but there's nothing that says you can talk to your GP about your sexual orientation or you know, so maybe had I seen something there, saying well I don't know, saying that you can discuss um these kind of issues with your doctor, then I'd have felt yes I could because I could go in there and I could talk to him and I wouldn't be dismissed because it says here that you know, my GP will point me in the right direction, give me, give me somewhere to go, or you know, someone, at least give me somebody else to talk to.

Experiences of Being Pathologized

A number of participants who disclosed their sexual identity in mental health care settings recounted experiences of having their sexuality pathologized. It was seen in the preliminary analysis of the first six interviews that Mandy described a health care experience in which her lesbian identity was seen as an abnormality caused by childhood sexual abuse. Both Jane and Julie described similar experiences, in which mental health care practitioners seemed to view their lesbian identity as an abnormality caused by childhood sexual abuse:

> I've had the "Oh you're just gay because your dad abused you." ( ). I've had it suggested by Community Psychiatric Nurses who've been try-ing to counsel me. "Do you think that might just be because (...) because of your father?

> Well everybody blames (the childhood sexual assault) ( ). I won't argue about it with anybody, my parents or my psychiatrist because I think that's ( ) that's what he believes, he thinks I'm frightened of men, so he's that's what he says: "You're not gay, you've got, you've got a men phobia" ( ). (My psychiatrist says that) because of what happened to me when I was very young and being afraid of men, I've just been spending all this time afraid of men, and then I started being worried about my, or confused about my identity and then I became ill and that's when I got my sexuality back to front.

Alice said that she was told quite directly by a counselor that it was abnormal to have same-sex attraction or relationships. Charlotte also expe-rienced a sense that her counselor viewed homosexuality as something abnormal or unhealthy, for which a cause could be found, such as having a difficult relationship with her mother:

> (She) just made me question it so much in a negative sense that you know and the cause and um, just where I was going to go with it and is it really healthy and maybe I will get over it. ( ) and almost trying to relate it to the fact that my (relationship with my) mother is a result of this, and I just thought well no ( ) it was like yeah she wanted to get to the bottom of why I like women.

The previous extract from Charlotte's interview also shows how she expe-rienced the counselor's suggesting that her lesbian identity was something that could be cured or grown out of ("maybe I will get over it"). Julie had a similar experience, in that her psychiatrist seemed to be suggesting to her that "she was not really gay" but simply had not yet developed enough to be able to have mature heterosexual relationship because she was "afraid of men." Other participants had similar experiences, in which they felt that their sexual identity was seen as a phase. Nicki's experience with her psychi-atrist gave her a clear message that homosexuality was seen as an immature and possibly attention-seeking phase:

The psychiatrist (said) ( ) I'm not really (gay but) I'm just fooling myself with shock tactics.

Nicki had further experiences of having her certainty about her sexual identity questioned as if it was something which might be a temporary phase which she would grow out of:

> Some of the nurses were a bit sort of like "Are you sure?"—I was like yes thank you. Then they'd say "Would you like a chat, would you like a chat."

Charlotte also experienced her counselor's implying that her lesbian identity was a phase she would grow out of and that she would eventually meet someone and have a heterosexual relationship:

> I don't think (the counsellor) really took me very seriously with me being so young. You know I think she sort of said to me "Well look wait a couple of years you know, you might meet someone."

Roger also felt that his GP viewed his gay identity as something he should just be able to get over:

> I saw the GP and when I said you know "I'm er gay" and er sort of mentioned it to him, he he was just sort of was very dismissive and said "How long have you been like this?" and I said "Always" ( ) and then he said "Well you want to sort yourself out" he said "Your problem is you're shy of women." ( ). He said "Pull yourself together and go and get a girlfriend."

It can be seen from the above extracts that the way in which lesbian and gay identities were pathologized was primarily through its being viewed as a developmental abnormality caused by either childhood sexual abuse or difficult relationships with parents. Within this, it was seen as an immature phase, with an implication that people would grow out of it or that they could in some way be helped to become heterosexual.

The other aspect to pathologization was that other potential causes of mental illness were not explored. Wayne described how when he was suffering from severe depression, his illness was attributed to his confusion about being gay, even though he felt that he had accepted his sexual identity:

They were bothered if there didn't seem to be a valid reason to be depressed but the only valid reason they saw in my case was to be confused about my sexuality ( ). It may have helped if the psychiatrist actually listened to what I was saying. Didn't just listen out for what they wanted me to say. And if I was referred to some type of counselling or therapy, some sort of talking therapy to try and iron things out. Even they may have found they were totally right, my whole problem was "coming out" but I didn't think so and I still don't think so now. But we could have sorted things out, dealt with different areas individually with what was wrong and how they all affected each other. I certainly think that would have helped.

Wayne felt that much of his depressive illness could be attributed to his experiences of bullying at school and having to take on caring responsibilities as a child rather than any confusion about or lack of acceptance of his gay identity. However, his experience was that his gay identity was perceived as the cause of his mental illness:

With the nurses and the doctors, their answer to it all was me being gay ( ) It was Wayne the gay—that's really the sum total of it.

Wayne's experience parallels the concerns expressed by Simone and cited in the previous section, where she said she did not disclose her sexual identity for fear that she would be seen only in the light of this. There were thus two kinds of pathologizing stance operating in people's health care experiences. The first was where sexual identity was seen as a problem that needed attention, in the sense that it was seen as having a cause and therefore a cure. The second one, experienced by Wayne, was where confusion about sexual identity, rather than sexual identity per se, was seen as the problem, with the solution being acceptance of gay identity. In both types of pathologization, the focus on sexual identity overrides any attention to other potential causes of people's mental health problems, such as childhood sexual abuse, bullying, and other kinds of stress. For instance, childhood sexual abuse is seen as the cause of homosexuality rather than a possible direct cause of mental illness.

Experiences of Being Silenced

I noted in the preliminary analysis that Alec experienced the feeling that his counselor did not want to discuss his gay identity or any associated concerns. Further analysis of the other interviews showed similar experiences for a number of participants. Sandra, like Alec, found that the health care practitioner she saw did not seem to want to discuss any issues relating to lesbian or gay identity:

> I did have um, I think it was, fifteen weeks CAT Therapy (cognitive analytic therapy), that was the NHS stuff that I got um (...) and (...) my being Gay was literally sort of noted down and passed over. It didn't figure in anything that was subsequently said. It just didn't figure. (It was like they said) "Yea, OK fine ( ) I don't have a problem with that."

Another participant, who was suffering from depression, had approached her GP and requested a referral to see a counselor to talk about her sexuality. She knew that her GP had made this clear in his referral letter to the counselor, but during the counseling sessions, she felt that all her attempts to broach the subject were ignored:

> The GP had written a referral letter to that counsellor which actually said I wanted to talk about issues of sexuality and that counsellor must have known from the beginning yet didn't bring it up or didn't enable me ( ). I think she could have explored it because I hinted so much, there were lots of things I hinted about.

For Sarah, Sandra, and Alec, their attempts to explore what they saw as a link between their mental health problems and their difficulties in adjusting to a lesbian or gay identity were ignored. Julie's experience of this was being told not to discuss her sexual identity rather than being ignored. She was initially encouraged by one nurse to discuss her concerns relating to her sexual identity in group therapy. However, another nurse then told her that this was not an appropriate place to discuss her sexual identity:

> Well the male nurse encouraged me to talk about it, to bring the issue up in group therapy but you see this other female nurse said "Well you know it's not really applicable to the group is it?" Which I, I was so shocked by I couldn't really argue because he had specifically said you know band it out in the group, that's what it's for, you know, and it would have been very difficult for me to say well this is one of my real problems. But I thought oh well no, I'll ask the female nurse about it and she just said "Well you know it's not, not really anyone else here with that problem."

A further way in which participants were silenced about their concerns about their sexual identity was through trivialization. Roger and Julie had similar experiences, in that they both felt that they needed help coping with their sexual identity, but when they tried to raise this and get help, they felt that their concerns were dismissed and trivialized:

> I think there's things, lots of things that I want to talk about and I'll always get shut up when I see one of the psychiatrists or whatever about the OCD (obsessive compulsive disorder) because by the time I've spoken to them about the OCD there's never time really to speak about the sexuality and if I do try to talk about it there's never enough time because it's always at the end of the interview and they say well just get on with it, you know I need to talk about it, you know?

> Well, one nurse said "Look why don't you just go somewhere and sort yourself out, all this business" you know all this business, it's like a fundamental part of my life ( ) but I couldn't come to terms with what was going on as far as I was concerned, my identity and stuff and ( ) a lot of nurses used the word "responsibility" to me, I wasn't being responsible, I've had to take it all on board for myself to sort out.

What these extracts show is that health care practitioners seemed not to understand the impact of homophobia, gay-related stress, and internalized homophobia on people's ability to adjust to a lesbian or gay identity and the impact that this has on their mental health.

One further shared experience that also had the effect of silencing was perceived distancing from health care providers after a disclosure about sexual identity. Julie regretted disclosing to one nurse, who, she felt, became hostile toward her and more difficult to talk to afterward:

> I spoke to a female nurse about it but I instantly regretted it ( ) at the time that I discussed it with her I was on my re-feeding programme and I felt afterwards that she was grilling me a bit more than the other girls, we used to eat together, about six of us at dinner and um I used to think that she picked up on my little tricks more than everybody else's, but you don't know how much of it is you know, your own paranoia. I'm sure she did, um but you know you can't really be sure ( ) and I just thought she, you know, maybe she thinks that I fancy her and er you know she's too understanding, maybe she's really worried about coming back to talk to me now because she thinks I'm going to leap

on her or something. Um you know it was probably completely unreasonable to think that but ( ).

What Julie was describing here was a sense that the nurse to whom she had disclosed had become less friendly toward her and was now less likely to spend time talking with Julie about anything, including her concerns about her sexual identity. This experience also fed into Julie's concerns about being seen as abnormal or as the kind of person who would be sexually predatory toward the nurse she had disclosed to. In another case, the counseling sessions were abruptly terminated just after Sarah disclosed her sexual identity to a nurse who was counseling her. Sarah experienced this as a rejection, and it made her feel that the counselor had ended the sessions because of negative views about lesbians and gay men, even though the reason given was that the nurse was leaving her current post:

Part of me believed that she wasn't really going to another job she just, it was because I was gay and I was an awful person and it had to stop.

These experiences of being pathologized, silenced, ignored, and rejected left participants feeling angry, upset, let down, disappointed, vulnerable, insecure, and confused about their sexual identity. Jane, Julie, and Sarah describe how being ignored or feeling that they had been silenced made them feel:

I mean to be honest, when people ignore it it's worse than saying that it's bad.

It made me think "God, why am I such a complete bag of nuts then, I must be, must be really weird if these people can't do anything for me."

I think she could have explored it because I hinted so much, there were lots of things I hinted about ( ). Whether that was about prejudice towards gay people or not wanting to talk about it I don't know but ( ) for me because it was quite close to that time of just coming to terms with it and accepting it, I guess the first thing I was thinking of was oh, it was because she, it was because I was gay and she didn't want to talk about it ( ) so there must be something wrong.

In the above extracts, both Julie and Sarah identify how the silence on the part of their counselor led to them feeling that there was something wrong with them because of their sexual identity.

Nicki and Charlotte describe how they felt as a consequence of their sexual identity's being viewed as an immature phase that they would grow out of. Nicki felt that her integrity and authenticity as a person were being undermined, and Charlotte was left feeling confused by the experience:

> When they turn around and say that all you're planning is complete sham, (it's) not so good, it doesn't help. It doesn't help at all. It makes me really, really upset.

> I was in a clinical situation and it was nice to sort of talk to someone that I thought could help but unfortunately it did the opposite, made me question maybe more, you know which isn't very good.

Mandy describes how she felt angry and let down when her lesbian identity was pathologized by being linked to childhood sexual abuse:

> I was really, really pissed off that he said it and it really left me ( ) confused ( ) and then I was left with even more questions because he'd made me really confused and I was angry with the fact that he was able to do that. And it was being seventeen it wasn't very helpful. It was an issue which was coming up a lot in my life as well at the time. I was having great difficulty feeling that I was a survivor ( ). I was going to see the counsellor ( ) and then it turned into a great big flop, it was not very helpful at all. A pretty big let-down.

Julie, who was also pathologized in this way by her psychiatrist, felt that this led to her being more confused about her sexual identity and unable to accept it:

> He's the one person who says "You're not gay you know" and I think how can he say that? But it's quite interesting to know his opinion, because er you know I've been seeing him for two years so he must know me pretty well but so that confuses me when I'm just sort of trying to find my feet myself, and because of the sort of, because of the way I've grown up doubting myself and worrying about what I am, who I am, my identity and stuff, as soon as someone says something different I start thinking well, and questioning myself you know, so I don't know if I could give a really true account of how I really did feel. So because every time I get to accepting it, something happens and I become depressed again.

In the previous extract, Julie attributes her mental illness in part to the denial and lack of validation of her lesbian identity by her psychiatrist and other mental health care workers. Some participants identified that these experiences led to their avoiding further mental health care encounters or maintaining a silence within health care encounters, which meant that they could not get help with some of the problems they were experiencing. This was the case for Mandy and Jane, who both felt that this effect on their access to mental health care had led to a worsening of their mental health problems. In the following two extracts, it can be seen that the effect of being pathologized for Mandy was to delay seeking any further help for another 2 years, and it led Jane to her not talking to the people from whom she should have been getting therapeutic interventions and support:

He just said that he thought that the reason why I was gay was the fact that I was a survivor. I mean, he basically said do you want to come back and have a specialised talk about it so I said "Fuck off" and then walked out left it at that ( ). I didn't get any other help for quite a while, about a year or so. ( ) I mean it put me off going to get more help. And it really put me off counselling. So he really did put me off looking for help for a long time—eighteen months to two years.

I've had it suggested by CPNs who've been trying to counsel me. "Do you think that might just be because...because of your father?" Just like yeah, okay, goodbye there. As soon as I hear that it's like I know it's not even worth it any more talking to them so.

Mandy and Jane both felt that this lack of access to appropriate mental health care led to an exacerbation of their mental health problems:

I've done a lot of things because I didn't have the support from my GP enough or from my counsellor ( ). I've had a lot of suicidal feelings and I've had an alcohol problem and I had that when I was seventeen actually. ( ) I've suffered from bulimia, I've had eating disorders, cutting myself up ( ) and if he hadn't have said what he said I might have got the help I needed so I wouldn't have gone through that.

I overdosed when I was in hospital at various times. I was doing it because I needed somebody to talk to me and to listen to what I had to say. Part of the fact, part of what I had to say was that I was gay. Just the fact of saying it, because it was a part of me that I couldn't ignore any more.

Wayne felt that the effect on his mental health of being pathologized and the insistence by medical and nursing staff that his problems all related to his confusion and lack of acceptance of his gay identity, along with side effects from medication, were actually making his life more difficult. However, unlike Mandy and Jane, he felt that he had benefited from avoiding further encounters with the mental health care system:

There are all sorts of other side effects and I just decided that I thought I'm blowed if I'm going to take these for the rest of my life, gave them up, didn't go back to the doctor and I basically thought bollocks to it and I'm going to get on with my life. Well I've done that for four and a half years now. ( ) I can remember my actual encounters with the medical profession caused me as much stress as the symptoms I was going along with. I thought let's cut this out, it really got to seem like a load of rubbish. Let's cut this cycle, let's stop it. If I don't go along to the doctors I won't get any support but at the same time I won't get any stress. If I don't have the medication it won't give me a miracle cure but at the same time it won't give me any of the side effects which are just as bad as the original problem. Really I just thought I'm fed up at the time I was 22 or 23 and I thought I'm not going to have this caper for the rest of my life. And I just gave up the medication, felt a lot better, tried to think positive, didn't see doctors so I didn't get stressed, just carried on really. ( ) I had to make the best of a bad situation ( ) and there really was no help in finding myself sorting myself out as Wayne not as a gay person. Sorting out my confidence and things like that so I had no choice but to do it. I had to do it myself or I'd be a victim forever, you know. Victim of the system.

CONCLUSION

The thematic analysis of the data set identified three themes in relation to lesbians' and gay men's mental health care experiences when they are coming out. These three themes of nondisclosure, pathologization, and silencing will be explored further in the next chapter in the light of previous research and theory.

ENDNOTES

[1] All names are pseudonyms.

2 Verbatim extracts from the interviews are shown as indented quotations in italics; empty parentheses indicate that material has been omitted, information in parentheses has been added to provide clarification and ellipsis points (...) indicate a pause in the flow of speech following the convention by Golsworthy and Coyle (1999).

Chapter 6
Mistaken Identities through a Phenomenological Lens

The three themes that emerged from the interpretative phenomenological analysis (IPA) were nondisclosure of sexual identity, experiences of being pathologized, and experiences of being silenced. Following discussion of each of the themes, and through relating these themes to prior theory, we now undertake the final stage of IPA to arrive at a superordinate organizing device. This lends further understanding to the shared aspects of people's mental health care experiences.

NONDISCLOSURE OF SEXUAL IDENTITY

We saw in the previous chapter that several participants did not feel able to disclose their sexual identity to their mental health care practitioner, even though they felt that anxiety about their sexual identity was contributing to their mental health problems. The participants who described this experience were Josh, Oscar, Len, Jane, Simone, and Sarah. The experiences of feeling unsafe to disclose lesbian or gay identity to health care practitioners have been found in other studies of lesbians' and gay men's experiences of health care in relation to general health care (Paroski, 1987; Stevens, 1994b) and mental health care (Bradford & Ryan, 1987; Golding, 1997; Hetrick & Martin, 1987; MacFarlane, 1998). Bradford and Ryan (1987) found in their survey that 10% of their sample had seen counselors to whom they had felt unable to come out. Golding (1997) found in her survey that 84% of the sample had concerns about disclosing their sexual identity to mainstream mental health service providers. Like the research participants in this study, they were concerned about being pathologized or experiencing other forms of stigmatization or prejudice. MacFarlane (1998) also found that a number of participants in her study did not feel able to disclose their sexual identity because of worries about being pathologized or stigmatized. In Hetrick and Martin's (1987) study, 9 of the lesbian and gay youth who were under treatment within mainstream services for suicide attempts had not told their therapist that they were lesbian or gay and that they felt their sexual identity was a factor in their suicide attempt.

A number of researchers have looked at the effects of nondisclosure, although none of these studies relate specifically to people who are in mental health care settings. There might be some psychological benefits from nondisclosure (e.g., Healy, 1993), and this becomes particularly important when individuals are negotiating their sexual identity in hostile environments (e.g., Clarke, 1996). However, nondisclosure is also associated with psychological strain (Berger, 1990; Cain, 1991). Griffin (1991) has discussed the effects of tensions between the fear of disclosure and wanting self-integrity and feelings of authenticity that can come only from disclosure, with isolation resulting from strategies involving passing, deception, and secrecy. Markowe (1996) also found that lesbian women identified a need for feelings of authenticity that could be acquired only through disclosure. Another study of lesbian physical education teachers found that the continual need for identity management led to emotional distress, including self-blame, internalized homophobia, and apologetic, passive acceptance of a subordinate role (Squires & Sparkes, 1996). Squires and Sparkes went on to describe how daily fear of detection leads to potential stress and how the willingness to compartmentalize falsely dichotomized private and public lives reflects powerlessness and oppression. Clarke (1996) has argued that although lesbian identities can be successfully concealed, the cost of maintaining a coherent but false heterosexual identity was dissonance, personal turmoil, anxiety, and the inability to form close relationships with colleagues, leading to isolation, lowering of self esteem, and self-destructive behavior.

This nondisclosure of sexual identity can be further understood by looking at the experiences of those who did disclose. This sets the fear of nondisclosure in its social context of likely homophobic reactions from health care practitioners and other reactions. These reactions serve to convey the message that lesbian and gay identities are somehow undesirable and can somehow be discouraged. It will be seen that it is not only homophobia that operates here but also heterosexism; in this worldview, homosexuality is not necessarily pathologized, nor is overt hatred directed toward lesbians and gay men. However, heterosexism operates through processes of invisibility, in which the message that heterosexuality is superior, more highly valued, and more desirable is conveyed. These concepts will be explored in more detail later in this chapter.

EXPERIENCES OF BEING PATHOLOGIZED

It can be seen that the fear of being pathologized in those who did not disclose their sexual identity was realized by several of those who did disclose. The participants who described this experience were Roger, Wayne, Mandy, Jane, Julie, Charlotte, and Nicki. As with nondisclosure, this experience of being pathologized has also been found in other studies of lesbians' and gay men's experiences of mental health care (Golding, 1997; Hetrick & Martin, 1987; Koffman, 1997; MacFarlane, 1998). In this study, there were similar reports of experiences of lesbian and gay identity being seen as an immature or attention-seeking phase; something that would be grown out of; something that had a cause and, therefore, presumably, a cure; or something that led in and of itself to mental health problems. It is not surprising that lesbians and gay men have such experiences if we look at the training that mental health care providers have and the pathological model of homosexuality that underpins their training. Homosexuality was not declassified as a mental illness in the ICD (International Classification of Diseases), the disease classification system used by British psychiatrists and psychologists, until 1992. At that time, however, a further category was established called "psychological and behavioral disorders associated with sexual development and orientation." Within this are listed "sexual maturation disorder" and "egodystonic sexual orientation." These new classifications incorporate ideas that mental illness arises from confusion and uncertainty about sexual orientation. Such classifications continue to pathologize lesbian and gay identities (Davies & Neal, 1996; Parker et al., 1995).

These psychiatric classifications are underwritten by a psychoanalytical model of homosexuality (Parker et al., 1995). Furthermore, many mental health care practitioners are influenced and trained within a psychoanalytical model of homosexuality (Bartlett et al., 2001; Ellis, 1994; Milton, 1998) and have not received any training to counter negative social attitudes toward lesbians and gay men (Annesley & Coyle, 1995). The extent to which homophobic attitudes are embedded within some of the leading training institutions is epitomized in their policy of not admitting openly lesbian or gay candidates for training (Ellis, 1994; Phillips et al., 2001).

Malley and Tasker (2001) have stated that psychoanalytic thinking about homosexuality filters down to the psychiatric profession and also other health care practitioners. In a similar vein, Markowe (1996) has pointed out the profound impact of psychoanalytic thinking on commonsense ideas. This dominant thinking, which is influenced by psychoanalysis, views lesbian and gay identities as immature, developmentally inferior to heterosexuality, and arising from a failure to resolve pre-Oedipal wishes (Coyle, 1998; Stevens & Hall, 1991; Taylor, 2002). This translates into ideas that childhood sexual abuse will lead to such a state of "arrested development." It has been argued that this stance also underpins a pathologizing model (Coyle et al., 1999; Milton, 1998). Pathologization is part of the dominant discourse. (The nature of discourses and dominant discourses was introduced in Chapter 3 and is revisited in Chapter 7, following the thematic exploration of experience in this chapter.)

In previous studies, research participants who have been pathologized describe experiences in which they were told that they were mistaken about their lesbian or gay identity, or that they could become heterosexual and that their mental health problems would dissipate if they did so (Golding, 1997). In this study, Roger was quite clearly given the message that he should be able to leave his gay identity behind him and choose to be heterosexual. In previous research, it has been found that young lesbians and gay men were likely to be told that their lesbian or gay identity was a phase that they would grow out of and that they were saying they were lesbian or gay only because they were seeking attention (Hetrick & Martin, 1987; Koffman, 1997; M. Schneider, 1991). In this study, Nicki's experience was very much cast within that psychoanalytical model, whereby a lesbian identity is seen as immature and attention seeking and is similar to some of the cases described by Schneider. Nicki was also questioned about her certainty about her sexual identity, implying that she could be mistaken. Charlotte also had the experience of having it suggested to her that her lesbian identity was a phase she would grow out of, and at one point, Julie was told that she had mistakenly believed she was a lesbian because of her mental illness.

Hetrick and Martin (1987) noted a number of years ago that to suggest to young people that they are too young to know that they are lesbian or gay, or that it is a phase that they will grow out of serves to

reinforce the denial of membership in the hated group, partly through confirmation of the belief that to be homosexual is not a thing to be desired. The difficulty with such reinforcement is that it postpones and complicates the whole process of dealing with a stigmatised social identity. (p. 38)

The apparent practice of not taking young people seriously and dismissing their sexual identity as a phase is particularly worrying in light of other research that shows that the younger people are when they become aware of their lesbian or gay identity, the more likely they are to make a serious suicide attempt or have serious mental health problems (Remafadi et al., 1991; Schneider, 1991).

Another common experience reported in other studies was that of being told by mental health care practitioners that lesbian or gay identity had been caused by past sexual trauma or abuse (Golding, 1997; Koffman, 1997; Milton, 1998). Again, this finding was also replicated in this study, with Mandy, Jane, and Julie describing health care encounters with psychiatrists and mental health nurses in which this assertion was made. Charlotte also had a sense that her counselor was searching for a cause for her lesbian identity. I noted earlier that this stance underpins a pathologizing approach to lesbian and gay identity formation, and it is important to consider the effect this will have on the therapeutic encounter. As with approaches that convey the message that homosexuality is an immature phase, assertions that it is an abnormality caused by developmental problems are equally damaging to the self-esteem of someone trying to integrate an identity that is socially stigmatized. Julie described how she relied on the support of her consultant, but his stance toward her lesbian identity made it difficult for her to accept herself, and she felt that this contributed to her mental illness. The finding that this unmet need for acceptance can influence mental health comes from Vincke and Bolton's (1994) study. They found empirical evidence that low self-acceptance follows depression contingent on low social support rather then low self-acceptance precipitating depression.

Furthermore, this focus on the presumed etiology of homosexuality by practitioners means that life events that might explain people's mental health status are not considered and people are not offered support in relation to them. Mandy, for example, who identified her experiences of childhood sexual abuse as something with which she needed help, was not offered help in relation to this. In previous studies, it was also found that practitioners focused on the cause of homosexuality rather than other potential factors that might have affected people's mental health (Golding, 1997; MacFarlane, 1998). Furthermore, in Golding's study, people reported being told that they were confused about their sexuality when they did not feel that they were. Mandy's experience echoes these findings, and Wayne also experienced being told he was confused about his sexuality when he felt that he was not. Again, that other factors might have contributed to mental health problems was not considered. It would seem from Wayne's account that he was probably diagnosed as suffering from "egodystonic sexual orientation," which, as noted earlier, is listed in the ICD. Although Wayne said that he felt quite positive about his sexual identity and was living openly with his male partner, he said that all the mental health staff caring for him were convinced that his severe depression arose from nonacceptance of his sexuality. He was never offered any therapeutic space in which to explore other possible reasons for his depression, such as homophobic bullying, which Rivers's (1997a, 1999, 2000) recent study showed to be linked to long-term mental health problems.

EXPERIENCES OF BEING SILENCED

In this study, lesbians and gay men found that they were silenced about their sexual identity in a number of ways during mental health care encounters: having issues relating to sexual identity ignored or trivialized, being told not to discuss such issues, and seeing caring relationships withdrawn. The participants who described this experience of being silenced were Alec, Roger, Sandra, Sarah, and Julie. Again, these findings are similar to those from other recent studies of lesbians' and gay men's experiences of mental health care (Annesley & Coyle, 1998; MacFarlane, 1998; G. Proctor, 1994). The silencing of lesbian and gay voices has also been noted in relation to psychotherapeutic training, texts, and practice (Coyle, 1998; Milton & Coyle, 1999). Some of the experiences of being silenced were ones such as Sandra's, in which the health care practitioners made a statement to the effect that they were not prejudiced but failed to pick up on whether there were any issues relating to sexual identity that might need to be explored. Such displays of liberalism, it has been argued, can serve to deny differences and are oppressive, in that they fail to acknowledge the stress related to being lesbian or gay in a homophobic culture (Annesley & Coyle, 1998; Burns, 1992; Hardman, 1997; C. Kitzinger, 1989; Seidler, 1994). They have also been identified as a subtle form of prejudice (Coyle et al., 1999; Peel, 2002).

A deeper understanding of liberal discursive practices in society might help to illuminate these reported health care experiences and the associated feelings of blame and responsibility. In the context of psychiatry, Parker et al. (1995) have remarked that this "rhetoric on the individuality (of the patient) functions to wrench the person from the various social contexts that have contributed to their distress" (p. 8). Furthermore, the discursive practices inscribed by the dominant value system of liberal humanism are only one short step away from victim blaming (Nightingale & Cromby, 1999; Parker et al., 1995). Such victim blaming was seen in the accounts of Julie and Roger, who were told by nurses and doctors to "sort themselves out" or "pull themselves together." It is important to consider this further, as liberal humanism underpins the dominant value system and ethic in nursing, and any advances made in the depathologization of homosexuality are followed by the re-entrenchment of homophobia through the erasure, invisibility, and silencing of lesbian and gay experience. There could perhaps be no more ripe a site for such reinscription of homophobia than in nursing, which is thoroughly immersed in a liberal humanist discourse of individualized patient care, with its inherent dualisms of same/different, public/private, and self/society.

The approach of individualized patient care has been noted to fail remarkably when applied to groups that do not fit within dominant cultural norms (e.g., Gerrish, 2000; Marshall, Woollett, & Dosanjh, 1998). Where the concept of individualized patient care has been problematized, it has been in the context of critical social theory (Wilson-Thomas, 1995), in the application of postmodern ideas to understanding the disciplining and positioning of the nursing profession (Lister, 1997), or, most saliently, through work on inequalities in health care (Hart & Lockey, 2002). Gerrish (1997), in her observational study of community nurses, found that cultural difference, and nursing care responsive to such difference, was not easily accommodated within the ideology of individualized patient care. She claimed that the whole concept was ethnocentric and in practice served to disadvantage minority groups further. A parallel argument can be made here that the individualized patient care approach is also profoundly heterocentric and serves to reinforce the oppression that, in many cases, has brought people to mental health care settings in the first place. The denial of difference (see the slippage from "we treat everyone the same" to "we are not bothered by homosexuality" to "don't talk about that here because it is of no concern to anyone else") reproduces the violence of erasure and the violence of Othering on the outside that has brought this person to the inside of a mental health care setting; that this denial of difference can be so disingenuously framed within an apparently humanist and holistic approach to care makes it profoundly damaging and disempowering, leaving little room to resist pathological positioning for the person who is presenting with mental health problems relating to their struggle with their sexual identity.

Hart and Lockey (2002), following on from their study of disadvantaged groups of women in relation to midwifery care, claimed that the concept of individualized care enshrines a liberal approach to inequality that rarely takes into account structural issues. Most important, they argued that health care workers, socialized into this individualistic way of practicing, are rarely able to understand the relationship between difference and disadvantage. In a similar vein, C. McDonald and Anderson (2003) have stated that individualism and heteronormativity within nursing have led to "resistance within the discipline to value and research social determinants of health [which] raises questions about our complicity in dominant ideologies of health and healthcare" (p. 698).

They went on to state, "When nurses have an increased knowledge and awareness of power structures in the health care system, they can more effectively participate in disrupting them" (C. McDonald & Anderson, 2003, p. 709), and taking material-discursive research into health care experience as an example, they said that such research can be used to disrupt heteronormativity in nursing discourse.

EFFECTS OF PATHOLOGIZATION AND SILENCING

It can be seen from the previous discussion that in different ways, lesbians and gay men receive a clear message in their mental health care encounters that their sexual identities are abnormal, undesirable, and not to be encouraged. For those who fear disclosure, there is no clear message to counter concerns about such reactions. It is important to ask what the effect of these messages is likely to be on someone's mental health. As discussed before, Hetrick and Martin (1987) have reasoned that such reactions in health care providers will inflict further damage on the self-esteem of someone who is trying to integrate a stigmatized identity. It is apparent that some research participants, such as Mandy, Nicki, Charlotte, and Wayne, disclosed their sexual identity with relative ease because they did not feel that it was related to their mental health problems and they had felt quite positive about their lesbian or gay identity up until this point. However, for some participants, being questioned about their certainty about their sexual identity and possible (pathologizing) reasons for it led to confusion and distress.

Breakwell (1986) has argued that if people's coping mechanisms are disrupted when their identity is threatened, it is likely that mental illness will ensue. Both Giddens (1991) and Breakwell (1986, 1992) have assumed a position that threats to identity require some kind of work and psychic reorganization. Some of the coping mechanisms described by Breakwell that are relevant to people coping with a stigmatized sexual identity are changes in self-definition and support structures that allow reevaluation of a previously learned negative social representation. In the mental health care encounters described in this study, negative messages about lesbian and gay identities disrupted existing coping mechanisms or failed to encourage the development of effective coping mechanisms. Research participants such as Mandy, Charlotte, and Wayne, who had started off in their mental health care encounters feeling positive about their sexual identity, found their coping mechanisms disrupted, leading to uncertainty and distress. For those who did not feel as positive about their gay or lesbian identity, such as Julie, these negative messages reinforced their feelings that there must be something wrong with them. Giddens (1991) has also argued that shame can result from feelings of not living up to ideals. Implicit or explicit messages from health care providers about the undesirability of lesbian and gay identities, through either pathologization or silencing, will reinforce any feelings that lesbians and gay men have about failing to live up to ideals imposed by society's dominant values.

To understand this process better, it will be useful to consider the broader social context in which these negative messages about lesbian and gay identities are heard in relation to dominant values and the processes that operate to reinforce dominant values. It is not only active discrimination through homophobia and pathologization that is at work here but also heterosexism and the way it operates through silencing and invisibility. This takes us forward to a further analysis of the data to arrive at what J. Smith, Osborn, et al. (1999) have called a superordinate device for understanding the shared experience of the research participants. The experiences of being pathologized and silenced can be understood as shared experiences in the wider social context of how minority and stigmatized groups are marginalized and oppressed. As Breakwell (1986, 1992) has said, these threats to identity and related coping strategies make sense only when seen in the light of dominant social beliefs and cultural expectations, and it is the subjective knowledge of the social world that is important. Both the process of pathologization and that of being silenced render groups of people as Other from the dominant norms and values of society. This process of Othering and the way it operates for lesbians and gay men in their mental health care encounters will now be explored further.

EXPERIENCES OF OTHERING

Two of the main categories that emerged from the data were being pathologized and being silenced. It can also be argued that nondisclosure was a form of silencing, as it occurred in a context in which no clear message was conveyed that it would be safe to disclose. For the further analysis, then, being silenced will include self-silencing and nondisclosure of sexual identity as well as being silenced or ignored following disclosure. What is common about these experiences of being pathologized and being silenced is that they both had the effect of casting lesbians and gay men as outside, or Other, in relation to dominant social norms and values. It is useful at this juncture to see how both pathologization and silencing have been theorized in relation to this process of Othering and the ways in which it is considered to be oppressive. Pathologization as a form of Othering will be discussed first.

Rutherford (1990b) has argued that it is characteristic of the modern Western world that identities are forged through polarities such as Black/White or heterosexual/homosexual, in which one term is dominant and the other subordinate. He indicated that through binarism, which operates in the same way as splitting and projection, the center, or dominant, position expels anxieties, contradictions, and irrationalities onto the subordinate position. This process of marginalizing the Other is at the core of the violence and aversions of dominant discourses and identities as seen in practices such as racism and homophobia. Sibley (1995) further explored this process of creating the Other to show how those who are different are rendered deviant and excluded. This is often signified through representations of dirt, disease, pollution, and ugliness, in which negative stereotypes are created that simultaneously provoke feelings of repulsion and desire (Rutherford, 1990b).

Such splitting, in which the acceptable is divided from the unacceptable, often uses the strategy of stereotyping. Negative feelings are associated with such stereotypes, and those assigned to stereotyped groups are excluded, marginalized, and oppressed (Hall, 1997b). Stereotypes accorded to groups that do not fit with or are different from dominant norms rely on symbolism that renders difference pathological, deviant, or unacceptable (Hall, 1997b). We saw in Chapter 5 that lesbians and gay men experienced being cast as Other in their mental health care experiences through being pathologized. Rendering someone who is different from societal norms and expectations as Other can be done through casting that person or group of people as sick or diseased (Sibley, 1995), and the pathologization of homosexuality in medicine, psychiatry, and psychology has a long and continuing history (D. Davies & Neal, 1996; McColl, 1994; Stevens & Hall, 1991). This representation of homosexuality as an illness has been part of the systematic oppression of lesbians and gay men (King & Bartlett, 1999) that marginalizes lesbian and gay voices and casts them as Other (Coyle, 1998).

This particular version of Othering, which operates through the pathologization of lesbian and gay identities, can be understood as a subset of homophobia. However, Othering also takes place through less obvious forms of discrimination, which are better explained by the concept of heterosexism. Plummer (1992b) has defined heterosexism as

a diverse set of social practices—from the linguistic to the physical, in the public sphere and the private sphere—in an array of social arenas (e.g., work, home, school, media, church, courts, streets, etc.), in which the homo/hetero binary distinction is at work whereby heterosexuality is privileged. (p.19)

Garnets et al. (1990) have described heterosexism as "an ideological system that denies, denigrates and stigmatizes any non heterosexual form of behavior, identity, relationship or community" (p. 369). Butler (1993) has explained heterosexism further to show the way in which it operates to make it appear as if heterosexuality is natural and superior to lesbian and gay sexuality. It is thus a system that both privileges heterosexuality and makes it normative; that is, heterosexuality is seen as a better, more desirable, and more normal state. It can be seen from this that the pathologizing of lesbian and gay identities renders them less normal, less desirable, and inferior. Butler went on to argue that the privileging of heterosexuality relies on the specter of the Other, which involves the full-scale rejection and repudiation of homosexuality. The effect of such a worldview on those who do not or cannot fit into these norms is best explained by Segal (1997), who linked this to identity, arguing that we live in subjective worlds, in which discourses about gender, tied inextricably to ideas about heterosexuality and the naturalness of both, are central to our sense of self.

Whereas homophobia and pathologization operate through stereotyping and explicit actions and statements that imply deviance, heterosexism can also operate through what is not said and through what it taken for granted. Lesbians' and gay men's experiences of mental health care in which they were silenced are more within this realm. Butler (1991) has said that the oppressive process of Othering can also take place through erasure, invisibility, and "the production of a domain of unthinkability and unnameability" (p. 20). Absence and silence impart a message that something is unimportant or shameful, or does not exist (Wilton, 2000). They can be seen in research participants' accounts—such as Alec's, in which he felt rebuffed, in Sarah's, in which all of her hints were ignored, and in Julie's, when she was told not to raise certain issues in group therapy—that erasure of lesbian and gay identities is operating. They were being given a clear message that this is a realm that cannot be spoken about and that is implicitly unacceptable.

In health care, this domain of unthinkability and unnameability means that lesbians and gay men have little in the way of reliable information to help them manage their identity. If invisibility is sustained, then the only information available to most lesbians and gay men is based on negative cultural stereotypes. A possible consequence of invisibility is that the most readily available negative images become internalized, leading to a negative view of one's self (Richardson, 1981). This introjection is often referred to as internalized homophobia (Malyon, 1982; Meyer & Dean, 1998; Sophie,

1987). A further consequence of silencing is that it leads to and contributes to the isolation of lesbians and gay men, who are unable to find images with which they can identify (Markowe, 1996). Such isolation is thought to contribute further to lowering self-esteem (Wilton, 2000) and to symptoms of emotional disturbance that resolve rapidly once lesbians and gay men are exposed to nonstereotypical role models and peer support (Hetrick & Martin, 1987). Robertson (1992) has discussed how assumptions of heterosexuality in health care contribute to the invisibility of lesbians and the perpetuation of negative experiences. Silencing has also been found to disrupt coping mechanisms (Flowers & Buston, 2001) and to lead to the exacerbation of mental health problems (Proctor, 1994). Garnets et al. (1990) have described the task of coming out as part of the interrelated challenge of overcoming internalized homophobia created by heterosexist stigma, which involves a "process of reclaiming disowned or devalued parts of the self, and developing an identity into which one's sexuality is well integrated" (p. 369). It can be seen, however, that many people's mental health care experiences of being Othered, through pathologization and through being silenced, will have the opposite effect and will reinforce internalized homophobia rather than helping lesbians and gay men to overcome it.

What is most useful about Butler's (1991, 1993, 1995) understanding of the ways in which lesbians and gay men are Othered is that it shows how pathologization and silencing operate together to marginalize and oppress. As noted earlier, homophobia operates through explicit prejudice and discrimination, in which lesbian and gay identities are repudiated, whereas heterosexism operates through what is assumed and also what is not said. Fuss (1989) has observed that much theory to date has looked at either homophobia or heterosexism, but there is a need to understand how they operate together to account for both the social and the psychological. It can be seen from the previous analysis that some research participants in this study experienced pathologizing and silencing simultaneously; for instance, Julie was given the message by her psychiatrist that her ideas about her sexuality were mistaken because of her illness and previous childhood experiences but was also given the message that her sexual identity was not something that she could explore or try to come to terms with. Her lesbian identity was negated and silenced by her being told that she was mistaken at the same time as being pathologized. Other research participants, such as Nicki, Alec, and Charlotte, were simultaneously pathologized and silenced; they were pathologized by being told their sexual identity was a phase or had been caused by abuse, and at the same time, they were silenced by being told that they might yet discover that they were heterosexual by being encouraged to focus on heterosexual relationships.

RESISTANCE TO BEING OTHERED

We have seen that several participants did not disclose their sexual identity, stopped discussing it, or avoided further health care interactions because of feelings that they had been pathologized. Again, this confirms findings from previous studies (MacFarlane, 1998; Stevens, 1994b). This can be seen in a broader context of resistance to being Othered. Most of the work on resistance to being Othered has taken place in the context of understanding how alternative lesbian and gay communities and lesbian and gay identity politics develop (e.g., D. Bell & Valentine, 1995; Butler, 1993; Duncan, 1996; Fuss, 1991). This space is not generally available to people who have mental health problems associated with the coming-out process. However, studies in other areas of health care might help us to understand this process of resistance. Heaphy (1996) has considered the ways in which the identities of people with AIDS or HIV (PWA/HIV) are negotiated in relation to interactions with medical practitioners and health care professionals. He suggested that Giddens's (1991) work provides a clearer way of understanding how such resistance comes into play and describes the ways in which PWA/HIV resist the dominant discourse of the health care professionals and its attendant policing and judging. The main strategy identified by Heaphy in his study of PWA/HIV was silence, which was used to resist medical practitioners' attempts to know them and place them in terms of categories of normality, which are, arguably, part of a process of pathologizing and disciplining.

Huby (1997) has suggested that silence in medical encounters might be an effort by the patient to prevent the powerful and invasive medical system from disrupting his or her coping strategies. Bloor and MacIntosh (1990) observed a number of strategies of resistance to medical surveillance by health visitors among working class mothers and within therapeutic communities. They noted that concealment was a common strategy that provided a way of gaining control without confrontation. Others have argued that non-utilization of services and noncompliance to professional advice by minority-ethnic populations can also be interpreted as a form of resistance to the dominant culture and its "imposed and stigmatizing cultural and community identities" (Abdulrahim, 1998, p. 42).

Self-silencing and nondisclosure serve to act as protective strategies. However, in the context of presenting for health care with the very thing that cannot be spoken about, it is important to ask what the effect of this is and whether any further understanding and analysis of the data can help to illuminate a path toward improving access to care. The whole process of being Othered, whether it is through pathologization or through erasure, relies on a dualistic framework of binary opposites, in which one position is subordinate and inferior. In this case, heterosexuality is seen as normal and privileged over other forms of sexuality, whereas lesbian and gay identities are cast as deviant, abnormal, undesirable, and unspeakable (Fuss, 1991). It is at this point that a more discursive analysis, which explores how dualisms operate, will help us to understand more fully the difficulties research participants had in negotiating a path in which it was possible to explore uncertainties, any negative feelings about their sexual identity, and their impact on their mental health. I will explore this further in the next chapters through a discursive analysis, using deconstruction and positioning theory.

If nurses and other health care professionals are to engage with the findings from this study thus far, we must not only repudiate pathologizing inscriptions of lesbians and gay men, which includes unsubscribing to arguments that suggest homosexuality is a phase that patients will (one hopes) grow out of, but also engage with and disrupt heteronormative discourses. In the absence of overt pathologization, these discourses continue covertly to pathologize lesbian and gay identities through invisibility, silencing, and erasure. Without this further step, the overturning of one dualism through which oppression operates will simply be replaced by another. The discursive practices that will step into any void created by the abandonment of pathologization are encoded within liberal and individualized approaches to care and are not easily shaken off. These practices are those that deny difference and the impact of the social but, at the same time, claim to be treating patients as individuals.

Chapter 7
A Discursive Analysis of Resistance to Mistaken Identities

In Chapters 5 and 6, the thematic analysis using IPA led to three broad categories related to nondisclosure of sexual identity in mental health care encounters and the pathologization and silencing of those who did disclose. These three broad categories were organized under a superordinate theme of experiences of being Othered. It was clear in the thematic analysis that lesbians and gay men were subjected to the dominant discourse of homosexuality as mental illness (i.e., a pathologizing discourse) in their mental health care encounters. Dominant discourses operate through institutional bases such as medicine or the family, and they "may be considered as regimes of truth that determine what counts as important, relevant or truthful" (Manias & Street, 2000, p. 53). The dominant discourse, in which homosexuality is seen as a mental illness, has been well documented as a feature of society in general and medicine in particular (Parker et al., 1995; Taylor, 2002; Wilton, 2000). To make more sense of how people negotiate health care when pathologization is the dominant discourse, it is necessary to ask how lesbians and gay men are positioned and how they position themselves in relation to this. I did this using Parker's (1992) framework of steps in the analysis of discourse, as outlined in Chapter 3.

The coding of interview data into categories and themes, which I covered in Chapter 5, fulfilled the requirements of the first stage of the analysis of discourse. While conducting the IPA, I was mindful of the further layer of analysis to be conducted and remained sensitive to "the connotations, allusions and implications which the texts evoke[d]" (Parker, 1992, p. 7) to achieve this. The next stage of the discursive analysis, again following Parker's (1992) framework, involved looking at the data to identify the discursive meanings that participants constructed in relation to lesbian and gay identities and then to look at how they were positioned and positioned themselves in relation to available discourses. I then analyzed the data to identify the discursive meanings that participants constructed in relation to lesbian and gay identities. The next stage, following Parker's steps, was to look at the way in which discourses contain subjects and to consider the ways in which subjects were positioned by the discourses identified so far; Parker stated that in Althusserian terms, we have to ask how a discourse is hailing us and what rights we have to speak when positioned by a discourse.

CALLED INTO POSITION

The discursive meanings for participants about being lesbian or gay were embedded in their concerns about disclosure, seen in Chapter 5; most participants had concerns about being seen as a freak, as disgusting, as sexually predatory, or as immature. There were many examples in Chapter 5 of how lesbians and gay men reported being directly pathologized as a result of disclosing their sexuality in a health care encounter. Some participants also talked about their awareness of this as a general discourse within psychiatry, even if they did not disclose their sexual identity:[1]

I'd also heard in hospital psychiatrists talking about homosexuality as if it was an illness. You know, okay, she's got psychosis, she's delusional, she can't sleep—and she's gay. ( ). Again it was another symptom.

This dominant discourse of homosexuality as illness was also experienced by lesbians and gay men in their interactions with their families. Max talked about how his grandmother suggested that he be taken for a cure for his homosexuality, and Jack talked about how his mother suggested that he could be cured in relation to his sexual identity:

My Nan, you know, she turned round to my mum and said "Oh there's injections for being gay ( ) take him down the hospital and get him sorted out."

(My Mum) said "If there was a problem with your washing machine you'd go out and fix it." She said "It's obviously something you ( ) if something goes wrong in nature, try and heal it."

As well as these discursive meanings, in which lesbian and gay identities were constructed as unnatural and perverted, participants were concerned about being rejected, ostracized, and punished. Oscar's account reflects these concerns when he talks about why he did not disclose his sexual identity to his GP, even though he felt it was implicated in his mental health problems at the time:

If my parents found out they would probably have crucified me, then it could have gotten back to school, where I was already having problems ( ) and as was proved at college, these things have a nasty habit of getting round. There's nothing people like better than a piece of tittle-tattle. And really fear of alienating myself even further from those people who possibly weren't too bad. Not that there were very many of those, but certainly mates at school.

Patrick suffered from physical and sexual abuse from two different nurses when he was an inpatient in a psychiatric hospital. He felt that this was some sort of punishment, suggesting further that the discursive meanings associated with homosexuality are that it is bad and punishable:

And I did feel, especially after the incident (of being sexually abused by a nurse) ( ) I did feel that there was probably, I was probably being punished for my sexuality. Um I mean, he took advantage of me and then when it appeared that I was going to come up and say something he knocked me senseless, you know. (And then with the other nurse who sexually abused me) I thought, well is he trying to teach me some sort of lesson. Is this supposed to put me off from being gay. It did appear that he might have been doing that.

Julie's account of how she perceived her parents to find mental illness less stigmatizing and shameful than homosexuality is another powerful example of the negative discursive meanings attached to lesbian and gay identities:

When I got really thin and I didn't really care about anything, couldn't really think about—that's why I became anorexic I think, you know I was so thin I couldn't think about anything let alone have any feelings, sexual feelings so ( ). I just wanted to disappear so you know, that seemed to be a good way of doing it, and er my parents found that much more acceptable to focus on than my sexuality, so instead of them just being embarrassed about it all they could say oh our daughter, you know, she's mentally ill, she's got anorexia, you know?

Ranjit also talked about how homosexuality was constructed as something shameful:

I feel very, very ashamed of myself ( ). I will feel very, very guilty that (...) I let my family down and most importantly I've let my children down

The discursive constructions of homosexuality as bad and sinful were particularly strong for participants who were part of faith communities. They were particularly concerned with being cast out by their families and communities and being rejected and punished. Simon, Tim, and Jane had grown up within Christian faith communities, and they felt very strongly that they would be ostracized by their communities if anyone knew about their sexual identity. Anwar was part of a Muslim community and also felt that he would be cast out. Ranjit, who was part of a Sikh community, feared for his life and thought that if people in his community found out, they would find him and possibly kill him:

I thought I would have to give up my Christianity (...) um (...) I suppose I wouldn't have actually have given up everything of it. I, I probably would have stopped going to church um and I would have lost contact with a lot of people that I've known for a long time.

And so, I was worried that that I would, um be rejected from the church and um rejected from my friends and that I'd find myself in an isolated position.

It was like in my head when I was like fifteen and stuff, it was either you're straight or you're completely on your own. People turn their backs on you in the street, spit at you, stuff like that. And that was horrible, really isolating, but fit with what I knew with church as well about being punished and all that.

Oh it's so sad, it really, really is. And how it affects your state of mind because the way I felt is that I came from this huge extended family so yeah, I never really needed to have friends for external support, I had two wonderful parents and all these siblings and all these cousins and I actually think that that kind of environment is brilliant to grow up in and I wouldn't change it for the world and I was in that and I was loving it and it's incredibly supportive and it's incredibly stable, generally speaking, but it's only those things as long as you conform.

If people in my Gurdwara, in my Sikh temple found out I think they would probably, they would probably want to execute me or something. ( ) I think they would probably want to exterminate me ( ). (My friend) says to me "The way you defend gay people I think you're gay" ( ) he says that if he found out that anybody, any of my friends were gay (...) he'd shoot the hell out of them and I've been friends with him for five or six years. ( ) I feel (...) trapped in a cage ( ) wherever I went, wherever I go we've got cousins in almost in every city in the UK and Wales and Scotland. People would hunt me down.

TAKING UP AVAILABLE POSITIONS

On many occasions, participants in this study were positioned as Other in terms of discursive positions in which homosexuality is constructed as mad or bad, with consequences of rejection and punishment or "treatment." In the context of mental health encounters, this positioning was more likely to occur within the dominant discourse of homosexuality as mental illness; in other words, mental health care practitioners saw participants' homosexuality as a mental illness or psychological maladjustment. As discussed in Chapters 3 and 4, such positions within discourses can be accepted, rejected, or resisted. There were few examples in the data of people accepting the dominant discourse of homosexuality as psychopathology but many examples of rejection and resistance.

Impositions and suppositions

One striking example of being positioned and positioning oneself within the dominant discourse of homosexuality as a mental illness was found in Patrick's account. Patrick was admitted to a psychiatric hospital as a teenager, and he had this to say about how he viewed his situation at that time:

It was kind of like um it didn't matter if I was gay there because I was mad anyway so you know, what did it matter. It was kind of ( ) it was almost like I was in the right place.

This part of Patrick's account suggests that at the time, he accepted the positioning of homosexuality as mental illness. Earlier, part of Max's account showed how he was positioned by a member of his family as ill. He went on to recount how being positioned as mentally ill by his family led to his also positioning himself within that pathologizing discourse:

> My Nan said "There's injections for being gay," do you know what I mean, "take him down the hospital and get him sorted out," do you know what I mean. ( ) and that's when I thought I was a real, I was ill, do you know what I mean ( ) because I didn't, you know, they were my family, I looked up to them anyway, do you know what I mean.

Julie and Fiona also gave accounts in which they positioned themselves as having a mental illness that was related to their sexual identity:

> I'm sure that if I wasn't confused about my sexuality I'd have a clearer identity and I wouldn't have become depressed, I don't think that would have happened. ( ) I just cannot merge the two lives, and just, maybe it will come with time, but when I do try to merge them I get really unsettled and a bit mad.

> I think my life would be a lot easier if I was straight ( ) I'm not happy being gay ( ) Why do I have to be gay? ( ). I just think for the rest of my life really I'll suffer from depression, I'll suffer from anxiety, anxiety I think is my problem, not depression sorry, and you know and I, I wish I didn't, and I know a lot of that is to do with being gay, I know it is, and of course you just feel like giving up, I mean I feel like giving up.

Oppositions

In stark contrast, other accounts suggest a wholesale rejection of such positioning. Charlotte was quite clear that her mental health problems were unrelated to her sexual identity:

> I knew that that wasn't the reason why I was depressed, I've always been positive to the fact that no, my sexuality's got nothing to do with the fact.

Mandy was also quite clear that her mental health problems related to her experiences of childhood sexual abuse and were unrelated to her sexual identity:

I was quite secure about the way I felt about men. I was quite secure about my sexuality.

She vehemently rejected being positioned within a pathologizing discourse, as seen in Chapter 5, when she described how she walked out of the health care encounter. Wayne also was clear in his rejection of being positioned as having a mental illness because of his sexual identity:

I developed quite severe depression at that time which the health care profession were quite worried about but at the same time they would only deal with the fact that I was gay and they were a little bit worried that I would deny that I was gay so they wanted to make sure I was. It was slightly the opposite to what I thought. ( ). There are all these professionals telling you you've got to leap from chandeliers and shout about it. ( ) I was very fed up with the word gay, fed up with talking about it, and it seemed to be the be all and end all. It seemed to hide me.

It was clear from Chapters 4 and 5 that the dominant discourse of homosexuality as mental illness was a significant factor in the mental health care experiences of lesbians and gay men. A further dimension to the normalizing and disciplining nature of the expert discourse of homosexuality as pathology can be understood through a further exploration of its dichotomies. Polarities are chronically embedded in discursive structures that are unconsciously reproduced to maintain expert systems and preserve the social order (Merttens, 1998). There were polarized positions that could be taken by participants. They could position themselves as being lesbian or gay with their sexual identity being unrelated to their mental health problems, as seen in the accounts of Wayne, Mandy, and Charlotte. Alternatively, they could accept the dominant discourse, as seen in Patrick's, Julie's, Fiona's, and Max's cases.

Another polarized set of opposing positions was reflected in the stances taken by practitioners. From participants' accounts, it would seem that practitioners either saw homosexuality as the cause of mental illness (the pathologizing position seen in the accounts of Mandy, Jane, Julie, Charlotte, Nicki, Roger, and Wayne) or seemed to dismiss it as completely unrelated (reflected especially in Sandra's account). Therefore, the accounts point to positioning and positions' being taken up or rejected that are polar opposites.

Juxtapositions

Further interrogation of the data, in which contradictions and tensions in the data were analyzed, showed where participants resisted rather than rejected or accepted the positioning of the dominant discourse. In this stage of the data analysis, I used Parker's (1992) approach to identifying positions available within a discourse by asking what kind of space the discourse makes available for particular kinds of self to step in. It also involved using Willig's (2000) understanding of how discursive positions are appropriated or resisted by individuals and how they come to form part of an individual's subjectivity. To conduct this stage of the analysis, I paid particular attention to silences, hesitations, contradictions, and awkward moments during interviews (Gillies & Willig, 1997; Harden & Willig, 1998; Willig, 1998a; Yardley, 1997b, 1998).

I noted in Chapter 4 that some interviews gave an overall impression of how a person presented him- or herself in terms of "coming out" and her or his mental health; in some interviews, participants gave accounts that suggested they were confident about their sexual identity, but on some occasions, new material was introduced at the end of or after an interview that contradicted this. For instance, after an interview, participants (who had suggested throughout the interview that they had disclosed their sexual identity to all the significant people in their life) might express concerns about telling their housemates or one of their parents about the research interview, as they had not yet "come out" to those people. Notable silences were also observed early on in the research process. This noting of contradictions and silences was among the reasons I took an epistemological position and sought a method of analysis that would allow closer examination of these tensions in the data.

INTERPRETING SILENCE

Silences were noted during some participants' accounts, and these often happened at times during the interview when participants were talking about an episode in their life when they were likely to be positioned within a pathologizing discourse, either by mental health care practitioners or by friends and family. For instance, Mandy was talking about a friend who had recently had a baby and how the baby's father refused to let her be involved with the baby. The following extract from the interview shows how Mandy became silent when asked to speculate on why she had not been allowed to look after the baby:[2]

> *M:* He wouldn't even let me look after their little girl, despite the fact that I'd been there all the way through the pregnancy, all the way through the birth and was looking after her all that time but he wouldn't let me see their little girl and that was quite hurtful. ( )
> *H:* What did he think would happen if you looked after his little girl?
> *M:* Um, to be honest, I don't know, I don't know. I don't think he knew, that was something that he had to explore to find out, which was fair play to him, he wanted to protect his little girl (...). But it was (...) he realised in the end that he didn't need to protect her from (...).

Notable silences can be found in this part of the interview: Mandy does not finish her sentence when she refers to what the baby might need to be protected from. In a similar way, Mandy became silent again when asked to discuss further how she had felt when the psychologist she had seen said that her lesbian sexual identity was caused by childhood sexual abuse:

> I don't know. I don't know, I didn't go down that (...) I don't know what the consequence is going to be.

Simon had a similar response when he was asked during his interview about what his concerns were about disclosing his anxieties about his sexual identity to his doctor:

> I probably thought that (...) um (...) Don't really know. Can't think about it (...) Anyway um (...).

Jane's account clearly shows how she used silence as a strategy of resistance to pathologization when she was an inpatient in a psychiatric hospital:

> It was one of those things that I knew but I had to deny. ( ) I mean I was sat in a psychiatric hospital and I didn't want to face that one because it would have just (...). It had such a big impact that I would have found it really difficult to cope with, but because of the stigma and people, everybody else's opinions, they would have found it difficult to cope with as well, so it's not like I would have just had to face up to it, they would have had to face up to it and I would have had to face up to their reactions and protect myself against them as well. I

couldn't do that. It was too difficult. ( ) I just remember at the time how I felt, it made me feel so isolated because it was like I knew but I couldn't know, because if I did it was just going to be another one of my symptoms.

Charlotte's account also suggests silence as a strategy of resistance to a pathologizing discourse:

The reason I didn't tell my mum or anyone in my life was that I'm afraid that people are going to say to me it's just a phase, you'll get over it.

INTERPRETING CONTRADICTION

These silences in people's accounts, and Jane's account of using silence, can be seen as strategies of resistance to being positioned within a pathologizing discourse. As well as these silences in people's accounts, and their accounts of using silence, there were also contradictions both within and across accounts, which are a reflection of the polarized discursive positions available. The contradictions within accounts can also be taken as signs of resistance to being positioned within a pathologizing discourse. Those contradictions across accounts were found where some participants firmly positioned themselves as having mental health problems that were unrelated to sexual identity issues (e.g., Wayne and Mandy), whereas others, such as Patrick, Julie, and Fiona, positioned themselves as having mental health problems more directly related to sexual identity issues. The contradictions within participants' accounts included that of Nicki, who positioned herself as both confused and not confused about her sexuality:

The confusion about it has stayed and got worse. I don't doubt myself anymore, I just doubt absolutely everything else. ( ) it doesn't bother me, it's just me ( ). I'm not confused now about my sexuality anymore. Did I just say that? It's true anyway. I'm not confused about that anymore. I know that bit.

Len also positioned himself differently at various points in his interview. Early on, he positioned himself as suffering from depression because of his sexual identity, but later in the interview, he says that they were unrelated:

I was depressed and I didn't know why, but I think deep down it was all to do with my sexuality, and the doctor was actually very concerned um because I think at the time I felt suicidal as well ( ). I can't explain it, I don't know why I suffer, like I say I think we're all potential candidates for depression, it's just—I just think it's, it's an illness and it's something that you can get treatment for ( ). So I mean I don't blame me being gay for my depression.

We saw earlier that Charlotte was very definite that her sexual identity and her depression were unrelated; that is, she positioned herself against the pathologizing discourse. However, again, when her account is analyzed further, we see contradictions within it. Charlotte alternatively attributes her mental health problems to her parents' divorce when she was a teenager or to her struggles with coming out. She positions herself as having mental health problems unrelated to her sexual identity but then goes on to position herself as needing a lesbian help line. In these extracts, in which she refers to "suppression" and "questions asked in my head," Charlotte is referring to her sexual identity:

I had to go on anti-depressants unfortunately, um that was when I was about sixteen ( ). I went to see my doctor and he just didn't really understand and I hadn't told him, I haven't sort of come out to him ( ). He prescribed me anti-depressants, and I mean it just seemed that that's what I was going through, depression, just you know sort of belated depression due to the divorce (of my parents) ( ) and er my just my general well-being just went, just downhill, I don't know if it was a result of the questions being asked in my head all the time and the suppression, I don't, I think I might have struggled with it a little bit, um, whether it was the underlying problem or not I don't know, I don't think so. ( ) I think that it doesn't help when you're harbouring, when you're bottling things up. ( ) Well the doctor mentioned the counselling, but he didn't give me a name of, of anyone, um, er, you know I mean, I suppose if he had said to me, personally or given me like you've given me a list of helplines you know, is there anything on this helpline list that you might, might think might help you,, and if I had just maybe pointed out yeah, maybe that one, you know, may, the Lesbian helpline or anything like that.

RESISTING THE DUALISMS

There is another aspect in the dominant discourse on homosexuality that might have an impact on the way in which participants positioned themselves and struggled to negotiate their mental health care. In the dominant discourse, homosexuality is seen as fixed and determined, and part of a bipolar dichotomy against its opposite, heterosexuality (Butler, 1990, 1991; Fuss, 1989; Richardson, 1996; Weeks, 1991). This is usually referred to as essentialism, and the pathologizing discourse can be part of it, in that lesbian and gay sexual identities are seen as being fixed and determined by either genetic or early childhood experiences.

It can also be seen that in resisting pathologizing positions, participants seeking mental health care also resisted essentializing positions. Both Lauren and Michael described mental health encounters in which they were asked about their sexual fantasies as a way of ascertaining what their sexual identity was:

> I started to go and see this psychiatrist but he was very very bizarre, very weird, and he just got straight into the um, like towards the end of the first session it was like straight into like masturbation and I was like "Where are you coming from?"

> (The psychiatrist) was sort of saying, he said, what you fantasise about when you masturbate is a really good sort of sign about how you feel. ( ) I think at that point I was just sort of like after a distinct answer: yes or no. And from that I think I actually got the answer I was looking for. ( ) And I thought well, okay, cos it's sort of coming from somebody that's sort of trained in that sort of field.

Again, it can be seen that a polarized discursive positioning is taking place here: People are either lesbian or gay, or they are not. This can make the whole process of disclosure much more threatening to people's identities. Furthermore, the polarized positionings available within the dominant essentializing discourse can make it difficult for people to negotiate health care when they feel uncertain about their sexual identity. In the first extract, Lauren is talking about an episode in her life when she saw a psychiatrist. In the second, Kate is talking about how she had attempted suicide at the age of 10 and why she had been reluctant to seek any help with her concerns about her sexual identity:

> I think, part of me was worried that he was going to turn round and say "Yes you are gay," because then that would be admitting to it, um and part of me was frightened that he was going to turn round and say "No, you're not really, it's just a phase you're going through and it will be OK." Because I didn't want that either, so it was like I was just really sort of stuck that I didn't actually want to hear anything he said,

because it was either going to confirm something or it was going to not confirm something and I didn't want anything confirmed. I wanted to stick along the middle there, like not really being anything, just there, not admitting to anything. Because then it wasn't reality, it wasn't the truth.

I knew I was but I didn't really want to admit it. ( ) I think it was more the fact that if I turned round and said I'm gay then I am gay, ( ) It would have confirmed it yeah I suppose and it was something that I didn't really want to do.

Len also talked about how disclosing his sexual identity to his GP or his psychiatrist would have positioned him as definitely gay within a discourse in which it is seen as something fixed and definite:

I couldn't tell him, I could not tell him, so I guess I still hadn't accepted it myself ( ). If I had looked up and told the psychiatrist that yes I'm gay, that's the problem, um mm, I'm not quite sure what I'm trying to say now, because I mean I knew, I knew I was gay ( ). I guess confirming it was um a lot harder because of the way I was brought up I guess.

We have shown, then, that the people in this study who were seeking mental health care could accept or reject the polarized positionings available in the dominant discourse of homosexuality as something essentialized and fixed and homosexuality as pathology. It has also been demonstrated that these positionings can be resisted through silence and nondisclosure. Resistance was also seen in the contradictions within and across accounts. However, resistance to being positioned as pathological is particularly problematic for those participants who did have mental health problems that they, in part, attributed to their conflict about their sexual identity and the associated stress in terms of being victimized or ostracized. Much of the work on resistance to dominant discourses about homosexuality has looked at how such resistance is played out in the forming of lesbian and gay communities (e.g., D. Bell & Valentine, 1995; Butler, 1995; e.g., Duncan, 1996; Rutherford, 1990a; Valentine, 1993).

To date, no work has been done on how individuals might resist this discourse when they have no alternative community with which to identify, as would be the case when individuals are still negotiating their sexual identity and when they do have mental health problems that they associate with their sexual identity. As noted in Chapter 3, current research on the mental health care experiences of lesbians and gay men takes as given that mental health and sexual identity are unrelated and that any attempt to connect them is necessarily a form of pathologization. There is no room within the polarized positions available for lesbians and gay men to deal with their uncertainties and conflicts about their sexual identity. This is reflected both in the current literature on health care experience and in these accounts of people's health care experiences. This is not surprising, and a material-discursive approach can be drawn on to interpret these experiences. Parker et al. (1995), drawing on the work of Cixous (1975), say that the ubiquity of particular types of discourse makes its impossible for their subjects to "think or even imagine an 'elsewhere.'" For the participants in this study, many of their silences could be interpreted as the inability to imagine an elsewhere. The polarized positioning available within dominant discourses is difficult to resist.

IMAGINING AN ELSEWHERE

However, further analysis of participants' accounts shows resistance that does begin to point to the "elsewhere" that can be so difficult to imagine. Parker et al. (1995) noted that people can resist being positioned by discourse,

> for those who are able to grasp the action function of discourse, and are able to reflect upon themselves as the objects of a scientific discourse, there is the possibility of successfully resisting marginalization or devaluation. (p. 89)

Parker and colleagues (Parker, 1998b; Parker et al., 1995) have also said that successful resistance requires an overturning of polarities to make other spaces available. Through further interrogation of the data, it is possible to begin to see how the polarities can be overturned so that lesbians and gay men would be able to negotiate their mental health care from a position of uncertainty and conflict about their sexual identity. Annie talked about how she was confused about her sexual identity but at the same time was clear that she wanted to resist being pathologized and wanted help to deal with her concerns about her sexual identity:

> It's like if somebody told me it's a phase or it's a difference, you know, like that's a part of you that's not healed, and especially because I feel confusion about it. And yes, if I did, you know, come with like I've had this confusion and yes it's going to be about that (...). They're not

going to ( ) understand the subtleties of that to help me negotiate that in an empowering way rather than telling me what (...).

Fiona also talked about how she felt that her mental health problems stemmed from her conflict about her sexual identity and her difficulties in adjusting to life as a member of a group that is stigmatized and marginalized. In an earlier extract, it could be seen that she positioned herself as having mental health problems that were related to her sexual identity. However, she also resisted the pathologization that might go with such an admission, but that meant that she felt unable to work through these concerns.

If somebody said to me "I'm gay and I'm feeling a bit depressed—I think I might go and see the doctor," I'd be going "no, because they'll think it's because you're gay."

Fiona went on to say later in her account that to be able to deal with her conflicts, she would first have to be sure that a mental health practitioner was not going to position her within a pathologizing discourse:

I think it's, like I say if GPs or doctors or whatever had the attitude that being gay wasn't all there was to you then it would be so much easier to say to them you know I, I'm not comfortable being gay. And their attitude would then be gay is normal would be fine, OK, well we do have somebody who helps people come to terms with them being gay um. ( ) I think you know attitudes have got to be you know gay is normal but if you're not happy being gay or you've got a little bit of a problem coming to terms with being gay for whatever reason, you know then we do have somebody who will help you.

Nicki also said in her interview that she did feel she needed to work through her conflicts about her lesbian identity but could not do this unless she also knew that she was not going to be positioned within the pathologizing discourse:

There probably are a few things that I could do with sorting out. But it's not something, it's something I would probably only talk about with (someone I already trust) if I knew (they weren't) going to make an issue of it, but having had so many people make an issue of it, it's really hard to try and do. ( ) It just becomes—like if everything's put on the gay thing, then being gay is just part of you and everything's just part of you and nothing can be dealt with the way you are, and it makes it really hard to blow away a few cobwebs and get rid of some of your garbage, next to impossible to do it. I don't think it's really fair to put that on someone, decidedly off to make someone feel like that. But it happens all the time.

Both Fiona's and Nicki's resistance to being positioned as pathological meant that they did not disclose their concerns about their sexual identity in mental health care encounters. Max also talked about the need to be depathologized but how this did not happen when he was referred to a counselor:

I suppose really all I wanted somebody to do was to turn round and say you know oh it's not horrible to be gay, do you know what I mean, it's not unusual, do you know what I mean, it's normal, do you know what I mean, but no one did.

In a similar way, Michael and Eve talked about how their mental health encounters left them without any further reference points with which to find out more about their sexual identities:

There could have been more feeling—somebody to associate with, rather than sort of just getting a cold yes or no answer from the psychiatrist. ( ) I think that would have sort of put my mind at ease, would have sort of made me feel a lot better about myself, if I'd sort of known that somebody else had gone through those same sort of problems.

Well, although she helped me sort of come to terms with things, I don't think she really provided me with any sort of further reference, like she could have, I mean even giving me say a rape crisis centre phone number or even an LGB switchboard number, or anything like that, there was no further information given, so both in terms of the rape and in terms of my sexuality most of the things I've, er, sort of learnt, have been through you know literature and materials because I wasn't given any other option.

Ashley talked about this need for normalization, which would allow an exploration of the specific stresses gay people experience, in relation to getting more understanding from a gay counselor:

You need like a gay counsellor ( ) just to make you look at things in a different way because I mean I was looking at things in a negative way all the time and like oh, do you know what I mean, and never being told that wasn't my fault, you know, you shouldn't be feeling like this, you haven't done that to deserve that and that's, yeah, if I had that, I think I would have been a lot better than I am now ( ) it's just, yeah, it seems to be a bit more sympathy, not sympathy, sympathy's not the right word, more empathy, because when you sort of going through things, and yeah being gay you are exposed to a lot more crap than so-called straight people go through.

TOWARD A RENEGOTIATION OF NORMALIZED IDENTITIES

There were no examples in the participants' accounts of being able to overturn the polarities and dominant discourses about homosexuality in mental health care encounters successfully. This is important in terms of accessing health care. In the previous extracts, it can be seen clearly that participants resisted pathologizing positioning and expressed a need for lesbian and gay identities to be normalized. Although there were no examples of this happening in health care, some participants talked about how gay or lesbian community support (usually through an LGB youth group) had helped them to resist dominant discourses in which their identities were pathologized or Othered.

Possibly I would have benefited from meeting other gay people earlier. ( ), just knowing that they were normal ordinary people because I was never too sure, I only had what I saw on TV or what my dad told me to take into account, and I never had any real proof and I wanted to know what they were like, I had, I knew that they were ordinary people but I needed to meet them in order to be um to have my expectations proven.

I just felt really depressed about the whole thing. I felt like I hadn't really answered any questions and I just felt that I didn't fit in to society, I just felt really, oh, um,(...) very different and stuck out like a, you know, sharp stick, or something like that. I just (...) I hadn't been (...) Nobody had explained anything to me about the history of the gay community or anything like that—Stonewall. I just needed loads of questions answered. I needed to speak to somebody, just be with people, you know. And I hadn't had any of that. Just literally going to (the

LGB youth group) and being with other people just gave me reassurance, you know.

(The lesbian and gay youth group) is a good project because it, it supports people, you know people are very young when they come out. They say that pub environments are the best place for—but it isn't necessarily the best place for them to erm arrive and be on their own and em it's much better to be able to, to ask questions and to be in a safe, completely safe environment and that's the key is it's safe.

And then I met these two women from the helpline and I thought these are true lesbians and I'm like, am I going to be scared of them? And I wasn't. You know I thought like you were saying, like the stereotype, I thought I might be scared of them like they'd be quite hard or wouldn't want to know a little old sixteen year old sort of want to talk to me. But they were just really nice and just fun, friendly and chatty. You know we weren't always talking about gay issues, we were talking about everything really, college life and just stupid things, the weather and that, and it was like humanising the situation.

The idea that lesbian and gay identities need to be normalized before care can be accessed is explored further in the next chapter in relation to internalized homophobia, gay-affirmative therapy, and further theory on how people cope with threatened identities. As has been seen in this chapter, many lesbians and gay men who are trying to cope with a threatened identity and who are seeking mental health care to try and integrate their sexual identity do not get this sort of help from the helping professions.

I think it was like um, like cracking an egg with a sledge hammer kind of, a nut with a sledge hammer, it was like I didn't need to go and see the GP or a psychiatrist, you know that wasn't the problem, getting you know it wasn't, again I was sort of thinking like "Why a psychiatrist, like am I sick in the head?" That kind of thing, and it was counselling I needed. ( ) I could have done that myself, I could have gone and found a counsellor, and done it that way, but I didn't know how to. So it was probably me I did it wrong in the first place anyway and then the doctor carried it on by sort of like sending me to the wrong place.

In beginning to theorize and understand resistance, it can be seen that the health care experience is not something that is done to people—people bring expectations, fears, and hopes with them to the mental health care encounter—they are already struggling, resisting, and negotiating their sexual identity in a social-cultural-political context, and health care is an extension of that context. The success of that negotiation depends partly on what the "patients" bring to that encounter and their resilience; it also depends on what they find when they get there. The "what they find when they get there" is the health care practitioner and the health care setting. A homophobic and/or heterosexist context and practitioner will make this negotiation of sexual identity all the more difficult and will reinforce dominant discourses about normality and acceptability. In the next chapter, I explore further how problematic access to care is for this vulnerable group by bringing together the different layers of analysis of the mental health care experiences of lesbians and gay men.

ENDNOTES

1 For details on transcription, see Chapter 5, Endnote 2 (p. 107).

2 In extracts where the interviewer's talk is included, it is prefixed by "H" with that of the participants prefixed by the initial of their first name (pseudonym).

Chapter 8
Disintegrating the Dualisms and Reintegrating Identities

In this chapter, I set out to bring the different layers of analysis together and further develop theoretical understanding about how material and related discursive practices influence health care. I bring together the phenomenological experiences of pathologization and silencing in health care with an understanding of how such practices are resisted and negotiated through further theoretical discussion about threatened identities and oppression, and through further exploration of how material differences such as the age, social class, or culture of participants mediated the discursive practices of pathologization and erasure.

The overall aim of this study was to investigate the mental health care experiences of lesbians and gay men when they are negotiating their sexual identity (or coming out). In Chapters 5 and 7, we saw clear accounts of lesbians and gay men being both silenced and pathologized in their mental health care encounters. The second aim of this research study was to explore how heterosexism and homophobia affect lesbians' and gay men's access to mental health care when they are coming out. It is abundantly clear from this study that silencing and pathologization act as barriers to accessing health care. The more complex ways in which homophobia and heterosexism can affect access to mental health care were found through a further layer of analysis, discussed in Chapter 7 and involving analysis of discourse, which provided a multilayered account of the data.

I contend that that the mental health care experiences of silencing and pathologization described by participants were deleterious to their mental health and affected their access to care. To understand this, it is useful to turn to the literature on gay-affirmative therapy and to revisit, in more depth, some of the literature already explored on internalized homophobia, minority stress, and threatened identities.

A first reading of the data, using IPA, pointed to deficiencies in clinical practice arising from ignorance and prejudiced attitudes. This signals a clear indication that health care professionals need further training to update their knowledge and skills: a point that has already been made on a number of occasions (see Annesley & Coyle, 1995; D. Davies, 1996; Milton, 1998). However, there is a further layer to the process of making practice more emancipatory that can come from a deeper understanding of the data. This deeper understanding comes from interrogating the data further to explore the contradictions and tensions in participants' accounts. A closer reading of the texts does reveal some insight into how practices need to change to allow the space to negotiate a nonpathologized sexual identity in mental health care encounters. This was done through the analysis of discourse, which allowed an exploration of the tensions in participants' accounts, and through understanding the data as both representing some concrete experience and revealing something about aspects of that experience that were ineffable and unsayable.

SPEAKING OF THE UNSPEAKABLE

By sampling a group that was more diverse than many in other studies that have sought to explore this issue, these unsayable aspects of experience came to the fore. By taking a material-discursive approach to the analysis, I enabled further understanding by simultaneously treating the data as both material and discursive; that is, there was a material aspect to people's accounts as well as an element to these accounts that operated in a more discursive way. Participants were giving accounts of their material experiences, and also, simultaneously, their accounts could be understood as operating at a discursive level; in other words, their talk was doing something as well as telling something. The participants were giving accounts of their experiences of threatened identities and, at the same time, were resisting threats to their identity. In the same way that Heaphy (1998) saw interviews as accounts of resistance to medicalization both within the health care experience and within the research interview itself, these accounts could be understood as also operating at both levels. Thus, the IPA revealed something about the health care experience, and the discursive analysis revealed something about resistance to what was happening during those health care experiences and resistance within the interview itself.

As noted earlier, a return to the literature on internalized homophobia, minority stress, and threatened identities and a turn to the theory developing in relation to gay-affirmative therapy helps us to understand this more fully. It is vital to do this to move beyond a position that highlights only the grosser manifestations of homophobia and heterosexism in health care.

Those who seek to apply discourse analysis have argued that interventions have to be tactical and provisional (Parker et al., 1995; Willig, 1999a) but with continued vigilance, as new practices can "reassert the old problems in new guises" (Harper, 1999, p. 128). Clarke (1996), for instance talked about how new kinds of homophobia have emerged in ostensibly less oppressive times under the guise of liberal democratic pseudotolerance. Others have also argued that liberal ideologies can uniquely reassert homophobia and that they do so principally through the way in which difference is ignored (e.g., C. Kitzinger, 1989; Seidler, 1994). We will return to this danger of unwittingly reproducing homophobia while endeavoring to improve practice later in this chapter and in Chapter 9, where I make recommendations arising from the research. The key to developing practice lies in understanding the binaries and polarities that position people; such an understanding can be informed by the material-discursive approach to analysis that was conducted, in which I sought to find ways of understanding the dualities that discursively produce experience. An analysis of tensions and contradictions in the data gave a particularly useful lever for doing this.

The main tension observed in the data was the part played by conflict over one's sexual identity and its relationship to presenting mental health care issues. The obvious polarity, revealed through my use of deconstructive methods and positioning theory to analyze the data, was that both participants and practitioners see sexual identity as either totally related to mental illness or completely unrelated to it. Markowitz (1991) has referred to this as the twin errors of assuming that homosexuality has everything or nothing to do with the presenting problem in therapy. As noted in Chapter 6, there is an assumption embedded in the mental health care experience literature that homosexuality has nothing to do with the presenting problem; that is, participants' accounts are accepted uncritically when they say that they feel that their sexual identity has been pathologized and the possible relationship between sexual identity and mental health is not problematized. This reproduces an unhelpful polarity, which can be moved beyond only through the adoption of a material-discursive approach to analyze and interpret the contradictions and tensions in participants' accounts. This further layer of analysis suggested that sexual identity was implicated in a complex way with the mental health of those participants who were coming out when they presented with mental health issues.

It is perhaps significant that most of the research on the mental health care experiences of lesbians and gay men has not really focused on participants who are coming out at the time of the health care experience. Furthermore, the gay-affirmative literature on coming out tends to focus on the clinical expertise of practitioners rather than the experiences of clients. It is possible that this arises from the difficulties of researching this particular topic and the relative lack of methodological approaches that allow analysis of data within the realm of the unsayable. That this research topic is within the realm of the unsayable is illustrated by a quote from a participant in Milton and Coyle's (1999) study of psychologists. The participant (a practicing psychotherapist) was commenting on how difficult it is to challenge the homophobia and silencing embedded in psychotherapy training courses:

It makes it more unspeakable, you know it makes it more unthinkable, it's [ ] seen as [ ] something you simply can't ask, because it's too appalling to ask. (p. 55)

The ineffability of many topics of sensitive research, and, in particular, the unspeakability of lesbian and gay identities, was discussed in Chapters 3 and 4 (Altheide & Johnson, 1998; Brannen, 1988; Heaphy, 1998; Holland & Ramazanoglu, 1994; Huby, 1997; Sedgwick, 1994) and became evident in research participants' accounts in Chapter 7. The unspeakability of people's experiences can be understood in the light of Butler's (1995) work on how discursive practices define what can and cannot be spoken about: "Discourses not only constitute the domains of the speakable, but are themselves bounded through the production of a constitutive outside, the unspeakable, the unsignifiable" (p. 238). Butler (1991) also argued that silencing is part of the process of oppression:

Here it becomes important to recognise that oppression works not merely through acts of overt prohibition, but covertly through the constitution of viable subjects and through the corollary constitution of a domain of unviable (un)subjects—*abjects*, we might call them—who are neither named nor prohibited...Here oppression works through the production of a domain of unthinkability and unnameability. (p. 20)

In this research study, I attempted to engage with these ineffable and unsayable aspects of people's experiences by using sampling methods and analytic approaches that enter this realm. Of particular note here were the accounts of Mandy, Simon, and Jane, presented in Chapter 7, in which it was clear that there were realms of experience that they were unable to articulate or, perhaps, even think about.

SHAME AND BLAME

I noted in Chapter 5 that the pathologizing and silencing of lesbians and gay men, in general and in their mental health care encounters, can reinforce internalized homophobia and delay the process of integrating a positive sexual identity. The literature on gay-affirmative therapy is helpful in understanding this further. Internalized homophobia, the introjection of negative feelings about lesbians and gay men, is a cause of mental health problems such as depression, low self-esteem, and psychological distress (DiPlacido, 1998; Meyer & Dean, 1998; Shidlo, 1994). Similar findings also apply to the effects of nondisclosure or concealment of sexual identity (DiPlacido, 1998). Gonsoriek (1982) has also noted that the stress of coming out can produce florid symptoms of severe emotional disturbance. However, a number of gay-affirmative practitioners have noted that internalized homophobia rarely manifests itself overtly (Davies, 1996; Gonsoriek, 1988; Mair, 2000; Tasker & McCann, 1999). Given that internalized homophobia affects mental health, it follows that any behavior on the part of mental health care practitioners that reinforces internalized homophobia will be injurious (Meyer & Dean, 1998; Shidlo, 1994) and can even lead to further self-pathologization (Milton, Coyle, & Legg, 2002). This tendency toward self-pathologization was noted in Sarah's and Julie's accounts in Chapter 5.

Furthermore, it can be very difficult for lesbians and gay men to disclose their concerns that relate to internalized homophobia (Mair, 2000). Shidlo (1994) observed that there can be shame about shame. Seu (1998), in her research into women's experiences of shame, found that silence is often used as a way of coping with shame. There was one explicit reference to feeling shame in Ranjit's account. However, in more cases, as seen in Chapter 7, the interpretation of silences and conversational awkwardnesses showed that internalized homophobia or feeling negative about one's (emergent or current) lesbian or gay identity was, indeed, a very difficult topic to bring up with a mental health care practitioner. It was also difficult for participants to discuss this within the context of the research interview. As previously mentioned, silence and conversational awkwardness was particularly noticeable in the accounts of Mandy, Simon, and Jane.

An interpretation of variation and contradictions in accounts also led to a further understanding of how participants resist their identities' being constructed in relation to homophobic discourses, whether internalized or external. In resisting potential pathologizing positions, they are unable to access appropriate care to help them manage their conflict and the consequences of their sexual identity. These contradictions, interpreted as resistance, were notable in the accounts of Charlotte, Len, Fiona, and Nicki.

To further our understanding of what might be happening in these mental health care encounters and the nature of the added burden created by the reinforcement of homophobia, it is useful to continue an exploration of the theory on identity work that was introduced in Chapter 6. Giddens (1991) has argued that the integrity of the self is maintained through the ability to maintain a feeling of biographical continuity. This autobiography at the core of self-identity in modern life has to be worked at and is both robust and stable. Shame can result from feelings of not living up to ideals, and anxiety results from feelings about the adequacy of one's narrative for sustaining a coherent biography. Giddens suggested that fateful moments, such as receiving a medical diagnosis, become transition points that have major implications for self-identity. Breakwell (1986, 1996) has said that threats and coping strategies make sense only when seen in the light of dominant social beliefs and cultural expectations, and it is the subjective knowledge of the social world that is important. Both Giddens and Breakwell have assumed a position that threats to identity require some kind of work and psychic reorganization. Saari (2001), drawing on the identity theory of Lichtenstein, has referred to the need for biographical continuity but has also emphasized the damaging effects of trying to maintain an identity under conditions of negative evaluation and prohibition—Lichtenstein referred to this set of conditions as the "malignant NO" (Saari, 2001, p. 648). For lesbians and gay men who are coming out, there is a threat to identity because of the way in which negative and prohibitive social values will affect their sense of continuity and of living up to ideals. This can then influence self-esteem and lead to feelings of shame. If homophobia or heterosexism occurs in the mental health care encounter, there is an added threat to identity.

In terms of the effects of shaming—and I have argued here that homophobia and heterosexism in health care encounters have that effect—Butler (1993) has claimed that discourses are injurious. Although she did not use the term material-discursive, it can be seen from her writing that there is a theorized relationship between the discursive and the material: She argued that power acts materially on our bodies and minds, even if the discourse that produces that power is abstract (Butler, 1990). Butler (1995) went on to argue that categories tend to be instruments of regulatory regimes and that the subject (in this case, the lesbian or gay man) is produced through the shaming interpellation. In theorizing this relationship, Butler is drawing on the work of Althusser, who argued that a subject is constituted through being hailed, addressed, or named. In the case of lesbian and gay identities, where homophobia and heterosexism are intrinsic to the dominant discourse, Butler said,

> If, then, we understand certain kinds of interpellations to be identity-conferring, then those injurious interpellations will constitute identity through injury. (p. 246)

Butler (1995) also explored the way in which being hailed or interpellated as a member of a social category can be paralyzing through the violence of its totalizing reduction of identity. The hesitations and resistance that research participants described in relation to their difficulties of making a disclosure about sexual identity in mental health care encounters can be interpreted in this context. In the extracts in Chapter 7, this reluctance to disclose, because it would have brought them into being as that kind of subject, was expressed in Kate's, Lauren's, and Len's accounts.

Whereas Butler (1991, 1995) went on to draw on the work of Foucault to theorize how such injurious interpellations can be resisted through occupation, such modes of resistance cannot really be seen in the accounts of participants describing their mental health encounters. Such resistance to homophobia and heterosexism can be seen in the many studies of identity politics and development of lesbians and gay communities (e.g., Bell & Valentine, 1995; Duncan, 1996; Hart et al., 1981; Munt, 1998; Richardson, 1992; Sampson, 1993; Shotter & Gergen, 1989), but is important to note that such spaces were not available to the lesbians and gay men in this study who were coming out, who were isolated, and who were experiencing mental health problems that they associated in some way with their sexual identity. As Sophie (1987) observed, from research and clinical experience, it can be difficult to identify with the terms *lesbian* or *gay* until one has managed to feel at least neutral, if not positive, about the category. For lesbians and gay men, then, who have no attachments or support from alternative lesbian and gay communities and who have mental health problems associated with coming out, the only form of resistance available was self-silencing, which serves only to produce a further barrier to accessing appropriate health care.

Butler (1995) and other writers on lesbian and gay identities (e.g., Clark, 2002; Clarke, 1998; hooks, 1990; Myslik, 1996; Weeks, 1991) have theorized a relationship between homophobia, heterosexism, identities, and communities, and have looked at how injurious interpellations are resisted. However, these theorists have not explored this in relation to those lesbians and gay men who have emergent identities and who are struggling, in a psychological sense, with those identities, although some recent work has started to focus on how sex education might need to be rethought for those groups of gay men who are in the process of coming out (e.g., Flowers et al., 1998; Watney, 1993). Cosgrove (2000) has stated that resistance needs to be theorized, if we are to develop our understanding of lived experience. In the absence of developed theory around resistance in this context, some parallels can be drawn by looking at studies in which people negotiate their identities in relation to illness and in relation to health care encounters.

MAKING IDENTITY WORK

A number of psychological and sociological studies have explored how people have to manage their identities in relation to illness and medical encounters (e.g., Charmaz, 1987; Faircloth, 1998; Mathieson & Barrie, 1999; Mathieson & Stam, 1995; Nochi, 1998; Sparkes, 1998; Squires & Sparkes, 1996; Yardley, 1998). Mathieson and Stam have reasoned that the psychosocial experience of chronic illness can be understood in terms of a readjustment of the person's whole identity. This requires identity work entailing biographical work and evaluating meaning in a social context; cancer patients have to renegotiate their identity, which is threatened by physical changes, changes in social relationships, and encounters with medical institutions. They argued that an added psychological strain is imposed by medical encounters in which there is a discrepancy between patients' lived experiences of illness and the way in which they are constructed in their health care encounters by their disease state. In a later work, Mathieson and Barrie (1999) stated that one of most common themes in research participants' experiences

> speaks to unsatisfactory patient-health care provider interactions. Its common presence suggests that, of all the roles patients must navigate, negotiating one's identity with health care providers may be the most constant and difficult one and this story may not be easily constructed, or listened to. (p. 599)

Mathieson and Barrie's (1999) work is informative, as it elucidates the problematic nature of the health care encounter as well as the illness in terms of the implications for identity work. Although not explicitly drawing on some of the theoretical approaches to identity previously discussed (e.g., Breakwell, 1986; Butler, 1995; Giddens, 1991), it is consistent with these

approaches in terms of recognition of the need for continuity, psychic reor-
ganization, and psychological burden when identity is threatened. Much of the research to date on illness and identity has focused on physical illness rather than mental illness. These studies are useful for informing
this research, insofar as they speak of the need for negotiation of identity in
relation to illness and health care encounters, but the negotiation of identities in relation to mental health care encounters might be more fraught.
Research on the negotiation of identity and mental health care experience
has not been conducted to date, but the studies by Yardley (1996, 1998,
1999), Ussher (2003; 1996; 1997a), and Heaphy (1996) are salient to this
current study. Both Yardley and Ussher have looked at experiences in relation to illnesses thought to have a strong "psychological" component (where
there is potential for pathologization), and Heaphy has examined the experience of an illness that is very much constructed within homophobic discourses.

Ussher (2003, 1996, 1997a) has used material-discursive approaches to
understand the experiences of women with premenstrual syndrome (PMS),
arguing that social constructionist approaches to understanding PMS tend
to dismiss the "real" experiences and suffering of women with PMS, whereas more realist approaches tend to misattribute (or position) unrelated difficulties of a social and emotional nature to PMS, resulting in pathologization.
There are parallels here for this study, with the similar overemphasis on a
unitary cause of illness. In this case, sexual identity was seen as the cause of
mental illness, with the negation of other potential causes of psychological
distress, such as bullying and other major life events. This was particularly
evident in the accounts of Wayne, Mandy, Jane, and Charlotte. Ussher
(2003) argued that some stresses in women's lives might be inappropriately
positioned as PMS; this bears a striking resemblance to the inappropriate
positioning of sexual identity as the (sole) cause of mental distress for some
participants in this study.

There are also some striking parallels between the findings of this study
and those in Yardley's (1996, 1998, 1999) work. Yardley has used a material-discursive approach to understanding the health care experiences of people who suffer from chronic dizziness. It is particularly salient in relation to
this study, as Yardley has looked at an illness in which people are struggling
to cope with a debilitating condition. They are placed in a dilemma between
getting recognition and support for their illness and not appearing passive
and, therefore, undeserving of sympathy or assistance. This creates a delicate
balancing act between coping and getting help to manage the illness. Yardley
(1998) has claimed that these dilemmas and the resulting resistance to, and
negotiation of, an illness identity account for the tensions and contradictions

in people's accounts of coping with this particular illness. She also contended that these dilemmas are, in part, materially produced by the inadequacies of dominant discourses available to people with chronic illness. There is a parallel here for people struggling with their mental health when they are coming out: The inadequacy of dominant discourses around sexual identity and mental health make it difficult for people to position themselves in a way that allows for both uncertainty and conflict about one's sexual identity and the positive management of that identity.

Yardley and Beech (1998) also observed a common thread in the nature of these health care experiences and encounters, saying that people who have to negotiate their identity in relation to chronic illness are disempowered in a way that is comparable to the disadvantage experienced by lesbians and gay men. In this study, this disadvantage was multiplied, in that participants were having to negotiate their sexual identity and their mental illness simultaneously, making then especially vulnerable to the material effects of discursive practices that Yardley (1998) has dubbed "cruel dichotomies" (p. 324).

A further understanding of these cruel dichotomies is central to our thinking about how practice can be improved and making recommendations as a result of this research. However, before exploring this in more detail, I will discuss the relevance of Heaphy's (1998) work, which was introduced in Chapter 7, as it is one of the few studies that has really addressed the issue of how silence in health care encounters is used to resist dominant, and often dichotomized, discourses.

Heaphy (1996) has considered the ways in which the identities of people with AIDS or HIV (PWA/HIV) are negotiated in relation to interactions with medical practitioners and health care professionals. Again, it is important to locate the discursive context in which these health care experiences take place:

> We should not underestimate the effectiveness of the rarely questioned proposition that AIDS is primarily medical. While dominant medico-scientific discourses may be challenged from various positions, they retain a privileged position in defining what is rational, sane and true. (p. 158)

Heaphy (1996) argued, drawing on Foucauldian ideas about the relationship between dominant discourse and power, that PWA/HIV will be subjected to the dominant biomedical discourse about AIDS and HIV. His study showed that in that subjection, practitioners go beyond giving information and managing the illness to police moral issues and to act as judges and teachers of self-discipline.

Heaphy (1996) then went on to look at how such disciplining and regulation can be resisted, drawing on Foucault's idea of reverse, or counter, discourse, and said that the dominant medical discourse is continually contested and challenged. He suggested that Giddens's (1991) work provides a clearer way of understanding how such resistance comes into play and how PWA/HIV are active agents in the creation of their own identities through reskilling, or empowerment, which can take place at fateful moments. Such empowerment can develop as a result of interaction with expert systems, such as in the use of counseling or therapy. Such resistance is akin to that theorized by Butler (1995), in that it depends on some kind of counteridentification, but, as noted previously, in the mental health care encounter for lesbians and gay men who are coming out, such types of resistance might not be possible. Furthermore, although Giddens and Heaphy have both suggested that fateful moments can lead to empowerment as a result of interactions with expert systems such as counseling, in the context of this research, it was these very expert systems that constituted the fateful moment and further threats to identity.

The other kind of identity work observed by Heaphy (1996, 1998), which is more pertinent to understanding the mental health care experiences of the lesbians and gay men in this study, was the strategy of silence as resistance to pathologizing and disciplining:

From my own research it is clear that PWA/HIV often employ silence in an effort to resist medical practitioners' attempts to know and place them in terms of categories of normality. (Heaphy, 1998, p. 33)

In the same way that Heaphy (1996) argued that PWA/HIV are subjected to medical discourses and that the medical discourse retains a privileged position, the lesbians and gay men in this study were subjected to the dominant medical pathologizing discourse about homosexuality, which likewise occupies a privileged position. The dominance of medical and psychoanalytical discourses about homosexuality is such that they pervade the practice of all health care professionals, not just those who are medically or psychoanalytically trained (Malley & Tasker, 2001). There was a suggestion in some of the participants' accounts that nurses were caught up in medical discourses and practices, apparently passively following the pathologizing approach set in motion by the diagnostic practices of psychiatrists involved in the same "case." A number of writers have commented on how inseparable much nursing practice is from dominant medical discourses, resulting in patterns of interaction and power dynamics between patients and nurses similar to those often seen between patients and doctors (Manias & Street, 2000; May, 1992; Porter, 1996; Wilson-Thomas, 1995). May has also observed that patients resist these power relations with nurses and other health care providers through silence. In this study, resistance to pathologizing and disciplining was seen in the silences in people's accounts and the accounts of their silences in mental health care encounters.

In summary, then, in terms of the two main research questions posed, it can be seen that homophobia and heterosexism operate in particular ways in mental health care encounters for people who are coming out. The silencing and pathologization of lesbian and gay identities in these settings compound the vulnerability of this particular group and create further harm and injury. This makes it difficult for lesbians and gay men to access appropriate mental health care. The harm and injury encountered in mental health care is an extension of the harm and injury of homophobic and heterosexist oppression already encountered in day-to-day life.

VULNERABILITY IN THE MATERIAL WORLD

Mental health care practitioners cannot be held to account for oppression arising from social conditions, but they can reflect on their practices and look at how they support such oppression. As Willig (1999b) has argued, there is also a need to challenge material and social structures that support limiting and oppressive discourses. It is clear from the study so far that the oppression of lesbians and gay men is reproduced in mental health care encounters, and discussion follows about how such practices can be overturned. However, before doing this, we can also interrogate the experiences of participants in this study to look in more detail at other material and social conditions that add to the vulnerability of lesbians and gay men who are coming out and seeking mental health care.

Ussher (1996) has stated that material aspects of people's experience, such as social class, often get neglected in constructionist approaches, and it is important not to omit consideration of such factors in this analysis. The particular sampling methods used in this study allowed such an exploration, as a diverse group of participants was included. In particular, analysis of the data suggested that factors such as social class, religious identity, cultural identity, youth, and lack of lesbian/gay community attachment added to the vulnerability of those lesbians and gay men who sought mental health care and increased the barriers to accessing appropriate care. These observations are linked to the extant literature and are offered cautiously, as the method chosen does not allow for a robust analysis of difference based on factors such as social class. However, in-depth data about participants' degrees of community attachment, religious and cultural identities, and social class were collected during the interviews, and I observed some powerful trends in relation to material conditions that add to vulnerability.

A remarkable number of participants who had grown up within fairly closed fundamentalist Christian communities came forward for inclusion into the study without purposeful sampling techniques in relation to this. Purposive sampling also included participants from other religious communities. It seemed from these participants' accounts that they were more vulnerable to isolation from positive lesbian and gay role models, and found it more difficult to access alternative lesbian or gay community support. They were also more prone to being offered psychological techniques for curing their homosexuality (by religious groups, not health care professionals) and more fearful about their physical safety should their sexual identity be discovered. They were also more concerned about disclosing to their health care practitioners because of fears about confidentiality within closed communities and further taboos within such communities about seeking external help with mental health problems. These concerns were particularly reflected in the accounts of Simon, Jane, Tim, Anwar, and Ranjit, seen in Chapter 7. The conflict between religious and sexual identities has been noted in other studies. Coyle and Rafalin (1999) indicated that such conflict relates not only to religious identity but also to cultural identity, wherein family values and community ties are salient. This has also been suggested by other authors (Abdulrahim, 1998; Chan, 1995; Greene, 1994). It has also been suggested that what is often salient about cultural difference in the nature of collective and family ties is the way in which individual identities are not privileged over expected social roles (Abdulrahim, 1998; Chan, 1995).

Working-class participants in this study also seemed to have an added vulnerability in terms of being less likely to be attached to lesbian and gay communities and less likely to be able to access talking treatments once they had presented for health care. It is known that social class makes a difference in how people negotiate their sexual identities and their access to gay communities, which, in turn, affects sexual health (Dowsett et al., 1992; Flowers et al., 1997b, 1998; Weatherburn et al., 1999). It seems likely then that there will be some kind of social class vulnerability in relation to mental health and lesbian and gay identity. Although some research has been conducted that explores the relationship between mental health and lesbian or gay community attachment (e.g., Coyle, 1992; Geraghty, 1996), less research has been done to explore the relationship between social class, lesbian and gay identities, and mental health. However, Bridget and Lucille (1996) have suggested a model of multi-oppression, in which factors such as lower socioeconomic status and minority ethnic status add to the vulnerability of young lesbians when they are coming out, making them more prone to serious mental health problems. Social class is a known indicator affecting mental health and access to mental health care (Pilgrim & Rogers, 1999), and both social class and sexual identity can affect access to talking treatments (NHS Executive, 2000). Practitioners might construct the symptoms of working-class patients in more biomedical and pathologizing terms, thus seeing types of severe mental illness thought to be less amenable to talking treatments (Pilgrim & Rogers, 1999). In this study, there was an apparent trend for working-class participants to be referred to psychiatrists and more middle-class participants to be referred or self-refer to counseling. This was aptly reflected in Lauren's account at the end of Chapter 7, in which she likened her psychiatric referral to "using a sledge hammer to crack a nut" (p. 140).

Finally, youth created an added vulnerability because of the way it intersected with dominant pathologizing discourses, in which homosexuality is seen as an immature phase. This made it difficult for young people to disclose any conflict or worries they had about their sexual identity for fear of being dismissed as being attention seeking or "too young to know"; if they did disclose, they were more likely to be subjected to this pathologizing discourse. They were also worried about being made to self-doubt when they had struggled on their own to form a positive identity and identified how their young age made them more predisposed to rely on the authority of parental and medical accounts. These concerns and experiences were noted in the accounts of Nicki, Charlotte, Alec, Max, and Sarah.

The multilayered material-discursive analysis of the data in this study showed that lesbians and gay men who were coming out experienced continued oppression in their mental health care encounters. These oppressive practices can be seen as part of the wider discursive practices of disciplining and regulating gender and sexuality in a hetero-patriarchal society (Adam, 1998; Plummer; Ussher, 1997b; Wilkerson, 1994), with added vulnerabilities created by other oppressive practices in relation to class, culture, community, and age. What is critical to a study of this kind is to find ways of overturning the polarities and dualisms that lie at the heart of these oppressive practices; otherwise, as noted earlier, such oppressive practices can be easily reasserted in new guises. Some of these potential overturnings were discussed in Chapter 6 in relation to liberal humanism in nursing practice. To develop this understanding, it is useful to look at other studies in which overturnings have been attempted and to reflect on the strengths and limitations of the methodological approaches used in this study.

DISRUPTING THE DUALISMS

Those who seek to apply discourse analysis have argued that interventions have to be tactical and provisional (Parker et al., 1995; Willig, 1999a) and that successful resistance requires an overturning of polarities to make other spaces available (Parker, 1998b; Parker et al., 1995). It is also necessary to challenge material and social structures that support limiting and oppressive discourses (Willig, 1999b); otherwise, we come full circle to victim blaming. What might such tactical interventions be, then, in this case?

The polarities identified through a phenomenological analysis of people's experiences and a discursive analysis using deconstruction and positioning theory were those of complete pathologization of sexual identity, at one end of the continuum, and the negation of minority stress related to sexual identity, at the other. These could be encapsulated in the epithets "mad to be gay" versus "glad to be gay" and are further elucidated in the binary identified by A. Smith (1997), in which the good homosexual is tolerated but the dangerous queer is not. A lesbian or gay man who is experiencing mental health problems, whether attributed to sexual identity or not, simply cannot qualify as a "good homosexual." As Yardley (1998) observed, people suffering from chronic dizziness simply cannot position themselves other than in relation to the cruel dichotomy of poor copers versus real victims. This polarization and dichotomization that discursively produced people's experiences does not allow for a position in between or outside these dualisms. In this study, such positioning made it impossible for participants to articulate their mental distress in relation to their sexual identity. In a similar vein, Boyle (1998) observed how the dominant social and medical discourses about abortion made it difficult for women to articulate their emotional distress and conflict about undergoing abortion.

Parker et al. (1995) have deconstructed discourses about psychotic illness and pathological speech to try to overturn the polarity between normality and abnormality that has the effect of marginalizing, pathologizing, and silencing. They have not attempted to deny the reality of psychotic illness but argued that more emancipatory realities could be arrived at if psychosis and pathological speech were seen as different rather than deviant. Such an overturning, they contended, would move us beyond the current denial of psychotic patients' experiences and the subsequent denial of a talking cure. In Parker's work on this, a discursive analysis is used to provide a critique and alternative account of how particular practices can be seen to open up a space for resistance (Willig, 1999c). Willig (1999b) has given another example of how discursive analysis can be used to overturn dominant discourses in relation to sex education, arguing that sex education tends to reproduce the dominant discourses about sexual activity that make it difficult for people to negotiate safer sex. She has maintained that for sex education to become more emancipatory, there must be explicit knowledge of desire (rather than the current constructions about loss of control and constructions of women as passive).

Yardley (1999) has talked in terms of side-stepping dualisms rather than overturning polarities. In her work on disorientation and chronic dizziness, she produced a material-discursive analysis of that experience in which she argued that dizziness and disorientation (following vestibular impairment) become chronic, disabling, and unmanageable because of a number of Cartesian dualisms that construct the experience of illness. In particular, the mind-body dualism of Western medicine is operating here. Other dualisms in this case relate to control, dilemmas concerning the "reality" of such illness, and expert knowledge, in which passive behavior is encouraged by social and environmental conditions that prevent the recovery of balance mechanisms. Yardley (1997a, 1999) side-stepped these dualisms to arrive at an alternative analysis and understanding, and suggested that these disabling practices can be overturned only by seeing the ways in which the mind and body are intimately linked and by shifting the focus of debate away from a futile discussion about primary etiology. She also argued that more attention needs to be given to the role of attitudes, social relations, and the built environment in terms of how these mediate the construction and experience of the "illness." The parallels between Yardley's work and this study, in terms of the clinician's obsession with the "cause of homosexuality" and the role of attitudes and social interactions in the production of illness and the experience of illness, are striking.

I have argued consistently that previous research on both the health care and the coming-out experiences of lesbians and gay men obscured the effects of discursive practices encoded in silences and silencing. This was also obscured in the first stage of analysis in this study. The presence of pathologizing discourses and the effects of pathologization are more accessible to researchers. Their starkness, although still not obvious to a practitioner who has reified psychoanalytic theory, is in the public realm. This means at least that the pathologization of homosexuality can be contested and can be spoken about, even if the ground still needs to be shifted much farther. However, conducting further analysis within the realm of the unsayable (which is embedded in heteronormative practices in nursing and medical discourse) has also made visible the effects of pathologizing and heterosexist discourses in mental health care.

In this study, material-discursive analysis has provided indications of how dualisms operate in the field of mental health care for lesbians and gay men when they are coming out. It has also provided some insights into how these dualisms can be side-stepped or how the polarities can be overturned to produce more emancipatory practice. Practitioners need to attend to how pathologization is resisted through silence and develop ways of facilitating disclosure about sexual identity and any associated concerns. It was clear from some of the participants' accounts that such disclosures can be facilitated by practitioners' first normalizing lesbian and gay identities to open up spaces where minority stress and its effects can be dealt with in a therapeutic environment.

The unfolding story embedded in the research participants' accounts and in their silences was a story of resistance to binary positioning and a refusal of pathologizing binaries. In this process of engagement with the heteronormative, and often homophobic, oppressive regime of mental health care (itself part of a homophobic and heteronormative society), lesbians and gay men were phased out, missed out, outclassed, cast(e) out, found out, kicked out, ruled out, rooted out, and whited out, but very rarely helped out. The mental health care professionals from whom these lesbians and gay men sought therapeutic help were outmoded and out of order, and the only morally acceptable response to this should be a collective outcry. In the process of trying to negotiate a stigmatized and threatened identity, lesbians and gay men have to undertake further negotiation to access the "helping" professions; it was their resistance to further pathologization and their refusal to have their identities mistaken, stolen, confiscated, or confuscated that lies of the heart of how homophobia and heterosexism affect access to mental health care. It is only when nurses and other health care professionals also refuse these binaries and pathologizations that they can truly engage in a therapeutic process.

TAKING UP NEW POSITIONS

What is required, then, is not only a shift in the practice of pathologization but a further step to enable disclosure and subsequent identity work. This would have to be an overt and courageous statement or "position" taken by nurses and other mental health care practitioners that they, too, were refusing the binaries that their patients are resisting to go together beyond the dualisms. Such a refusal of dualisms would lead toward a more emancipatory and therapeutic exchange that would not force people into binary positions of "definite lesbians and gay men with no uncertainty" versus those who were confused, arrested in their development, or "unaccepting" of their sexuality. It would be possible in this world of mental health care where constrictive dualisms had been overturned to be sad or mad as well as glad to be gay; to be sad about being rejected by one's peers or family but also proud of (or accepting of) one's identity, that is, to be enabled to traverse the shame/pride dichotomy rather than having it reinforced and being constrained, constricted, and constructed by it.

What this would mean in practice is that nurses and other health care professionals would help lesbians and gay men in the negotiation of their sexual identities; instead of lesbians' and gay men's having to be sure and certain and unconfused and definite and positive before it was (relatively) safe to come out in a mental health care setting, they could present for health care and be helped to work out their identity struggle. They would be able to do this without being told that their confusion was a sign that they were really heterosexual or, perversely (in some cases), that they had not come out enough, and without being told by a well-meaning liberal that their sexual identity was of no consequence or interest. Such a journey would demand a certain level of self-awareness, a politicization of nursing and medical knowledge, and an understanding of the relationship between medical and nursing knowledge. As well as calls for critical social theory to be applied within nursing knowledge (Cheek, 2000; Lister, 1997; Manias & Street, 2000; McDonald & Anderson, 2003; Wilson-Thomas, 1995), Hart et al. (2003) have suggested a model underpinned by reflective practice to enable this but have cautioned against trying to map this onto models of individualized care or cultural competence.

Unless that negotiation is framed in its social, cultural, and political context, dualistic thinking will reassert itself, re-inscribing new patterns of oppression. Individuals will be individualized: They will be wrenched from their social context, and if their negotiation is successful, it will be seen as a sign of individual resilience. If they are not successful, they will be repathologized, victim-blamed, and found deficient. Additional dualisms in relation to gender, social class, age, race, and ethnicity will be mapped onto the individual/society and heterosexual/homosexual binaries, creating further layers of oppression through erasure. If nurses (and other mental health care professionals) are to enter into a therapeutic relationship with lesbians and gay men who are negotiating their sexual identities in mental health care settings, they will have to disrupt the dominant discourses that pathologize and invisibilize lesbians and gay men, and they will have to disrupt the individualization embedded in nursing philosophy, which is itself embedded in liberal humanism. In particular, the shame/pride dichotomy must be disrupted, so that it is possible to be both ashamed and proud or neither of these. As practice currently stands, lesbians and gay men risk their mental health if they access mental health care without the certainty of pride. The irony of this, of course, should not be lost on the reader: A certain and proud lesbian or gay man is less likely to need to access mental health care than a shamed or uncertain one. However, certain and proud lesbians and gay men do have mental health problems that might be unrelated to conflict as such about their sexual identity, but even with the shame/pride dichotomy intact, access to care for such people is problematic, as they, too, become repathologized.

If the shame/pride dichotomy could be disrupted, it would be possible for lesbians and gay men to access mental health care regardless of where they were positioned in relation to this dichotomy, because health care practitioners would help them to negotiate that path; any repositioning could then emerge from a therapeutic engagement rather than a nontherapeutic reinscription of pathologization and/or marginalization. In disrupting this, essentialist questions about the etiology of homosexuality and its permanence would become redundant. The responsibility for this endeavor must lie with nurse educators, nurse researchers, and nursing organizations as well as individual practitioners: "If the potential constraining effect of a particular discursive frame's dominance in the health arena is recognized, then it is possible for space to be opened up for other discourses or ways of thinking" (Cheek, 2000, p. 25). De Lacey (2002) has applied this way of thinking to how nurses can either reproduce or disrupt pathologizing discourses of infertile women and has argued that nurses must and can rupture negative stereotypes through their practice and the way they interact with their patients. Such new ways of thinking will require a challenge to current models of training and the development of reflective practice.

Chapter 9
Negotiating Sexual Identities

Dualistic thinking, very much a product of modernity, makes it extraordinarily difficult for people to think of themselves or others in ways that do not immediately invoke a binary. I have argued throughout this book that such binaries restrict our ability to understand and investigate experience. This is particularly important when investigating experiences in relation to sexual identity, as identity formation tends to be experienced in either/or terms; thus, people tend to experience their sexual identity as something fixed and stable along a bipolar continuum. Similarly, they will tend to be positioned by others in relation to such a bipolar continuum or binary. Dualistic thinking has spawned a further set of binaries onto those with lesbian and gay identities through pathologization and criminalization: the good versus the bad "homosexual." In this scheme of things, which can be summed up as the dominant discourse, the normal (natural) heterosexual occupies the privileged side of the binary, and all that is bad, unnatural, and deviant is projected onto the Other side: in this case, the mad, bad, or sad (but always shameful) homosexual.

UNTHINKING THE BINARIES

These binaries and dualisms are reproduced further in the research on lesbians' and gay men's lives, leading to unresolved tensions and polarized positions around pathologization. There was a long period of research activity in which clinical and prison populations of homosexuals were studied to "prove" the theory that homosexuality was a form of psychopathology; this was followed historically, post Stonewall and a gay rights political movement, with its polar opposite—gay-affirmative psychology—which set out to disprove the pathologizing research preceding it and win the political and scientific argument in favor of the well-adjusted homosexual. Much of this early gay-affirmative research was fairly self-fulfilling, a prime example of which is the early research into coming out and stage models thereof. I critiqued this research in Chapter 2 and held out early warning signals about the need to pay careful attention to sampling issues, which I explored in considerable depth in Chapter 4. Following the gay-affirmative psychology period (an empirical body of literature that tended to be atheoretical) came a further wave of more theoretical literature on the formation of lesbian and gay identities and communities. What both of these bodies of literature have done has been to reinforce the dualism between the good and the bad, or the celebratory and the pathologized. Research on the celebratory side of the binary, although a necessary condition for the depathologization of homosexuality has not been a sufficient condition, and I have set out in this book to begin to address this.

These bodies of literature have ignored the tension created by the stark evidence that lesbians and gay men suffer from a much higher incidence of attempted suicide and other mental health problems than control groups of heterosexual people. This tension is reproduced in the literature on the mental health care experiences of lesbians and gay men; we have seen from the review of literature in Chapter 2 that there is considerable empirical evidence that health care practitioners hold homophobic attitudes and that their training neither counters such views nor allows space for them to understand the health care needs of lesbians and gay men. There is also considerable empirical evidence that these negative attitudes translate into poor practice, with many accounts of verbal, physical, and sexual abuse, hostility, withdrawal of care, and voyeurism in both general and mental health care settings. Within the mental health field in particular, there are accounts of experiences' of being pathologized and silenced. In addition, there is evidence of the experience of heterosexism in health care, often encoded within a more liberal and less pathologizing discourse.

The existing literature on mental health care experiences brings into play research evidence about the vulnerability of lesbians and gay men in terms of their mental health, evidence that was missing from the early lesbian and gay psychology literature, from the theory on lesbian and gay identities and communities, and from the pathologizing research that preceded both of these. A tension arises, then, when research participants and researchers make claims that sexual identity and mental illness are unrelated but, at the same time, present evidence of added vulnerability and a higher than expected incidence of mental health problems. This added vulnerability is reported to be associated with a period in lesbians' and gay men's lives when they are coming out; so although this tension can be ignored if research is being conducted into mental health care experiences that postdate coming out, these experiences cannot be ignored if research is to be undertaken about mental health care experiences at the time of coming out.

In this book, I set out to work with the tensions arising from such elision; in so doing, I have had to extend the available methods and their applications, tackling the limitations imposed by dualistic thinking in both theory and method. Although I make no grand claims to have gone beyond dualistic thinking, I do claims to have extended the limits of our knowledge through methodological innovation applied specifically to an area in which previous empirical research was sparse and theory limited. So although dualistic thinking has to some extent been side-stepped, allowing a further interrogation of data than would have otherwise been possible, it is probably currently beyond the capacity of either individual or collective imaginings to overturn completely the polarities that mediate our experience and our interpretations of experience.

Data that have been presented and analyzed in this book have been interpreted through different lenses that straddle epistemological divides. This relatively new and innovatory approach has been termed a *bricolage* in the methodological literature. In doing this, I have been able to go some way beyond the essentialism of so much lesbian- and gay-affirmative psychology, and the lesbian and gay health care experience literature, but to also pull back from the brink of nihilistic social constructionism. This brings these disparate bodies of thought together to inform theoretically and empirically our understanding of how homophobia and heterosexism in mental health care encounters affect the person who is struggling with his or her sexual identity.

The side-stepping of dualisms throughout this study allowed a more sophisticated approach to sampling than is often found with research into hidden populations and permitted more attention to be paid to the complex ways in which identities and community attachments are formed and mediated by material conditions such as social class, culture, and religion. By pushing the boundaries of sampling strategies with hidden populations and reaching a more diverse group in terms of how sexual identities interrelate with lesbian and gay community attachments, social class, and cultural differences, I was confronted with a data set that was not, in a sense, ready theorized or self-fulfilling. Instead, I entered the realm of the unsayable by extending the sampling to include those who "dared not speak their name." Had the "usual suspects" been interviewed (i.e., a snowball sample of White, middle-class, lesbian and gay community–attached, university-educated professionals), then it is highly likely that some of the complexities of how homophobia and heterosexism influence patient care would have been lost.

BREAKING THE SILENCE

Up until now, most applied researchers have been silent on the issue of silence, and research into the ineffable has remained at the margins of academic tolerance. By engaging in an analysis of the ineffable, I have also challenged the common practice of excising methodological detail when conducting sensitive research (Lee, 1995). Such excision does not occur here, and I have also challenged and refused the binaries of methodological purists (or, rather, what has been coined as "methodolatry"; Elliott, Fischer, & Rennie, 2000; Reicher, 2000).

By analyzing the data through multiple lenses, which allows a realist exploration of some aspects of people's experiences, alongside a discursive analysis of some of the contradictions and tensions in people's accounts of their mental health care experiences, it has been possible to come to a deeper understanding of the complex ways in which homophobia and heterosexism operate in mental health care encounters. This deeper understanding takes into account the discursive production of identities and of nursing and health care, and health care experience. It also considers the role of language in the production and maintenance of identities, and the role of language in the mental health care encounter as well as in the research interview. The discursive analysis, which drew on positioning theory, also allowed a deeper understanding and interpretation of the silences and contradictions in people's accounts, which mirrored their silences in their mental health care encounters. It was only through this kind of engagement, using innovative methods and theories that have rarely been applied to empirical enquiry, that I was able to go beyond a surface claim that homophobia and heterosexism in health care are harmful and to begin to understand the complexities of how they operate in mental health care and the ways in which they affect access to care.

The more realist lens through which the data were analyzed, interpretative phenomenological analysis (IPA), enabled the first research question to be addressed. This was How do homophobia and heterosexism manifest themselves in mental health care encounters when lesbians and gay men are coming out?

The analysis of the data using IPA clearly showed that lesbians and gay men experienced homophobia and heterosexism in their mental health care encounters. These experiences were commensurate with findings in the extant literature; that is, lesbians and gay men experienced hostility, abuse, withdrawal of care, pathologization, and silencing. The one feature in the literature on general health care experiences that does not seem to occur in mental health care settings was voyeurism. It is as if the spectacle of the Other in settings in which physical health is attended to is that of the physical freak, who must be looked at—hence the voyeurism—whereas in mental health care settings, the process of Othering is through pathologization of the mind—in this case, the mental freak.

Thus far, then, the research had confirmed what was already known from previous studies. However, the second research question had not really been addressed in the extant literature other than by passing reference to health care avoidance as a consequence of homophobia and the observation that in many cases, lesbians and gay men do not disclose their sexual identity in health care encounters. The second research question was more concerned with the effects of homophobia and heterosexism: How do homophobia and heterosexism affect lesbians' and gay men's access to mental health care when they are coming out?

It seemed vital to address this further question if health care professionals were to be convinced of the need to reflect on their practice. The existing research presents the evidence of homophobia and heterosexism in health care, and within that there is a self-evidentiary assumption that homophobia and heterosexism are harmful. However, many health care professionals remain to be convinced of this, and as the health care experience literature shows, those service users who complain about homophobia in mental health care are often told that they will have to get used to it; it is as if the fault lies in their deficient character being unable to cope with homophobia rather than homophobia being understood as an unacceptable and violating form of oppression. The key to understanding the way in which homophobia and heterosexism affect access to mental healthcare lay in the nondisclosure of sexual identity frequently reported in people's accounts. This nondisclosure occurred even when participants felt quite sure that their presenting issue was linked to their struggle with their sexual identity. Further understanding of the way in which homophobia affects access to care also lay in the contradictions within people's accounts about the extent to which they felt they had accepted their sexual identity and the extent to which they felt that their sexual identity was linked to their mental health problems. However, interpreting these data was not without its challenges, as many participants found this aspect of their care very difficult to articulate.

It was clear early on in the study that some aspects of people's experience required an epistemological position and a method of analysis that took into account these silences and contradictions. The methodological literature on conducting sensitive research was particularly helpful in this respect, as were theoretical understandings about identities. Of particular use was methodological reflection where researchers had undertaken work in areas that contained parallels, that is, in which people were talking about the experience of illness or health care in relation to a disease that was contested. Yardley's (1998) work on people's experience of chronic dizziness and Heaphy's (1996) work with people with AIDS were both oases in a methodological desert of silence about silence. Heaphy's (1998) reflections were all the more illuminating, as he commented on how silences in health care encounters mirror silences in research interviews. I had noted this phenomenon early on in the research process with this study; this observation, with Heaphy's work and the methodological literature on social constructionism, made it imperative to find another lens through which to analyze the data to make sense of this extra layer of meaning. What was needed was an approach to analysis that took into account the rhetorical aspects of language and the ways in which meaning is constructed through language.

Furthermore, experience is constituted through language; that is to say, I took a position in which I understood that language does not mirror reality but is constitutive of it; thus, an interview cannot necessarily be seen as a direct and true account of experience. What was noted in the interviews conducted for this study was that parts of people's accounts seemed at times to be rhetorical. Participants might present a particular account of their sexual identity, coming out, and mental health that could be understood to be rhetorical, in that it served a purpose in terms of constructing and presenting their identity in a particular way. I was alerted to this in a number of ways, but one definable way was when material was introduced into the interview that directly contradicted the previous "construction." It also seemed to be possible that these constructions within the interview process might mirror something that also happened in the health care encounter. It was at this point that Heaphy's (1998) reflections were particularly salient, but it also became clear that the most common method arising from the social constructionist framework (i.e., discourse analysis) would be difficult to apply to this kind of data.

Discourse analysis is usually used with text in which power relations and discursive meanings are analyzed, with the focus most often being on how people use dominant discourses to persuade others of their arguments or, perhaps, to justify their arguments; thus, Wetherell and Potter (1992), in their classic study, looked at how people talked about racism, that is, how their racist practices were embedded in and constructed through the way they talked. Similarly discourse analysis has been used to analyze and understand how other dominant practices, such as sexism and homophobia, are produced and reproduced in talk. What is specific about most discourse analysis empirical research is that it seeks to uncover the ways in which dominant discourses operate within the way people talk. Therefore, if one applied discourse analysis to an understanding of the dominant discourses in relation to the pathologization of homosexuality, it would make sense to analyze the talk of mental health care professionals. A discourse analysis could uncover the ways in which lesbians and gay men were constructed as pathological in the talk and diagnostic practices of professionals. To apply such an approach to an analysis of health care experience is immediately problematic, however, as the process becomes once removed from such practices: It is the experiences of such practices, not the practice of such practices, that are being analyzed. Discourse analysis does not lend itself to this enterprise, as it has developed around an analysis of the oppressor rather than the oppressed.

Where researchers have attempted to analyze health care experience or the experience of the oppressed using discursive analyses, these analyses have tended to be more theoretical and less empirical than those studies that have involved discourse analysis. Parker at al.'s (1995) work is a case in point, where a discursive analysis is applied to the experience of having an identity that is pathologized rather than focusing on the pathologizer; however, these studies are theoretical, not empirical. Willig (1999a) has argued that it is necessary to develop methods that allow for an empirical discursive analysis of experience so that it can be applied and used in such a way that practice can be challenged and developed. She has said that the only researcher who has managed to achieve this challenging task is Yardley (1996, 1997a), who applied such an analysis to an understanding of the experience of chronic dizziness. However, such approaches are necessary if we are to really understand nursing practice (Cheek, 2000). Willig (1999a) asserted that the theoretical approach that allows an understanding of how people experience the effects of oppressive discourses is positioning theory. Again, this has rarely been applied to empirical data, and, as in the case of Parker et al's (1995) work, it tends to hover above rather than engage with the text.

RENEGOTIATING NONPATHOLOGIZED IDENTITIES

In this study, I break new ground, in that I have applied a discursive analysis using positioning theory to an empirical data set about people's experiences of discursive practices. I have brought together and, therefore, take further two disparate sets of work; there is a body of empirical (but atheoretical) work about people's health care experiences or their coming-out experiences, and, on the other hand, theoretical work about identity that has not been applied or used to interrogate empirical data. Through the bringing together of these two approaches, more can be said about the nature of those experiences than could be said by using either approach alone. Furthermore, this combined approach, or bricolage, was applied to a topic that had, up until now, been neglected by both approaches—there was neither empirical investigation nor theoretical work specifically in relation to mental health care experiences and coming out.

Interpretation of data in this study (about silencing, nondisclosure, and being pathologized) through the discursive analysis led to a clearer under-standing of what was at stake. I illuminated this by uncovering the dualisms and binaries at work. Clear pairings, or binaries, through out this study are identified in the theory about identity and the process of Othering. These clearly link to the empirical data with regard to the research participants' experiences of mental health care. To reiterate, these binaries construct the pathological, deviant homosexual within a discourse of heteronormativity.

These findings, as they stand, if presented to the nursing profession as evidence of malpractice, would not be highly contested. With current policy shifts toward greater equality legislation and codes of professional practice about the fair and equal treatment of people regardless of race, religion, sex-ual orientation, and so on, this fairly hard evidence of homophobic abuse and pathologization would probably be considered unacceptable practice in most liberal circles. However, the underwriting of psychiatry by psychoanalytic thinking and psychiatry's enduring influence on nursing practice in mental health makes the task of presenting such evidence more problematic in men-tal health care contexts.

The findings from this study could be condensed to a statement about the need for mental health care practitioners to normalize lesbian and gay iden-tities so that lesbian and gay patients feel safe enough to disclose some of their ambivalences, uncertainties, and concerns about coping with, manag-ing, or negotiating a stigmatized identity. Although these findings might be accepted at face value, this seems unlikely. As noted earlier, overturning of dualisms is problematic, and power relations are all too often re-inscribed in a new form. The key to understanding where the danger lies in nursing of such re-inscription is also to be found within this book through an under-standing of one final and underpinning dualism.

This dualism, explored in Chapter 6, is the individual/society dualism embedded in liberal humanism. It underpins both nursing practice, in the guise of individualized patient care (Lister, 1997; Wilson-Thomas, 1995), and lesbian and gay psychology, through unproblematized use of the concept of internalized homophobia (C. Kitzinger, 1997). As noted in Chapters 2 and 3, in attempting to overturn dualisms, power relations reassert themselves in new guises; it is the guise of liberal humanism that is central to understanding where nursing practice erases difference through its dominant ethos of individualized patient care. This perspective enables sense to be made of those mental health care experiences in this study wherein participants described being silenced. It also helps to make further sense of some of those anomalous experiences whereby participants described being told that their problem was that they had not accepted their gay identity (i.e., they were not "well-adjusted homosexuals").

As we attempt to overturn the dualisms that pathologize lesbians and gay men, a danger arises that the re-inscription of homophobia will pathologize them in new ways. As dualistic thinking rears its head again, it threatens to subsume subtleties about the relationship between sexual identity and mental health by binarizing the confused homosexual. Research participants' accounts were replete with resistance to such positioning, and it is important to ensure that in our attempt to sum up the message from this research, "confusion" about sexual identity (as in stress associated with managing a lesbian or gay identity) is not conflated with the "confusion" of not knowing what or who one is. Research participants' accounts clearly showed that their nondisclosure was often a form of resistance to being positioned as confused, a binary position on which the pathological model of homosexuality relies.

It is this distinction between mental health problems that arise from having to deal with a stigmatized sexual identity and the notion that sexual identity is a sign in and of itself of pathology (whether that is assumed to be one that will be grown out of or one that is permanent) that is crucial to our understanding of nondisclosure in mental health care encounters and the pathologization of those who do disclose. There is also, of course, a relationship between these two phenomena, as the nondisclosers resist the pathologizing identity imposed by mental health care practitioners on many of those who do disclose. Furthermore, the individualism of nursing care threatens to erase difference and lead to victim blaming. For nursing practice to be emancipatory, it must disrupt these dualisms, and, in particular, it must disrupt the shame/pride dichotomy; it can do this through both normalizing lesbian and gay identities and tolerating, but not imposing, any uncertainties people bring to their mental health care encounters.

REFLECTING ON THE SITUATION

In this book, I have claimed to have straddled epistemological divides and produced a bricolage through mixed methods and interpretation of the data through different lenses. My main argument about method has been that I have worked as a bricoleur; to research any aspect of cultural practice, methodological purity must be eschewed (Brown, 1999). Concerns about undertaking such research are that it inflicts conceptual violence on theoretical systems (Parker et al., 1995) and lays the researcher open to charges of ontological gerrymandering (Harper, 1999). However, these concerns can be addressed by asking about the "quality of the results, how well they serve to inform us about the issue in question, (and) what kind of work they make visible" (Brown, 1999, p. 40). Harper (1999) says further that this judgment can be informed for the reader by asking, "Are my analysis and implications persuasive, taking what you know of my assumptions and politics into consideration?" (p. 140).

This requires the writing of a transparent account that demonstrates sensitivity to context, highlights the importance of the findings, and positions the researcher. The context and position of the researcher were given in Chapter 1 and then revisited throughout the book in terms of my insider status and use of innovative sampling strategies. These approaches disrupted my worldview, as discussed in Chapter 4, and these, alongside material-discursive methods of analysis, have made visible the kind of work that other researchers have, up until now, obscured. In doing this, I have made no grand claims to have completely overturned dualisms—in short, to have single-handedly reversed centuries of Cartesian thought—and any claim to have extended knowledge will be partial and situated. However, the claim made here is that the shame/pride dichotomy has been disrupted, as have a number of other supporting ontological, epistemological, and methodological dualisms. This process opens a window into how nurses and other mental health care professionals could make their practice more emancipatory through further disruption of individualism.

References

Abdulrahim, D. (1998). Power, culture and the "hard to reach": The marginalisation of minority ethnic populations from HIV prevention and harm minimisation. In R. Barbour & G. Huby (Eds.), *Meddling with mythology: AIDS and the social construction of knowledge* (pp. 37-53). London: Routledge.

Adam, B. D. (1998). Theorizing homophobia. *Sexualities, 1*(4), 387-404.

Ahmed, B. (1999). Reflexivity, cultural membership and power in the research situation: Tensions and contradictions when considering the researcher's role. *British Psychological Society Psychology of Women Section Newsletter, 7*, 35-40.

Altheide, D. L., & Johnson, J. M. (1998). Criteria for assessing interpretive validity in qualitative research. In N. K. Denzin & Y. S. Lincoln (Eds.), *Collecting and interpreting qualitative material* (pp. 283-312). Thousand Oaks, CA: Sage.

Andrade, S. J. (1995). Reaching "hidden populations" through qualitative research: Ethnographic street lessons from street children in Bolivia. In H. Kirsch (Ed.), *Drug lessons and education programs in developing countries* (pp. 61-79). New Brunswick, NJ: Transaction.

Annesley, P. (1995). *Dykes and psyches: Lesbians' experiences and evaluation of clinical psychology services.* Unpublished doctoral dissertation, University of Surrey, United Kingdom.

Annesley, P., & Coyle, A. (1995). Clinical psychologists' attitudes to lesbians. *Journal of Community and Applied Psychology, 5*, 327-331.

Annesley, P., & Coyle, A. (1998). Dykes and psyches: Lesbian women's experiences of clinical psychology services. *Changes: An International Journal of Psychology and Psychotherapy, 16*(4), 247-258.

Anzaldúa, G. (1990). How to tame a wild tongue. In R. Ferguson, M. Gever, T. T.Min-ha, & C. West (Eds.), *Out there: Marginalization and contemporary cultures* (pp. 203-212). Cambridge, MA: MIT Press.

Archer, S. (1988). "Qualitative" research and the epistemological problems of the management disciplines. In A. M. Pettigrew (Ed.), *Competitiveness and the management process* (pp. 265-302). Oxford, UK: Basil Blackwell.

Ayella, D. B. (1993). "They must be crazy": Some of the difficulties in researching "cults." In C. M. Renzetti & R. M. Lee (Eds.), *Researching sensitive topics* (pp. 108-124). London: Sage.

Bagley, C., & Tremblay, P. (1997). Suicidal behaviors in homosexual and bisexual males. *Crisis, 18*(1), 24-34.

Bartlett, A., King, M., & Phillips, P. (2001). Straight talking: An investigation of the attitudes and practice of psychoanalysts and psychotherapists in relation to gays and lesbians. *British Journal of Psychiatry, 179,* 545-549.

Bell, A., & Weinberg, M. (1978). *Homosexualities: A study of diversity among men and women.* New York: Simon and Schuster.

Bell, D., & Valentine, G. (1995). *Mapping desire: Geographies of sexuality.* London: Routledge.

Berger, R. M. (1990). Passing: Impact on the quality of same-sex couple relationships. *Social Work, 35*(4), 328-332.

Bhaskar, R. (1989). *Reclaiming reality: A critical introduction to contemporary philosophy.* London: Verso.

Bhugra, D. (1988, July 15). One in 10 GPs view gays as ill. *General Practitioner,* p. 2.

Bhugra, D., & King, M. (1989). Controlled comparison of attitudes of psychiatrists, general practitioners, homosexual doctors and homosexual men to male homosexuality. *Journal of the Royal Society of Medicine, 82,* 603-605.

Biernacki, P., & Waldorf, D. (1981). Snowball Sampling problems and techniques of chain referral sampling. *Sociological Methods and Research, 10*(2), 141-163.

Binnie, J. (1995). Trading places: Consumption, sexuality and the production of queer space. In D. Bell & G. Valentine (Eds.), *Mapping desire: Geographies of sexuality* (pp. 182-199). London: Routledge.

Black, D., Gates, G., Sanders, S. A., & Taylor, L. (2000). Demographics of the gay and lesbian population in the United States: Evidence from available systematic data sources. *Demography, 37*(2), 139-154.

Bloor, M., & McIntosh, J. (1990). Surveillance and concealment: A comparison of techniques of client resistance in therapeutic communities and health visiting. In S. Cunningham-Burley & N. P. McKegany (Eds.), *Readings in medical sociology* (pp. 159-181). London: Tavistock and Routledge.

Boatwright, K. J., Gilbert, M. S., Forrest, L., & Ketzenberger, K. (1996). Impact of identity development upon career trajectory: Listening to the voices of lesbian women. *Journal of Vocational Behavior, 48,* 210-228.

Bola, M., Drew, C., Gill, R., Harding, S., King, E., & Seu, B. (1998). Representing ourselves and representing others: A response. *Feminism and Psychology, 8*(1), 105-110.

Bond, S., Rhodes, T., Phillips, P., & Tierney, A. (1990). Knowledge and attitudes: HIV and community nursing staff in Scotland, 2. *Nursing Times, 86*(45), 49-51.

Boyle, M., & McEvoy, J. (1998). Putting abortion in its social context: Northern Irish women's experiences of abortion in England. *Health, 2*(3), 283-304.

Bradford, J. B., & Ryan, C. (1987). *National Lesbian Health Care Survey: Implications for mental health care.* Richmond: Virginia Commonwealth University, Survey Research Laboratory and The National Lesbian and Gay Health Foundation.

Bradford, J. B., & Ryan, C. (1988). *The National Lesbian Health Care Survey.* Richmond: Virginia Commonwealth University, National Lesbian and Gay Health Foundation and Survey Research Laboratory.

Bradford, J. R., Ryan, C., & Rothblum, E. (1994). National lesbian health care survey: Implications for mental health care, special section—Mental health of lesbians and gay men. *Journal of Consulting and Clinical Psychology, 62*(2), 228-242.

Brannen, J. (1988). Research note: The study of sensitive subjects. *Sociological Review, 36*, 552-563.

Breakwell, G. M. (1986). *Coping with threatened identities.* London: Methuen.

Breakwell, G. M. (1992, March). *The AIDS generation, Thatcher's children.* Identity, Social Representations and Action—Inaugural Lecture: University of Surrey, UK.

Breakwell, G. M. (1996). Identity processes and social changes. In G. M. Breakwell & E. Lyons (Eds.), *Changing European identities: Social psychological analyses of social change* (pp. 13-37). Oxford, UK: Butterworth/Heinemann.

Bridget, J., & Lucille, S. (1996). Lesbian youth support information service (LYSIS): Developing a distance support agency for young lesbians. *Journal of Community and Applied Psychology, 6*(386), 1-10.

Broadhead, R. S., Heckathorn, D. D., Grund, J. P. C., Stern, L. S., & Anthony, D. L. (1995a). Drug users versus outreach workers in combatting AIDS, Part I: Agency problems in traditional outreach interventions. *International Journal of Drug Policy, 6*(3), 178-188.

Broadhead, R. S., Heckathorn, D. D., Grund, J. P. C., Stern, L. S., & Anthony, D. L. (1995b). Drug users versus outreach workers in combatting AIDS, Part II: Preliminary results of a peer-driven intervention. *International Journal of Drug Policy, 6*(4), 274-288.

Brown, L. S. (1995). Lesbian identities: Concepts and issues. In A. R. D'Augelli & C. J. Patterson (Eds.), *Lesbian, gay and bisexual identities over the lifespan: Psychological perspectives* (pp. 3-23). New York: Oxford University Press.

Brown, S. D. (1999). Stress as regimen: Critical readings of self-help literature. In C. Willig (Ed.), *Applied discourse analysis: Social and psychological interventions* (pp. 22-43). Buckingham, UK: Open University Press.

Burman, E., & Parker, I. E. (1993). *Discourse analytic research: Repertoires and readings of text in action.* London: Routledge.

Burns, J. (1992). The psychology of lesbian health care. In P. Nicolson & J. M. Ussher (Eds.), *The psychology of women's health and health care* (pp. 225-248). Basingstoke, UK: Palgrave Macmillan.

Burr, V. (1995). *An introduction to social constructionism.* London: Routledge.

Burr, V. (1998). Overview: Realism, relativism, social constructionism and discourse. In I. Parker (Ed.), *Social constructionism, discourse and realism* (pp. 13-26). London: Sage.

Butler, J. (1990). *Gender trouble: Feminism and the subversion of identity.* New York: Routledge.

Butler, J. (1991). Imitation and gender insubordination. In D. Fuss (Ed.), *Inside/out: Lesbian theories, gay theories* (pp. 13-31). London: Routledge.

Butler, J. (1993). *Bodies that matter: On the discursive limits of "sex."* New York: Routledge.

Butler, J. (1995). Subjection, resistance, resignification: Between Freud and Foucault. In J. Rajchman (Ed.), *The identity in question* (pp. 229-249). New York: Routledge.

Cain, R. (1991). Stigma management and gay identity development. *Social Work, 36*(1), 67-73.

Calandrino, M. (1999). *Sexual orientation discrimination in the UK labour market.* Unpublished manuscript, St Anthony's College, University of Oxford, UK.

Cannon, L. W., Higginbotham, E., & Leung, M. L. A. (1991). Race and class bias in qualitative research on women. In J. Lorber & S. J. Farrell (Eds.), *The social construction of gender* (pp. 237-248). London: Sage.

Cass, V. (1979). Homosexual identity formation: A theoretical model. *Journal of Homosexuality, 4*, 219-236.

Caulfield, H., & Platzer, H. (1998). Next of kin. *Nursing Standard, 13*(7), 47-49.

Chan, C. S. (1995). Issues of sexual identity in an ethnic minority: The case of Chinese American lesbians, gay men, and bisexual People. In A. R. D'Augelli & C. J. Patterson (Eds.), *Lesbian, gay and bisexual identities over the lifespan: Psychological perspectives* (pp. 81-101). New York: Oxford University Press.

Charmaz, K. (1987). Struggling for a self: Identity levels of the chronically ill. In J. A. Roth & P. Conrad (Eds.), *Research in the sociology of healthcare* (Vol. 6, pp. 283-321). Greenwich, CT: JAI.

Charmaz, K. (1990). "Discovering" chronic illness: Using grounded theory. *Social Science & Medicine, 11*, 1161-1172.

Charmaz, K. (1995). Grounded theory. In J. A. Smith, R. Harré, & L. Van Langenhove (Eds.), *Rethinking methods in psychology* (pp. 27-49). London: Sage.

Cheek, J. (2000). *Postmodern and poststructural approaches to nursing research.* London: Sage.

Cheek, J., & Rudge, T. (1994). Nursing as textually mediated reality. *Nursing Inquiry*, *1*(1), 15-22.

Chouinard, V., & Grant, A. (1996). On not being even anywhere near "The Project." In N. Duncan (Ed.), *BodySpace: Destabilising geographies of gender and sexuality* (pp. 170-196). London: Routledge.

Citizenship 21. (2003). *Profiles of prejudice: The nature of prejudice in England—In-depth analysis of findings*. London: Stonewall.

Cixous, H. (1975). "Sorties." In E. Marks & I. de Courtivon (Eds.), *New French feminisms* (pp. 90-98). Hassocks, UK: Harvester.

Clark, V. (2002). Resistance and normalisation in the construction of lesbian and gay families: A discursive analysis. In A. Coyle & C. Kitzinger (Eds.), *Lesbian and gay psychology: New perspectives* (pp. 98-116). Leicester, UK: BPS Blackwell.

Clarke, G. (1996). Conforming and contesting with (a) difference: How lesbian students and teachers manage their identities. *International Studies in Sociology of Education*, *6*(2), 191-209.

Clarke, G. (1998). Working out: Lesbian teachers and the politics of (dis)location. *Journal of Lesbian Studies*, *2*(4), 85-99.

Cochran, S. D., & Mays, V. M. (1994). Depressive distress among homosexually active African American men and women. *American Journal of Psychiatry*, *151*(4), 524-529.

Coffey, A. (1999). *The ethnographic self: Fieldwork and the representation of identity*. London: Sage.

Cohen, K. M., & Savin-Williams, R. C. (1996). Developmental perspectives on coming out to self and others. In R. C. Savin-Williams & K. M. Cohen (Eds.), *The lives of lesbians, gays and bisexuals* (pp. 113-151). Fort Worth, TX: Harcourt Brace.

Copas, A. J., Wellings, K., Erens, B., Mercer, C. H., McManus, S., Fenton, K. A., et al. (2002). The accuracy of reported sensitive sexual behaviour in Britain: Exploring the extent of change 1990–2000. *Sexually Transmitted Infections*, *78*, 26-30.

Cosgrove, L. (2000). Crying out loud: Understanding women's emotional distress as both lived experience and social construction. *Feminism and Psychology*, *10*(2), 247-267.

Cottler, L. B., Compton, W. M., & Keating, S. (1995). What incentives are effective rewards for "hidden populations" interviewed as part of research projects? [Letter to the editor]. *Public Health Reports*, *110*(2), 178.

Coyle, A. (1991). *The construction of gay identity*. Unpublished doctoral dissertation, University of Surrey, UK.

Coyle, A. (1992). "My own special creation"? The construction of gay identity. In G. M. Breakwell (Ed.), *Social psychology of identity and the self concept* (pp. 187-220). London: Surrey University Press/Academic Press Harcourt Brace Jovanovich.

Coyle, A. (1998). Developing lesbian and gay identity in adolescence. In J. Coleman & D. Roker (Eds.), *Teenage sexuality: Health, risk and education* (pp. 163-187). London: Harwood Academic.

Coyle, A. (2000). Discourse analysis. In G. M. Breakwell, S. Hammond & C. Fife-Schaw (Eds.), *Research methods in psychology* (2nd ed., pp. 251-268). London: Sage.

Coyle, A., Milton, M., & Annesley, P. (1999). The silencing of lesbian and gay voices in psycho-"therapeutic" texts, training and practice. *Changes: An International Journal of Psychology and Psychotherapy, 17,* 132-143.

Coyle, A., & Rafalin, D. (1999, March). *Negotiating cultural, religious, and sexual identity: Jewish gay men's accounts of sexual identity development in their youth.* Paper presented at a conference on Gay and Lesbian Identities: Working with Young People, their Families and Schools, University College London.

Coyle, A., & Rafalin, D. (2000). Jewish gay men's accounts of negotiating cultural, religious, and sexual identity: A qualitative study. *Journal of Psychology and Human Sexuality, 12*(4), 21-48.

Coyle, A., & Wright, C. (1996). Using the counselling interview to collect data on sensitive topics. *Journal of Health Psychology, 1*(4), 431-440.

Creith, E. (1996). *Undressing lesbian sex.* London: Cassell.

Cunningham-Burley, S. (1985). Rules, roles and communicative performance in qualitative research interviews. *International Journal of Sociology and Social Policy, 5,* 67-77.

Dardick, L., & Grady, K. E. (1980). Openness between gay persons and health professionals. *Annals of Internal Medicine, 93*(1), 115-119.

D'Augelli, A. R., & Hershberger, S. L. (1993). Lesbian, gay and bisexual youth in community settings: personal challenges and mental health problems. *American Journal of Community Psychology, 21*(4), 421-448.

Davies, B. (1998). Psychology's subject: A commentary on the relativism/realism debate. In I. Parker (Ed.), *Social constructionism, discourse and realism* (pp. 133-146). London: Sage.

Davies, B., & Harré, R. (1990). Positioning: The discursive production of selves. *Journal for the Theory of Social Behaviour, 20*(1), 43-63.

Davies, D. (1996). Homophobia and heterosexism. In D. Davies & C. Neal (Eds.), *Pink therapy: A guide for counsellors and therapists working with lesbian, gay and bisexual clients* (pp. 41-65). Buckingham, UK: Open University Press.

Davies, D., & Neal, C. (1996). An historical overview of homosexuality and therapy. In D. Davies & C. Neal (Eds.), *Pink Therapy: A guide for counsellors and therapists working with lesbian, gay and bisexual clients* (pp. 11-23). Buckingham, UK: Open University Press.

Davies, P. M. (1990). *Some problems in defining and sampling non-heterosexual males.* London: Project Sigma.

Davies, P. M., Hickson, F., Weatherburn, P., Hunt, A. J. (with Broderick, P. J., Coxon, T. P. M., et al.). (1993). *Sex, gay men and AIDS*. London: Falmer.

de Lacey, S. (2002). IVF as lottery or investment: Contesting metaphors in discourses of infertility. *Nursing Inquiry, 9*(1), 43-51.

D'Emilio, J. (1993). Gay politics and community in San Francisco since World War II. In L D. Garnets & D. C. Kimmel (Eds.), *Psychological perspectives of lesbian and gay male experiences* (pp. 59-79). New York: Columbia University Press.

de Montflores, C. (1993). Notes on the management of difference. In L. D. Garnets & D. C. Kimmel (Eds.), *Psychological perspectives of lesbian and gay male experiences* (pp. 218-247). New York: Columbia University Press.

Denzin, N. K. (1998). The art and politics of interpretation. In N. K. Denzin & Y. S. Lincoln (Eds.), *Collecting and interpreting qualitative material* (pp. 313-344). Thousand Oaks, CA: Sage.

Denzin, N. K., & Lincoln, Y. S. (1998). Introduction: Entering the field of qualitative research. In N. K. Denzin & Y. S. Lincoln (Eds.), *Strategies of qualitative inquiry* (pp. 1-34). Thousand Oaks, CA: Sage.

Denzin, N. K., & Lincoln, Y. S. (Eds.). (1994). *Handbook of qualitative research*. Thousand Oaks, CA: Sage.

Deren, S. S., Stephens, R., & Davis, W. R. (1994). The impact of providing incentives for attendance at AIDS prevention services. *Public Health Reports, 109*(40), 548-554.

DiPlacido, J. (1998). Minority stress among lesbians, gay men, and bisexuals: A consequence of heterosexism, homophobia and stigmatization. In G. M. Herek (Ed.), *Stigma and sexual orientation: Understanding prejudice against lesbians, gay men, and bisexuals* (pp. 160-186). Thousand Oaks, CA: Sage.

Doll, L. S., Petersen, L. R., White, C. R., Johnson, E. S., Ward, J. W., & The Blood Donor Study Group. (1992). Homosexually and nonhomosexually identified men who have sex with men: A behavioural comparison. *Journal of Sex Research, 29*(1), 1-14.

Douglas, N., Warwick, I., Kemp, S., & Whitty, G. (1998). *Playing it safe: Responses of secondary school teachers to lesbian, gay and bisexual pupils, bullying, HIV and AIDS education and Section 28*. London: Health and Education Research Unit, Institute of Education, University of London.

Dowsett, G. W., Davies, M. D., & Connell, R. W. (1992). Working-class homosexuality and HIV/AIDS prevention: Some recent research from Sydney, Australia. *Psychology and Health, 6*, 313-324.

Duncan, N. (Ed.). (1996). *BodySpace: Destabilising geographies of gender and sexuality*. London: Routledge.

Dunne, G. (1997). *Lesbian lifestyles: Women's work and the politics of sexuality*. Basingstoke, UK: Macmillan.

Edwards, D., Ashmore, M., & Potter, J. (1995). Death and furniture: the rhetoric, politics and theology of bottom line arguments against relativism. *History of the Human Sciences, 8*(2), 25-49.

Edwards, R. (1993). An education in interviewing: Placing the researcher and the researched. In C. M. Renzetti & R. M. Lee (Eds.), *Researching sensitive topics* (pp. 181-196). London: Sage.

Edwards, R. (1996). White woman researcher—Black women subjects. In S. Wilkinson & C. Kitzinger (Eds.), *Representing the Other: A feminism and psychology reader* (pp. 83-88). London: Sage.

Eliason, M. (1996). *Who cares?: Institutional barriers to health care for lesbian, gay and bisexual persons.* New York: National League for Nursing.

Elliott, R., Fischer, C. T., & Rennie, D. L. (1999). Evolving guidelines for publication of qualitative research studies in psychology and related fields. *British Journal of Clinical Psychology, 38,* 215-229.

Elliott, R., Fischer, C. T., & Rennie, D. L. (2000). Also against methodolatry: A reply to Reicher. *British Journal of Clinical Psychology, 39*(1), 7-10.

Ellis, M. L. (1994). Lesbians, gay men and psychoanalytic training. *Free Association: Psychoanalysis, Groups, Politics, Culture, 4*(4), 501-517.

Faircloth, C. A. (1998). Epilepsies, identities, and difference: Horizons of meaning for individuals with an epilepsy. *Qualitative Health Research, 8,* 602-617.

Farquhar, C., with Das, R. (1999). Are focus groups suitable for "sensitive" topics? In R. S. Barbour & J. Kitzinger (Eds.), *Developing focus group research: Politics, theory and practice* (pp. 47-63). London: Sage.

Fassinger, R. E. (1991). The hidden minority: Issues and challenges in working with lesbian women and gay men. *Counseling Psychologist, 19*(2), 157-176.

Feldman, M. S. (1995). *Strategies for interpreting qualitative data* (Vol. 33). London: Sage.

Fenton, K. A., Johnson, A. M., McManus, S., & Erens, B. (2001). Measuring sexual behaviour: Methodological challenges in survey research. *Sexually Transmitted Infections, 77,* 84-92.

Finch, J. (1984). "It's great to have someone to talk to": The ethics and politics of interviewing women. In C. Bell & H. Roberts (Eds.), *Social researching: Politics, problems and practice* (pp. 70-87). London: Routledge Kegan Paul.

Fine, M. (1989). The politics of research and activism: Violence against women. *Gender and Society, 3*(4), 549-558.

Fine, M. (1992). *Disruptive voices: The possibilities of feminist research.* Ann Arbor, MI: University of Michigan Press.

Fine, M. (1994). Working the hyphens: Reinventing self and other in qualitative research. In N. K. Denzin & Y. S. Lincoln (Eds.), *Handbook of qualitative research* (pp. 70-82). Thousand Oaks, CA: Sage.

Fish, J. (1999). Sampling lesbians: How to get 1000 lesbians to complete a questionnaire. *Feminism and Psychology*, *9*(2), 229-238.

Fish, J. (2000). Sampling issues in lesbian and gay psychology: Challenges in achieving diversity. *Lesbian and Gay Psychology Review*, *1*(2), 32-38.

Fisher, E. (1990). *Behavioural sciences for nurses: Towards Project 2000*. London: Duckworth.

Fitzgerald, J. L. (1996). Hidden populations and the gaze of power. *Journal of Drug Issues*, 26(1), 5-21.

Flick, U. (1998). *An introduction to qualitative research*. London: Sage.

Flowers, P., & Buston, K. (2001). "I was terrified of being different": Exploring gay men's accounts of growing-up in a heterosexist society. *Journal of Adolescence*, *24*(1), 51-65.

Flowers, P., Smith, J., Sheeran, P., & Beail, N. (1997a). Health and romance: Understanding unprotected sex in relationships between gay men. *British Journal of Health Psychology*, *2*, 73-86.

Flowers, P., Smith, J. A., Sheeran, P., & Beail, N. (1997b). Identities and gay men's sexual decision making. In P. Aggleton, P. Davies, & G. Hart (Eds.), *AIDS: Activism and alliances* (pp. 192-212). London: Taylor and Francis.

Flowers, P., Smith, J. A., Sheeran, P., & Beail, N. (1998). "Coming out" and sexual debut: Understanding the social context of HIV risk-related behaviour. *Journal of Community and Applied Social Psychology*, *8*, 409-421.

Foster, C. (1998). Of tales, myth, metaphor and metonym. In R. Barbour & G. Huby (Eds.), *Meddling with mythology: AIDS and the social construction of knowledge* (pp. 146-161). London: Routledge.

Fox, R. C. (1995). Bisexual identities. In A. R. D'Augelli & C. J. Patterson (Eds.), *Lesbian, gay and bisexual identities over the lifespan: Psychological perspectives* (pp. 48-86). New York: Oxford University Press.

Franke, R., & Leary, M. R. (1991). Disclosure of sexual orientation by lesbians and gay men: A comparison of private and public processes. *Journal of Social and Clinical Psychology*, *10*(3), 262-269.

Fuss, D. (1989). *Essentially speaking: Feminism, nature and difference*. New York: Routledge.

Fuss, D. E. (1991). *Inside/out: Lesbian theories, gay theories*. London: Routledge.

Garnets, L. D., Herek, G. M., & Levy, B. (1990). Violence and victimisation of lesbians and gay men: Mental health consequences. *Journal of Interpersonal Violence*, 5(3), 366-383.

Geraghty, W. (1996). *An investigation into factors associated with psychological health in young lesbians*. Unpublished doctoral dissertation, Open University, Milton Keynes, United Kingdom.

Gergen, K. J. (1998). Constructionism and realism: How are we to go on? In I. Parker (Ed.), *Social constructionism, discourse and realism* (pp. 147-156). London: Sage.

Gerrish, K. (2000). Individualized care: Its conceptualization and practice within a multiethnic society. *Journal of Advanced Nursing, 32*(1), 91-99.

Giddens, A. (1991). *Modernity and self-identity: Self and society in the late modern age.* Cambridge, UK: Polity.

Gill, R. (1996). Discourse analysis: Practical implementation. In J. T. E. Richardson (Ed.), *Handbook of qualitative research methods for psychology and the social sciences* (pp. 141-158). Leicester, UK: BPS.

Gillett, G. (1995). The philosophical foundations of qualitative psychology. *The Psychologist, 8*(3), 111-114.

Gillies, V. (1999). An analysis of the discursive positions of women smokers: Implications for practical interventions. In C. Willig (Ed.), *Applied discourse analysis: Social and psychological interventions* (pp. 66-86). Buckingham, UK: Open University Press.

Gillies, V., & Willig, C. (1997). "You get the nicotine and that in your blood": Constructions of addiction and control in women's accounts of cigarette smoking. *Journal of Community and Applied Social Psychology, 7*(4), 285-301.

Glaser, B. G., & Strauss, A. L. (1967). *The discovery of grounded theory: Strategies for qualitative research.* Chicago: Aldine.

Goffman, E. (1963). *Stigma: Notes on the management of spoiled identity.* Englewood Cliffs, NJ: Prentice-Hall.

Golding, J. (1997). *Without prejudice: MIND lesbian, gay and bisexual mental health awareness research.* London: MIND.

Golsworthy, R., & Coyle, A. (1999). Spiritual beliefs and the search for meaning following partner loss among older adults. *Mortality, 4*(1), 21-40.

Gonsoriek, J. C. (1982). The use of diagnostic concepts in working with gay and lesbian populations. *Journal of Homosexuality, 7*(2/3), 9-20.

Gonsoriek, J. C. (1988). Mental health issues of gay and lesbian adolescents. *Journal of Adolescent Health Care, 9*(2), 114-122.

Gonsoriek, J. C. (1991). The empirical basis for the demise of the illness model of homosexuality. In J. C. Gonsoriek & J. D. Weinrich (Eds.), *Homosexuality: Research implications for public policy* (pp. 115-136). Newbury Park, CA: Sage.

Gough, B. (2002). "I've always tolerated it but": Heterosexual masculinity and the discursive reproduction of homophobia. In A. Coyle & C. Kitzinger (Eds.), *Lesbian and gay psychology: New perspectives* (pp. 219-238). Leicester, UK: BPS Blackwell.

Grammick, J. (1984). Developing a lesbian identity. In T. Darty & S. Potter (Eds.), *Women-identified women* (pp. 31-44). Palo Alto, CA: Mayfield.

Grbich, C. (1999). *Qualitative research in health: An introduction.* London: Sage.

Greene, B. (1994). Ethnic-minority lesbians and gay men: Mental health and treatment issues. *Journal of Consulting and Clinical Psychology, 62*(2), 243-251.

Griffin, C., & Phoenix, A. (1994). The relationship between qualitative and quantitative research: Lessons from feminist psychology. *Journal of Community and Applied Social Psychology, 4,* 287-298.

Griffin, P. (1991). Identity management strategies among lesbian and gay educators. *Qualitative Studies in Education, 4*(3), 189-202.

Griffiths, P. G., Gossop, M., Powis, B., & Strang, J. (1993). Reaching hidden populations of drug users by privileged access interviewers: Methodological and practical issues. *Addiction, 88,* 1617-1626.

Grund, J. P. C., Broadhead, R. S., Heckathorn, D. D., Stern, L. S., & Anthony, D. L. (1996). Peer-driven outreach to combat HIV among IDUs. In T. Rhodes & R. Hartnoll (Eds.), *AIDS, drugs and prevention: Perspectives on individual and community action* (pp. 201-215). London: Routledge.

Guba, E. G., & Lincoln, Y. S. (1994). Competing paradigms in qualitative research. In N. K. Denzin & Y. S. Lincoln (Eds.), *Handbook of qualitative research* (pp. 105-117). Thousand Oaks, CA: Sage.

Hall, S. (1997a). *Representation: Cultural representations and signifying practices.* London: Sage/The Open University.

Hall, S. (1997b). The spectacle of the "Other." In S. Hall (Ed.), *Representation: Cultural representations and signifying practices* (pp. 225-279). London: Sage/ Open University Press.

Hammersley, M. (1996). The relationship between qualitative and quantitative research: paradigm loyalty versus methodological eclecticism. In J. T. E. Richardson (Ed.), *Handbook of qualitative research methods for psychology and the social sciences* (pp. 159-174). Leicester, UK: BPS.

Harden, A., & Willig, C. (1998). An exploration of the discursive constructions used in young adults' memories and accounts of contraception. *Journal of Health Psychology, 3*(3), 429-445.

Hardman, K. L. J. (1997). Social workers' attitudes to lesbian clients. *British Journal of Social Work, 27,* 545-563.

Harper, D. (1999). Tablet talk and depot discourse: Discourse analysis and psychiatric medication. In C. Willig (Ed.), *Applied discourse analysis: Social and psychological interventions* (pp. 125-144). Buckingham, UK: Open University Press.

Harré, R. (1995). Discursive psychology. In J. A. Smith, R. Harré & L. Van Langenhove (Eds.), *Rethinking psychology* (pp. 143-159). London: Sage.

Harry, J. (1986). Sampling gay men. *Journal of Sex Research, 22*(1), 21-34.

Harry, J. (1989). Sexual identity issues. In Alcohol, Drug Abuse and Mental Health Administration (Ed.), *Report of the Secretary's Task Force on Youth Suicide<D>* (Vol. 2, pp. 131-142). Rockville, MD: U.S. Department of Health and Human Services.

Harry, J. (1990). Conceptualizing anti-gay violence. *Journal of Interpersonal Violence, 5*(3), 350-358.

Harry, J. (1993). Being out: A general model. *Journal of Homosexuality, 26*(1), 25-39.

Hart, A., Hall, V., & Henwood, F. (2003). Helping health and social care professionals to develop an "inequalities imagination": A model for use in education and practice. *Journal of Advanced Nursing, 41*(5), 480-489.

Hart, A., & Lockey, R. (2002). Inequalities in health care provision: The relationship between contemporary policy and contemporary practice in maternity services in England. *Journal of Advanced Nursing, 37*(5), 485-493.

Hart, J., & Richardson, D., (Eds.). (1981). *The theory and practice of homosexuality.* London: Routledge Kegan Paul.

Harvey, K. (1997). "Everybody loves a lover": Gay men, straight men and a problem of lexical choice. In K. Harvey & C. Shalom (Eds.), *Language and desire: Encoding sex, romance and intimacy* (pp. 60-84). London: Routledge.

Harvey, K., & Shalom, C. E. (1997). *Language and desire: Encoding sex, romance and intimacy.* London: Routledge.

Hatfield, L. D. (1989, June 5). Method of polling: Gay population impossible to count? *San Francisco Examiner*, p. 20.

Healy, T. (1993). A struggle for language patterns of self-disclosure in lesbian couples. *Smith College Studies in Social Work* [Special issue], *63*(3), 247-264.

Heaphy, B. (1996). Medicalisation and identity formation: Identity and strategy in the context of AIDS and HIV. In J. Weeks & J. Holland (Eds.), *Sexual cultures: Communities, values and intimacy* (pp. 139-160). Basingstoke, UK: BSA/Macmillan.

Heaphy, B. (1998). Silence and strategy: Researching AIDS/HIV narratives in the flow of power. In R. Barbour & G. Huby (Eds.), *Meddling with mythology: AIDS and the social construction of knowledge* (pp. 21-36). London: Routledge.

Heaphy, B., Weeks, J., & Donovan, C. (1998). "That's like my life": Researching stories of non-heterosexual relationships. *Sexualities, 1*, 453-470.

Heckathorn, D. D. (1997). Respondent-driven sampling: A new approach to the study of hidden populations. *Social Problems, 44*(2), 174-199.

Henderson, L., Reid, D., Hickson, F., McLean, S., Cross, J., & Weatherburn, P. (2002). *First, service: Relationships, sex and health among lesbian and bisexual women.* London: Sigma Research.

Henwood, K. L. (1993). Women and later Life: The discursive construction of identities within family relationships. *Journal of Aging Studies, 7*(3), 303-319.

Henwood, K., & Nicolson, P. (1995). Qualitative research. *The Psychologist, 8*(3), 109-110.

Henwood, K., & Pidgeon, N. (1994). Beyond the qualitative paradigm: A framework for introducing diversity within qualitative psychology. *Journal of Community and Applied Social Psychology, 4*, 225-238.

Henwood, K., & Pidgeon, N. (1995). Grounded theory and psychological research. *The Psychologist, 8*(3), 115-118.

Henwood, K. L., & Pidgeon, N. (1992). Qualitative research and psychological theorizing. *British Journal of Psychology, 83*, 97-111.

Herdt, G. (1990). Developmental discontinuities and sexual orientation across cultures. In D. P. McWhirter, S. A. Sanders & J. M. Reinsich (Eds.), *Homosexuality/heterosexuality: concepts of sexual orientation* (pp. 208-236). London: Oxford University Press.

Herdt, G. H. (1992). "Coming out" as a rite of passage: A Chicago study. In G. Herdt (Ed.), *Gay culture in America: Essays from the field* (pp. 29-67). Boston: Beacon.

Herek, G. M., & Berrill, K. T. (1990). Anti-gay violence and mental health: Setting an agenda for research. *Journal of Interpersonal Violence, 5*(3), 414-423.

Hershberger, S. L., & D'Augelli, A. R. (1995). The impact of victimisation on the mental health and suicidality of lesbian, gay and bisexual youths. *Developmental Psychology, 31*(1), 65-73.

Hetrick, E. S., & Martin, A. D. (1987). Developmental issues and their resolution for gay and lesbian adolescents. *Journal of Homosexuality, 14*(1), 25-43.

Hickson, F., Reid, D., Weatherburn, P., Henderson, L., & Stephens, M. (1998). *Making data count: Findings from the national gay men's sex survey 1997*. London: Sigma Research/ CHAPS Community HIV and AIDS Prevention Strategy.

Hitchcock, J. M., & Wilson, H. S. (1992). Personal risking: Lesbian self disclosure of sexual orientation to professional health care providers. *Nursing Research, 41*(3), 178-183.

Holland, J., & Ramazanoglu, C. (1994). Coming to conclusions: Power and interpretation in researching young women's sexuality. In M. Maynard & J. Purvis (Eds.), *Researching women's lives from a feminist perspective* (pp. 125-148). London: Taylor and Francis.

Hollway, W. (1989). *Subjectivity and method in psychology: Gender, meaning and science*. London: Sage.

Hooker, E. (1992). The adjustment of the male homosexual. In W. R. Dynes & S. Donaldson (Eds.), *Homosexuality and psychiatry, psychology and counseling* (pp. 142-155). New York: Garland.

hooks, B. (1990). Marginality as a site of resistance. In R. Ferguson, M. Gever, T. T. Min-ha, & C. West (Eds.), *Out there: Marginalisation and contemporary cultures* (pp. 337-340). Cambridge, MA: MIT Press.

Huby, G. (1997). Interpreting silence, documenting experience: An anthropological approach to the study of health service users' experience with HIV/AIDS care in Lothian, Scotland. *Social Science & Medicine, 44*(8), 1149-1160.

Hunter, J. (1990). Violence against lesbian and gay male youths. *Journal of Interpersonal Violence, 5*(3), 295-300.

Hunter, J., & Schaecher, R. (1987). Stresses on lesbian and gay adolescents in schools. *Social Work in Education, 9*, 180-190.

Jackson, S. (1996). Heterosexuality and feminist theory. In D. Richardson (Ed.), *Theorising heterosexuality: Telling it straight* (pp. 21-38). Buckingham, UK: Open University Press.

James, T., Harding, I., & Corbett, K. (1994). Biased care. *Nursing Times, 90*(51), 28-30.

James, T., & Platzer, H. K. (1999). Ethical considerations in qualitative research with vulnerable groups: A personal perspective. *Nursing Ethics, 6*(1), 73-81.

Jarman, M., Smith, J. A., & Walsh, S. (1997). The psychological battle for control: A qualitative study of healthcare professionals' understandings of the treatment of anorexia nervosa. *Journal of Community and Applied Social Psychology, 7*, 137-152.

Jay, K., & Young, A. (1977). *The gay report: Gay men speak about sexual experience and lifestyles.* New York: Summit Books, Simon and Schuster.

Jenness, V. (1992). Coming out: Lesbian identities and the categorization problem. In K. Plummer (Ed.), *Modern homosexualities: Fragments of lesbian and gay experience* (pp. 65-73). London: Routledge.

Johnson, A. M., Mercer, C. H., Erens, B., Copas, A. J., McManus, S., Wellings, K., et al. (2001). Natsal 2000: Sexual behaviour in Britain—Partnerships, practices, and HIV risk behaviours. *The Lancet, 358*, 1835-1842.

Johnson, A. M., Wadsworth, J., Wellings, K., Field, J., & with Bradshaw, S. (1994). *Sexual attitudes and lifestyles.* Oxford, UK: Blackwell Scientific.

Jones, S. (1985). Depth interviewing. In R. Walker (Ed.), *Applied qualitative research* (pp. 56-71). Aldershot, UK: Gower.

Kalton, G., & Anderson, D. W. (1986). Sampling rare populations. *Journal of the Royal Statistical Society, 149*(1), 65-82.

Kaplan, C. D., Korf, D., & Sterk, C. (1987). Temporal and social contexts of heroin-using populations: An illustration of the snowball sampling technique. *Journal of Nervous and Mental Disease, 175*(9), 566-574.

Kidder, L. H., & Fine, M. (1997). Qualitative inquiry in psychology: A radical tradition. In D. Fox (Ed.), *Critical psychology: An introduction* (pp. 34-50). London: Sage.

King, M., & Bartlett, A. (1999). British psychiatry and homosexuality. *British Journal of Psychiatry, 175*(106), 113.

Kitzinger, C. (1987). *The social construction of lesbianism.* London: Sage.

Kitzinger, C. (1989). Liberal humanism as an ideology of social control: The regulation of lesbian identities. In J. Shotter & K. J. Gergen (Eds.), *Texts of identity* (pp. 82-98). London: Sage.

Kitzinger, C. (1997). Lesbian and gay psychology: A critical analysis. In D. Fox & I. Prilleltensky (Eds.), *Critical psychology: An introduction* (pp. 202-216). London: Sage.

Kitzinger, C., & Coyle, A. (1995). Lesbian and gay couples: Speaking of difference. *The Psychologist, 8*(2), 64-69.

Kitzinger, C., & Wilkinson, S. (1995). Transitions from heterosexuality to lesbianism: The discursive construction of lesbian identities. *Developmental Psychology*, *31*, 95-104.

Kitzinger, C., & Wilkinson, S. (1996). Theorising representing the other. In S. Wilkinson & C. Kitzinger (Eds.), *Representing the Other: A feminism and psychology reader* (pp. 1-32). London: Sage.

Kitzinger, J. (1994). The methodology of focus groups: The importance of interaction between research participants. *Sociology of Health and Illness*, *16*(1), 103-121.

Klawitter, M. M., & Flatt, V. (1998). The effect of state and local antidiscrimination policies on earnings for gays and lesbians. *Journal of Policy Analysis and Management*, *17*(4), 658-686.

Koffman, N. (1997). *Lesbian, gay, and bisexual mental health needs assessment report*. London: Metro Centre.

Kramer, J. L. (1995). Bachelor farmers and spinsters: Gay and lesbian identities and communities in rural North Dakota. In D. Bell & G. Valentine (Eds.), *Mapping desire: Geographies of sexuality* (pp. 200-213). London: Routledge.

Krueger, R. A. (1994). *Focus groups: A practical guide for applied research* (2nd ed.). Thousand Oaks: Sage.

Kuebler, D., & Hausser, D. (1997). The Swiss hidden population study: Practical and methodological aspects of data collection by privileged access interviewers. *Addiction*, *92*(3), 325-334.

Lee, R. M. (1993). *Doing research on sensitive issues*. London: Sage.

Lee, R. M. (1995). *Dangerous fieldwork*. London: Sage.

Leonard, M. (1993, April). *Informal work and employment in Belfast: Researching a sensitive topic in a politically sensitive locality*. Paper presented at the Annual Conference of the British Sociological Association, University of Essex, UK.

Lister, P. (1997). The art of nursing in a "postmodern" context. *Journal of Advanced Nursing*, *25*(1), 38-44.

Lyons, A. (1999). Shaping health psychology: Qualitative research, evaluation and representation. In M. Murray & K. Chamberlain (Eds.), *Qualitative health psychology: Theories and methods* (pp. 241-255). London: Sage.

MacFarlane, L. (1998). *Diagnosis: Homophobic—The experiences of lesbians, gay men and bisexuals in mental health services*. London: PACE.

Mair, D. (2000). The enemy within. *Counselling*, *11*(7), 414-417.

Malley, M., & Tasker, F. (2001). Lesbians, gay men and family therapy: A contradiction in terms? *Journal of Family Therapy*, *21*, 3-29.

Malyon, A. K. (1982). Psychotherapeutic implications of internalized homophobia in gay men. *Journal of Homosexuality*, *7*(2/3), 59-69.

Manias, E., & Street, A. (2000). Possibilities for critical social theory and Foucault's work: A toolbox approach. *Nursing Inquiry*, *7*(1), 50-60.

Markowe, L. A. (1996). *Redefining the Self: Coming out as lesbian.* Cambridge, UK: Polity.

Markowitz, L. M. (1991). Homosexuality: Are we still in the dark? *Family Therapy Networker, 15*(1), 26-35.

Marshall, H., Woollett, A., & Dosanjh, N. (1998). Researching marginalised standpoints: Some tensions around plural standpoints and diverse "experiences." In K. Henwood, C. Griffin & A. Phoenix (Eds.), *Standpoints and differences: Essays in the practice of feminist psychology* (pp. 115-133). London: Sage.

Martin, A. D. (1982). Learning to hide: The socialization of the gay adolescent. *Adolescent Psychiatry, 10,* 152-165.

Martin, A. D., & Hetrick, E. S. (1988). The stigmatisation of the gay and lesbian adolescent. *Journal of Homosexuality, 15*(1/2), 163-183.

Martin, J. L., & Dean, L. (1993). Developing a community sample of gay men for an epidemiological study of AIDS. In C. M. Renzetti & R. M. Lee (Eds.), *Researching sensitive topics* (pp. 82-100). London: Sage.

Mathieson, C., & Barrie, C. M. (1999). Probing the prime narrative: Illness, interviewing and identity. *Qualitative Health Research, 8,* 581-601.

Mathieson, C., & Stam, H. J. (1995). Renegotiating identity: Cancer narratives. *Sociology of Health and Illness, 17*(3), 283-306.

May, C. (1992). Nursing work, nurses' knowledge, and the subjectification of the patient. *Sociology of Health and Illness, 4,* 472-487.

May, K. A. (1991). Interview techniques in qualitative research: Concerns and challenges. In J. M. Morse (Ed.), *Qualitative nursing research: A contemporary dialogue* (pp. 188-201). Newbury Park, CA: Sage.

Maynard, M. (1994). Methods, practice and epistemology: The debate about feminism and research. In M. Maynard & J. Purvis (Eds.), *Researching women's lives from a feminist perspective* (pp. 10-26). London: Taylor and Francis.

McCann, K., Clark, D., Taylor, R., & Morrice, K. (1984). Telephone screening as a research technique. *Sociology, 18*(3), 393-402.

McColl, P. (1994). Homosexuality and mental health services. *British Medical Journal, 308*(6928), 550-551.

McDonald, C., & Anderson, B. (2003). The view from somewhere: Locating lesbian experience in women's health. *Health Care for Women International, 24*(8), 697-711.

McDonald, G. J. (1982). Individual differences in the coming out process for gay men: Implications for theoretical models. *Journal of Homosexuality, 14,* 53-65.

McDowell, L. (1996). Spatializing feminism: Geographic perspectives. In N. Duncan (Ed.), *BodySpace: Destabilising geographies of gender and sexuality* (pp. 28-44). London: Routledge.

Merttens, R. (1998). What is to be done? (With apologies to Lenin!). In I. Parker (Ed.), *Social constructionism, discourse and realism* (pp. 59-74). London: Sage.

Meyer, I. H., & Dean, L. (1998). Internalised homophobia, intimacy, and sexual behavior among gay and bisexual men. In G. M. Herek (Ed.), *Stigma and sexual orientation: Understanding prejudice against lesbians, gay men, and bisexuals* (pp. 160-186). Thousand Oaks, CA: Sage.

Mills, S., & White, C. A. (1997). Discursive categories and desire: Feminists negotiating relationships. In K. Harvey & C. Shalom (Eds.), *Language and desire: Encoding sex, romance and intimacy* (pp. 222-244). London: Routledge.

Milton, M. (1998). *Issues in psychotherapy with lesbians and gay men: A survey of British psychologists* (Occasional Papers, Vol. 4). Leicester, UK: British Psychological Society for the Division of Counselling Psychology.

Milton, M., & Coyle, A. (1999). Lesbian and gay affirmative psychotherapy: Issues in theory and practice. *Sexual and Marital Therapy, 14*(1), 43-57.

Milton, M., Coyle, A., & Legg, C. (2002). Lesbian and gay affirmative psychotherapy: Defining the domain. In A. Coyle & C. Kitzinger (Eds.), *Lesbian and gay psychology: New perspectives* (pp. 175-197). Leicester, UK: BPS Blackwell.

Miranda, J., & Storms, M. (1989). Psychological adjustment of lesbians and gay men. *Journal of Counselling and Development, 68*, 41-45.

Morgan, M. (1999). Discourse, health and illness. In M. Murray & K. Chamberlain (Eds.), *Qualitative health psychology: Theories and methods* (pp. 64-82). London: Sage.

Morgan, M., & Coombes, L. (2001). Subjectivities and silences, mother and woman: Theorizing an experience of silence as a speaking subject. *Feminism and Psychology, 11*(3), 361-375.

Morse, J. M., & Field, P. A. (1996). *Nursing research: The application of qualitative approaches* (2nd ed.). London: Chapman and Hall.

Munt, S. R. (1998). *Heroic desire: Lesbian identity and cultural space*. London: Cassell.

Murphy, B. C. (1989). Lesbian couples and their parents: The effects of perceived parental attitudes on the couple. *Journal of Counseling and Development, 68*, 46-51.

Murray, M., & Chamberlain, K. (1999). Health psychology and qualitative research. In M. Murray & K. Chamberlain (Eds.), *Qualitative health psychology: Theories and methods* (pp. 3-15). London: Sage.

Myslik, W. (1996). Renegotiating the social/sexual identities of places: Gay communities as safe havens or sites of resistance? In N. Duncan (Ed.), *BodySpace: Destabilising geographies of gender and sexuality* (pp. 156-169). London: Routledge.

NHS Executive. (2000). *NHS psychotherapy services in England: Review of strategic policy*. London: Department of Health.

Nightingale, D. J., & Cromby, J. E. (1999). *Social constructionist psychology: A critical analysis of theory and practice*. Buckingham, UK: Open University Press.

Nochi, M. (1998). Struggling with the labeled self: People with traumatic brain injuries in social settings. *Qualitative Health Research, 8*, 665-681.

190

Office of National Statistics. (2000). [Untitled]. Retrieved March 20, 2000, from http://www.statistics.gov.uk/

Oguntokun, R. (1998). A lesson in the seductive power of sameness: Representing Black African refugee women. *Feminism and Psychology*, *8*(4), 525-529.

Osborn, M., & Smith, J. A. (1998). The personal experience of chronic benign lower back pain: An interpretative phenomenological analysis. *British Journal of Health Psychology*, *3*, 65-83.

Parker, I. (1992). *Discourse dynamics: Critical analysis for individual and social psychology*. London: Routledge.

Parker, I. (1996). Discursive complexes in material culture. In J. Howarth (Ed.), *Psychological research—Innovative methods and strategies* (pp. 185-196). London: Routledge.

Parker, I. (1998a). Realism, relativism, and critique in psychology. In I. Parker (Ed.), *Social constructionism, discourse and realism* (pp. 1-10). London: Sage.

Parker, I. (1999). Introduction: Varieties of discourse and analysis. In I. Parker & the Bolton Discourse Network (Eds.), *Critical textwork: An introduction to varieties of discourse and analysis* (pp. 1-12). Buckingham, UK: Open University Press.

Parker, I. (Ed.). (1998b). *Social constructionism, discourse and realism*. London: Sage.

Parker, I., & Burman, E. (1993). Against discursive imperialism, empiricism and constructionism: Thirty-two problems with discourse analysis. In E. Burman & I. Parker (Eds.), *Discourse analytic research: Repertoires and readings of text in action* (pp. 155-172). London: Routledge.

Parker, I., Georgaca, E., Harper, D., McLaughlin, T., & Stowell-Smith, M. (1995). *Deconstructing psychopathology*. London: Sage.

Paroski, P. A. (1987). Health care delivery and the concerns of gay and lesbian adolescents. *Journal of Adolescent Health Care*, *8*(2), 188-192.

Patrick, J. H., Pruchno, R. A., & Rose, M. S. (1998). Recruiting research participants: A comparison of the costs and effectiveness of five recruitment strategies. *The Gerontologist*, *38*(2), 295-302.

Patton, M. Q. (1990). *Qualitative evaluation and research methods* (2nd ed.). London: Sage.

Paul, J. P. (1996). Bisexuality: Exploring/exploding the boundaries. In R. C. Savin-Williams & K. M. Cohen (Eds.), *The lives of lesbians, gays and bisexuals* (pp. 436-461). Fort Worth, TX: Harcourt Brace.

Peel, E. (2002). Lesbian and gay awareness training: Challenging homophobia, liberalism and managing stereotypes. In A. Coyle & C. Kitzinger (Eds.), *Lesbian and gay psychology: New perspectives* (pp. 255-274). Oxford, UK: Blackwell.

Peterson, K. J. E. (1996). Health care for lesbians and gay men [Entire issue]. *Journal of Gay and Lesbian Social Services*, *5*(1).

Phillips, P., Bartlett, A., & King, M. (2001). Psychotherapists' approaches to gay and lesbian patients/clients: A qualitative study. *British Journal of Medical Psychology*, *74*, 73-84.

Phoenix, A. (1994a). Practising feminist research: the intersection of gender and "race" in the research process. In M. Maynard & J. Purvis (Eds.), *Researching women's lives from a feminist perspective* (pp. 49-71). London: Taylor and Francis.

Phoenix, A. (1994b). Research: Positioned differently? Issues of "race," difference and commonality. *Changes*, *12*(4), 299-305.

Pidgeon, N. (1996). Grounded theory: Theoretical background. In J. T. E. Richardson (Ed.), *Handbook of qualitative research methods for psychology and the social sciences* (pp. 75-85). Leicester, UK: BPS.

Pilgrim, D., & Rogers, A. (1997). Mental health, critical realism and lay knowledge. In J. M. Ussher (Ed.), *Body talk: The material and discursive regulation of sexuality, madness and reproduction* (pp. 33-49). London: Routledge.

Pilgrim, D., & Rogers, A. (1999). *A sociology of mental health and illness* (2nd ed.). Buckingham, UK: Open University Press.

Platzer, H. (1990). Sexual orientation: Improving care. *Nursing Standard*, *4*(38), 38-39.

Platzer, H. K. (1992). Chipping away at change. *Nursing Standard*, *6*(52), 46-47.

Platzer, H. K. (1993). Nursing care of lesbian and gay patients. *Nursing Standard*, *7*(17), 34-37.

Platzer, H. K. (1995). Lesbian and gay men's experience of nursing care. *Anthropology in Action*, *2*(1), 9-10.

Platzer, H. K., & James, T. (1997). Methodological issues conducting sensitive research on lesbian and gay men's experience of nursing care. *Journal of Advanced Nursing*, *25*, 626-633.

Platzer, H. K., & James, T. (2000). Lesbians' experiences of healthcare. *Nursing Times Research*, *5*(3), 194-202.

Plummer, D. Homophobia and health: Unjust, anti-social, harmful and endemic. *Health Care Analysis*, *3*(2), 150-156.

Plummer, K. (1981). Going gay: Identities life cycles and lifestyles in the male gay world. In J. Hart & D. Richardson (Eds.), *The theory and practice of homosexuality* (pp. 93-110). London: Routledge Kegan Paul.

Plummer, K. (1992a). *Modern homosexualities: Fragments of lesbian and gay experience.* London: Routledge.

Plummer, K. (1992b). Speaking its name: Inventing lesbian and gay studies. In K. Plummer (Ed.), *Modern homosexualities: Fragments of lesbian and gay experience* (pp. 3-28). London: Routledge.

Ponse, B. (1980). Lesbians and their worlds. In J. Marmor (Ed.), *Homosexual behavior: A modern reappraisal.* New York: Basic Books.

Porter, S. (1996). Contra-Foucault: Soldiers, nurses and power. *Sociology, 30*(1), 59-78.

Potter, J. (1996). Discourse analysis and constructionist approaches: Theoretical background. In J. T. E. Richardson (Ed.), *Handbook of qualitative research methods for psychology and the social sciences* (pp. 125-140). Leicester, UK: BPS.

Potter, J. (1998). Fragments in the realization of relativism. In I. Parker (Ed.), *Social constructionism, discourse and realism* (pp. 27-46). London: Sage.

Potter, J., & Wetherell, M. (1987). *Discourse and social psychology: Beyond attitudes and behaviour.* London: Sage.

Potter, J., & Wetherell, M. (1994). Analysing discourse. In A. Bryman & R. G. Burgess (Eds.), *Analysing qualitative data* (pp. 47-66). London: Routledge.

Potter, J., & Wetherell, M. (1995). Discourse analysis. In J. A. Smith, R. Harré, & L. Van Langenhove (Eds.), *Rethinking methods in psychology* (pp. 80-92). London: Sage.

Power, R. (1994). Some methodological and practical implications of employing drug users as indigenous fieldworkers. In M. Boulton (Ed.), *Challenge and innovation: Methodological advances in social research on HIV/AIDS* (pp. 97-109). London: Taylor and Francis.

Power, R., & Harkinson, S. (1993). Accessing hidden populations: The use of indigenous interviewers. In P. Aggleton, P. Davies & G. Hart (Eds.), *Social aspects of AIDS* (pp. 109-117). London: Falmer.

Prenzlauer, S., Drescher, J., & Winchel, R. (1992). Suicide among homosexual youth [Letter to the editor]. *American Journal of Psychiatry, 149*, 1416.

Proctor, C. D., & Groze, V. K. (1994). Risk factors for suicide among gay, lesbian and bisexual youths. *Social Work, 39*(5), 504-513.

Proctor, G. (1994). Lesbian clients' experience of clinical psychology: A listener's guide. *Changes, 12*(4), 290-298.

Pujol, J. (1999). Deconstructing and reconstructing: Producing a reading on "human reproductive technologies." In C. Willig (Ed.), *Applied discourse analysis: Social and psychological interventions* (pp. 87-109). Buckingham, UK: Open University Press.

Reicher, S. (1994). Particular methods and general assumptions. *Journal of Community and Applied Social Psychology, 4*, 299-303.

Reicher, S. (2000). Against methodolatry: Some comments on Elliott, Fischer, and Rennie. *British Journal of Clinical Psychology, 39*(1), 1-6.

Remafadi, G., Farrow, J. A., & Deisher, R. W. (1991). Risk factors for attempted suicide in gay and bisexual youth. *Pediatrics, 87*(6), 869-875.

Rennie, D. L., Phillips, J. R., & Quartaro, G. K. (1988). Grounded theory: A promising approach to conceptualization in psychology? *Canadian Psychology, 29*(2), 139-150.

Renzetti, C. M., & Lee, R. M. (1993). *Researching sensitive topics.* London: Sage.

Research and Decisions Corporation. (1984). *Designing an effective AIDS prevention campaign strategy for San Francisco.* San Francisco: San Francisco AIDS Foundation.

Richardson, D. (1981). Lesbian identities. In J. Hart & D. Richardson (Eds.), *The theory and practice of homosexuality* (pp. 111-124). London: Routledge Kegan Paul.

Richardson, D. (1992). Constructing lesbian sexualities. In K. Plummer (Ed.), *Modern homosexualities: Fragments of lesbian and gay experience* (pp. 187-199). London: Routledge.

Richardson, D. (1996). *Theorising heterosexuality: Telling it straight.* Buckingham, UK: Open University Press.

Richardson, D., & Hart, J. (1981). The development and maintenance of a homosexual identity. In J. Hart & D. Richardson (Eds.), *The theory and practice of homosexuality* (pp. 73-92). London: Routledge Kegan Paul.

Rivers, I. (1997a, November). *The long-term impact of peer victimization in adolescence upon the well-being of lesbian, gay and bisexual adults.* Paper presented at the Psychological Society of Ireland's Annual Conference.

Rivers, I. (1997b). Violence against lesbian and gay youth and its impact. In M. Schneider (Ed.), *Pride and prejudice: Working with lesbian and gay and bisexual youth* (pp. 31-47). Toronto, Canada: Central Toronto Youth Services.

Rivers, I. (1999, August). *The impact of homonegativism at school over the lifespan.* Paper presented at the 107th Annual Convention of the American Psychological Association Division, Boston.

Rivers, I. (2000). Long-term consequences of bullying. In C. Neal & D. Davies (Eds.), *Pink therapy 3: Issues in therapy with lesbian, gay, bisexual and transgender clients* (pp. 146-159). Buckingham, UK: Open University Press.

Rivers, I. (2002). Developmental issues for lesbian and gay youth. In A. Coyle & C. Kitzinger (Eds.), *Lesbian and gay psychology: New perspectives* (pp. 30-44). Oxford, UK: Blackwell.

Robertson, M. M. (1992). Lesbians as an invisible minority in the health services arena. In P. N. Stern (Ed.), *Lesbian health: What are the issues?* (pp. 65-74). Washington, DC: Taylor and Francis.

Roesler, T., & Deisher, R. W. (1972). Youthful male homosexuality: Homosexual experience and the process of developing homosexual identity in males aged 16 to 22 years. *Journal of the American Medical Association, 219*(8), 1018-1023.

Rose, L. (1994). Homophobia among doctors. *British Medical Journal, 308*, 586-587.

Rose, P., & Platzer, H. K. (1993). Confronting prejudice. *Nursing Times, 89*(31), 52-54.

Rothbart, G. S., Fine, M., & Sudman, S. (1982). On finding and interviewing the needles in the haystack: The use of multiplicity sampling. *Public Opinion Quarterly, 46*, 408-421.

Rothenburg, T. (1995). "And she told two friends": Lesbians creating urban social space. In D. Bell & G. Valentine (Eds.), *Mapping desire: Geographies of sexuality* (pp. 165-181). London: Routledge.

Rotherum-Borus, M. J., Meyer-Bahlburg, H. F. L., Nat, R., Rosario, M., Koopman, C., Haignere, C. S., et al. (1992). Lifetime sexual behaviors among predominantly minority male runaways and gay/bisexual adolescents in New York City. *AIDS Education and Prevention, Fall*(Suppl.), 34-42.

Rothfield, P. (1990). Feminism, subjectivity, and sexual experience. In S. Gunew (Ed.), *Feminist knowledge: Critique and construct* (pp. 121-144). London: Routledge.

Royal College of Nursing. (1994). *The nursing care of lesbians and gay men: An RCN statement* (Vol. 26). London: Author.

Royal College of Nursing. (1998a). *Guidance for nurses on "next-of-kin" for lesbians and gay patients or children with lesbian or gay parents* (Vol. 47). London: Author.

Royal College of Nursing. (1998b). *Sexual orientation and mental health* (Vol. 48). London: Author.

Royal College of Nursing. (2000). *Key issues in the nursing care of lesbians* (Vol. 51). London: Author.

Rust, P. C. (1993). "Coming out" in the age of social constructionism: Sexual identity formation among lesbian and bisexual women. *Gender and Society, 7*(1), 50-77.

Rutherford, J. (1990a). *Identity, community, culture and difference*. London: Lawrence and Wishart.

Rutherford, J. (1990b). A place called home: Identity and the cultural politics of difference. In J. Rutherford (Ed.), *Identity, community, culture and difference* (pp. 9-27). London: Lawrence and Wishart.

Saari, C. (2001). Counteracting the effects of invisibility in work with lesbian patients. *Psychotherapy in Practice, 57*(5), 645-654.

Saghir, M. R., & Robins, E. (1973). *Male and female homosexuality: A comprehensive investigation*. Baltimore: Williams and Wilkins.

Sampson, E. E. (1993). Identity politics: Challenges to psychology's understanding. *American Psychologist, 48*(12), 1219-1230.

Sapsford, R., & Abbott, P. (1998). *Research methods for nurses and the caring professions*. Buckingham, UK: Open University Press.

Saunders, J. M., Tupac, J. D., & MacCulloch, B. (1988). *A lesbian profile: A survey of 1000 lesbians*. West Hollywood, CA: Southern California Women for Understanding.

Saunders, J. M., & Valente, S. M. (1987). Suicide risk among gay men and lesbians: A review. *Death Studies, 11*(1), 1-23.

Savin-Williams, R. C. (1994). Verbal and physical abuse as stressors in the lives of lesbian, gay male and bisexual youths: associations with school problems, running away, substance abuse, prostitution and suicide. *Journal of Consulting and Clinical Psychology, 62*(2), 261-269.

Sayer, A. (2000). *Realism and social science.* London: Sage.

Scherzer, T. (2000). Negotiating health care: The experiences of young lesbian and bisexual women. *Culture, Health and Sexuality, 2*(1), 87-102.

Schmitt, J. P., & Kurdek, L. A. (1987). Personality correlates of positive identity and relationship involvement in gay men. *Journal of Homosexuality, 13*(4), 101-109.

Schneider, B. E. (1987). Coming out at work: Bridging the private/public gap. *Work and Occupations, 13*(4), 463-487.

Schneider, M. (1991). Developing services for lesbian and gay adolescents. *Canadian Journal of Community Mental Health, 10*(1), 133-151.

Schneider, S. G., Farberow, N. L., & Kruks, G. N. (1989). Suicidal behaviour in adolescent and young adult gay men. *Suicide and Life-Threatening Behaviour, 19*(4), 381-394.

Schwandt, T. A. (1994). Constructivist, interpretivist approaches to human inquiry. In N. K. Denzin & Y. S. Lincoln (Eds.), *Handbook of qualitative research* (pp. 118-137). Thousand Oaks, CA: Sage.

Scott, P. (1998). *Blind spots: A review of the literature on men who make sexual encounters in public sex environments and their HIV-related risk.* London: AIDS Education Unit, Barnet Healthcare Trust, London and Brent, and Harrow Health Promotion, Middlesex.

Sedgwick, E. K. (1994). *Epistemology of the closet.* London: Penguin.

Segal, L. (1997). Sexualities. In K. Woodward (Ed.), *Identity and difference* (pp. 183-238). London: Open University Press, Sage.

Seidler, V. J. (1994). *Recovering the self: Morality and social theory.* London: Routledge.

Seidman, S., Meeks, C., & Traschen, F. (1999). Beyond the closet?: The changing social meaning of homosexuality in the United States. *Sexualities, 2*(1), 9-34.

Seu, I. B. (1998). Shameful women: Accounts of withdrawal and silence. In K. Henwood, C. Griffin, & A. Phoenix (Eds.), *Standpoints and differences: Essays in the practice of feminist psychology* (pp. 135-155). London: Sage.

Shepherd, J. (1997). *Peer-led sexual health promotion work with young gay and bisexual men—A practical guide.* Southampton, UK: University of Southampton, Health education Unit, School of Education.

Shepherd, J., Weare, K., & Turner, G. (1997). Peer-led sexual health promotion with young gay and bisexual men—Results of the HAPEER Project. *Health Education, 6*, 204-212.

Shidlo, A. (1994). Internalized homophobia: Conceptual issues in measurement. In B. Green & G. Herek (Eds.), *Lesbian and gay psychology: Theory, research and clinical applications* (Vol. 1, pp. 176-205). London: Sage.

Shotter, J., & Gergen, K. J. E. (1989). *Texts of identity.* London: Sage.

Sibley, D. (1995). *Geographies of exclusion: Society and difference in the West.* London: Routledge.

Sinfield, A. (1994). *The Wilde century.* London: Cassell.

Smith, A. M. (1997). The good homosexual and the dangerous queer: Resisting the "new homophobia." In L. Segal (Ed.), *New sexual agendas* (pp. 214-231). London: Macmillan.

Smith, J. A. (1991). Conceiving selves: A case study of changing identities during the transition to motherhood. *Journal of Language and Social Psychology, 10*(4), 225-243.

Smith, J. A. (1995). Semi structured interviewing and qualitative analysis. In J. A. Smith, R. Harré, & L. Van Langenhove (Eds.), *Rethinking methods in psychology* (pp. 9-26). London: Sage.

Smith, J. A. (1996a). Beyond the divide between cognition and discourse: Using interpretive phenomenological analysis in health psychology. *Psychology and Health, 11,* 261-271.

Smith, J. A. (1996b). Evolving issues for qualitative psychology. In J. T. E. Richardson (Ed.), *Handbook of qualitative research methods for psychology and the social sciences* (pp. 189-201). Leicester, UK: BPS.

Smith, J., Flowers, P., & Osborn, M. (1997). Interpretive phenomenological analysis and the psychology of health and illness. In L. Yardley (Ed.), *Material discourses of health and illness* (pp. 68-91). London: Routledge.

Smith, J. A., Harré, R., & Van Langenhove, L. (1995a). Idiography and the case-study. In J. A. Smith, R. Harré, & L. Van Langenhove (Eds.), *Rethinking psychology* (pp. 59-69). London: Sage.

Smith, J. A., Harré, R., & Van Langenhove, L. (Eds.). (1995b). *Rethinking methods in psychology.* London: Sage.

Smith, J. A., Osborn, M., & Jarman, M. (1999). Doing interpretative phenomenological analysis. In M. Murray & K. Chamberlain (Eds.), *Qualitative health psychology: Theories and methods* (pp. 218-240). London: Sage.

Snape, D., Thomson, K., & Chetwynd, M. (1995). *Discrimination against lesbians and gay men: A study of the nature and extent of discrimination against homosexual men and women in Britain today.* London: Social and Community Planning Research.

Sophie, J. (1987). Internalised homophobia and lesbian identity. *Journal of Homosexuality, 14,* 53-65.

Sparkes, A. C. (1998). Athletic identity: An Achilles' heel to the survival of self. *Qualitative Health Research, 8,* 644-664.

Spink, M. J. P. (1999). Making sense of illness experiences. In M. Murray & K. Chamberlain (Eds.), *Qualitative health psychology: Theories and methods* (pp. 83-97). London: Sage.

Squires, S. L., & Sparkes, A. C. (1996). Circles of silence: Sexual identity in physical education and sport. *Sport, Education and Society, 1*(1), 77-101.

Stainton-Rogers, W. (1996). Critical approaches to health psychology. *Journal of Health Psychology, 1*(1), 65-77.

Stevens, P. E. (1992). Lesbian health care research 1970-1990. In P. N. Stern (Ed.), *Lesbian health: What are the issues?* (pp. 1-30). Washington, DC: Taylor and Francis.

Stevens, P. E. (1994a). Lesbians' health-related experiences of care and noncare. *Western Journal of Nursing Research, 16*(6), 639-659.

Stevens, P. E. (1994b). Protective strategies of lesbian clients in health care environments. *Research in Nursing and Health, 17,* 217-229.

Stevens, P. E., & Hall, J. M. (1988). Stigma, health beliefs and experiences with health care in lesbian women. *IMAGE: Journal of Nursing Scholarship, 20*(2), 69-73.

Stevens, P. E., & Hall, J. M. (1990). Abusive health care interactions experienced by lesbians: A case of institutional violence in the treatment of women. *Response, 13*(3), 23-27.

Stevens, P. E., & Hall, J. M. (1991). A critical historical analysis of the medical constructionism of lesbianism. *International Journal of Health Services, 21*(2), 291-307.

Stoppard, J. M. (1997). Women's bodies, women's lives and depression: Towards a reconciliation of material and discursive accounts. In J. M. Ussher (Ed.), *Body talk: The material and discursive regulation of sexuality, madness and reproduction* (pp. 10-32). London: Routledge.

Susman, J. (1994). Disability, stigma and deviance. *Social Science & Medicine, 38*(1), 15-22.

Tafoya, T. (1997). Native gay and lesbian issues. In B. Greene (Ed.), *Ethnic and cultural diversity among lesbians and gay men* (Vol. 3, pp. 1-9). London: Sage.

Tasker, F., & McCann, D. (1999). Affirming patterns of adolescent sexual identity: the challenge. *Journal of Family Therapy, 21*(1), 30-54.

Taylor, G. (2002). Psychopathology and the social and historical construction of male identities. In A. Coyle & C. Kitzinger (Eds.), *Lesbian and gay psychology: New perspectives* (pp. 154-174). Leicester, UK: BPS Blackwell.

Tremble, B., Schneider, M., & Appathurai, C. (1989). Growing up gay or lesbian in a multicultural context. *Journal of Homosexuality, 17*(3/4), 253-268.

Trenchard, L., & Warren, H. (1984). *Something to tell you: The experiences and needs of young lesbians and gay men in London.* London: London Gay Teenage Group.

Trippet, S. (1994). Lesbians' mental health concerns. *Health Care for Women International, 15,* 317-323.

Troiden, R. R. (1992). Becoming homosexual: A model of gay identity acquisition. In W. R. Dynes & S. Donaldson (Eds.), *Homosexuality and psychiatry, psychology and counseling* (pp. 288-299). New York: Garland.

Troiden, R. R. (1993). The formation of homosexual identities. In L. D. Garnets & D. C. Kimmel (Eds.), *Psychological perspectives of lesbian and gay male experiences* (pp. 191-217). New York: Columbia University Press.

Troiden, R. R., & Goode, E. (1980). Variables related to the acquisition of a gay identity. *Journal of Homosexuality, 5*(4), 383-392.

Turner, G., & Mallett, L. (1998). *A second survey of the health needs of gay and bisexual men in Southampton and South West Hampshire.* Southampton, UK: Southampton Gay Men's Health Project.

United Kingdom. (1988). *Local Government Act* (c. 9). London: HMSO. Retrieved February 3, 2006, from http://www.opsi.gov.uk/acts/acts1988/ Ukpga_19880009 _en_1.htm

Ussher, J. (2000). Women's madness: A material-discursive-intrapsychic approach. In D. Fee (Ed.), *Pathology and the postmodern: Mental illness as discourse and experience* (pp. 207-230). London: Sage.

Ussher, J. (2003). The ongoing silencing of women in families: An analysis and rethinking of premenstrual syndrome and therapy. *Journal of Family Therapy, 25,* 388-405.

Ussher, J. M. (1996). Premenstrual syndrome: Reconciling disciplinary divides through the adoption of a material-discursive epistemological standpoint. *Annual Review of Sex Research, 7,* 218-251.

Ussher, J. M. (1997a). *Body talk: The material and discursive regulation of sexuality, madness and reproduction.* London: Routledge.

Ussher, J. M. (1997b). Framing the sexual "other": The regulation of lesbian and gay sexuality. In J. M. Ussher (Ed.), *Body talk: The material and discursive regulation of sexuality, madness and reproduction* (pp. 131-158). London: Routledge.

Ussher, J. M. (1997c). Introduction: Towards a material-discursive analysis of madness, sexuality and reproduction. In J. M. Ussher (Ed.), *Body talk: The material and discursive regulation of sexuality, madness and reproduction* (pp. 1-9). London: Routledge.

Valentine, G. (1993). (Hetero)sexing space: Lesbian perceptions and experiences of everyday spaces. *Environment and Planning D: Society and Space, 11,* 395-413.

van de Goor, L. A. M., Garretsen, H. F. L., Kaplan, C., Korf, D., Spruit, I. P., & de Zwart, W. M. (1994). Research methods for illegal drug use in hidden populations: Summary report of a European invited expert meeting. *Journal of Psychoactive Drugs, 26*(1), 33-40.

Vincke, J. B., & Bolton, R. (1994). Social support, depression, and self-acceptance among gay men. *Human Relations, 47*(9), 1049-1062.

Waldorf, D., & Biernacki, P. (1981). The natural recovery from opiate addiction: Some preliminary findings. *Journal of Drug Issues, 11,* 61-74.

Watney, S. (1993). Emergent sexual identities and HIV/AIDS. In P. Aggleton, P. Davies, & G. Hart (Eds.), *AIDS: Facing the second decade* (pp. 13-27). London: Falmer.

Watters, J. K., & Biernacki, P. (1989). Targeted sampling: Options for the study of hidden populations. *Social Problems, 36*(4), 416-430.

Weatherburn, P., Davies, P. M., Hickson, F., & Hartley, M. (1999). *A class apart: The social stratification of HIV infection among homosexually active men—Briefing paper.* London: Sigma Research/CHAPS Community HIV and AIDS Prevention Strategy.

Weatherburn, P., Hickson, F., Reid, D. S., & Davies, P. M. (1998). Sexual HIV risk behaviour among men who have sex with both men and women. *AIDS Care, 10*(4), 463-471.

Weatherburn, P., Reid, D. S., Beardsell, S., Davies, P. M., Stephens, M., Broderick, P., et al. (1996). *Behaviourally bisexual men in the UK: Identifying needs for HIV prevention.* London: Sigma Research, Health Education Authority.

Webb, D. (1999). *Defining quality—Gay men's values in primary health care.* Southampton, UK: Wessex Institute for Health Research and Development Incorporating Public Health Medicine: University of Southampton.

Weeks, J. (1991). Questions of identity. In J. Weeks (Ed), *Against nature: Essays on history, sexuality and identity* (pp. 68-85). London: Rivers Oram.

Weeks, J., Heaphy, B., & Donovan, C. (2001). *Same sex intimacies: Families of choice and other life experiments.* London: Routledge.

Wellings, K., Field, J., Wadsworth, J., Johnson, A. M., & Bradshaw, S. A. (1990). Sexual lifestyles under scrutiny. *Nature, 348,* 276-278.

Wetherell, M., & Potter, J. (1988). Discourse analysis and the identification of interpretative repertoires. In C. Antaki (Ed.), *Analysing everyday explanation: A casebook of methods* (pp. 168-183). London: Sage.

Wetherell, M., & Potter, J. (1992). *Mapping the language of racism: Discourse and the legitimation of exploitation.* Hemel Hempstead, UK: Harvester Wheatsheaf.

Wiebel, W. (1996). Ethnographic contributions to AIDS intervention strategies. In T. Rhodes & R. Hartnoll (Eds.), *AIDS, drugs and prevention: Perspectives on individual and community action* (pp. 186-200). London: Routledge.

Wiebel, W., Biernacki, P., Mulia, N., & Levin, L. (1993). Outreach to IDUs not in treatment. In B. S. Brown, G. M. Beschner, with the National AIDS Research Consortium) (Eds.), *Handbook on risk of AIDS: Injection drug users and sexual partners* (pp. 437-444). Westport, CT: Greenwood.

Wilkerson, A. (1994). Homophobia and the moral authority of medicine. *Journal of Homosexuality, 27*(3/4), 329-347.

Willig, C. (1998a). Constructions of sexual activity and their implications for sexual practice: Lessons for sex education. *Journal of Health Psychology, 3*(3), 383-392.

Willig, C. (1998b). Social constructionism and revolutionary socialism: A contradiction in terms? In I. Parker (Ed.), *Social constructionism, discourse and realism* (pp. 91-104). London: Sage.

Willig, C. (1999a). Conclusion: Opportunities and limitations of applied discourse analysis. In C. Willig (Ed.), *Applied discourse analysis: Social and psychological interventions* (pp. 145-159). Buckingham, UK: Open University Press.

Willig, C. (1999b). Discourse analysis and sex education. In C. Willig (Ed.), *Applied discourse analysis: Social and psychological interventions* (pp. 110-124). Buckingham, UK: Open University Press.

Willig, C. (1999c). Introduction: Making a difference. In C. Willig (Ed.), *Applied discourse analysis: Social and psychological interventions* (pp. 1-21). Buckingham, UK: Open University Press.

Willig, C. E. (1999d). *Applied discourse analysis: Social and psychological interventions.* Buckingham, UK: Open University Press.

Willig, C. (2000). A discourse-dynamic approach to the study of subjectivity in health psychology. *Theory and Psychology, 10*(4), 547-570.

Willimack, D. K., Schuman, H., Pennell, B., E., & Lepkowski, J. M. (1995). Effects of a prepaid nonmonetary incentive on response rates and response quality in a face-to-face survey. *Public Opinion Quarterly, 59*, 78-92.

Willott, S., & Griffin, C. (1997). "Wham bam, am I a man?": Unemployed men talk about masculinities. *Feminism and Psychology, 7*(1), 107-128.

Wilson-Thomas, L. (1995). Applying critical social theory in nursing education to bridge the gap between theory, research and practice. *Journal of Advanced Nursing, 21*, 568-575.

Wilton, T. (1999). Towards an understanding of the cultural roots of homophobia in order to provide a better midwifery service for lesbian clients. *Midwifery, 15*(154), 164.

Wilton, T. (2000). *Sexualities in health and social care: A textbook.* Buckingham, UK: Open University Press.

Wooffitt, R. (1993). Analysing accounts. In N. Gilbert (Ed.), *Researching social life* (pp. 287-305). London: Sage.

Woolgar, S. (1996). Psychology, qualitative methods and the ideas of science. In J. T. E. Richardson (Ed.), *Handbook of qualitative research methods for psychology and the social sciences* (pp. 11-24). Leicester, UK: BPS.

Woollett, A., Marshall, H., & Stenner, P. (1998). Young women's accounts of sexual activity and sexual/reproductive health. *Journal of Health Psychology, 3*(3), 369-382.

World Health Organization. (1992). *International statistical classification of diseases and related health problems* (No. 10). Geneva, Switzerland: Author.

Wright, R., Decker, S. H., Redfern, A. K., & Smith, D. L. (1992). A snowball's chance in hell: Doing fieldwork with active residential burglars. *Journal of Research in Crime and Delinquency, 29*(2), 148-161.

Wyatt, G. E. (1991). Examining ethnicity versus race in AIDS related sex research. *Social Science & Medicine, 33*(1), 37-45.

Yardley, L. (1996). Reconciling discursive and materialist perspectives on health and illness: A reconstruction of the biopsychosocial approach. *Theory and Psychology, 6*(3), 485-508.

Yardley, L. (1997a). Disorientation in the (post) modern world. In L. Yardley (Ed.), *Material discourses of health and illness* (pp. 109-131). London: Routledge.

Yardley, L. (1997b). Introducing discursive methods. In L. Yardley (Ed.), *Material discourses of health and illness* (pp. 25-49). London: Routledge.

Yardley, L. (1997c). Introducing material-discursive approaches to health and illness. In L. Yardley (Ed.), *Material discourses of health and illness* (pp. 1-24). London: Routledge.

Yardley, L. (1998). "I'm not a doctor": Deconstructing accounts of coping, causes and control of dizziness. *Journal of Health Psychology, 3*(3), 313-327.

Yardley, L. (1999). Understanding embodied experience. In M. Murray & K. Chamberlain (Eds.), *Qualitative health psychology: Theories and methods* (pp. 31-46). London: Sage.

Yardley, L. (2000). Dilemmas in qualitative research. *Psychology and Health, 15*, 215-218.

Yardley, L. (Ed.). (1997d). *Material discourses of health and illness.* London: Routledge.

Index